METAPHYSICS
An Introduction

KEITH CAMPBELL
University of Sydney
Australia

Dickenson Publishing Company, Inc.
Encino, California   Belmont, California

THE DICKENSON SERIES IN PHILOSOPHY   JOEL FEINBERG, SERIES EDITOR

Copyright © 1976 by Dickenson Publishing Company, Inc. All rights reserved. No part of this book may be reproduced, stored in a retrieval system, or transcribed, in any form or by any means—electronic, mechanical, photocopying, recording, or otherwise—without the prior written permission of the publisher, 16250 Ventura Boulevard, Encino, California 91436.

ISBN-0-8221-0175-0
Library of Congress Catalog Card Number: 76-1312

Printed in the United States of America
Printing (last digit): 9 8 7 6 5 4 3 2 1

Cover by Marshall Licht

Preface

This book is a text, not a treatise; it is distinctive in its selection and arrangement, rather than the novelty of its material. It is designed for students taking their first courses in metaphysics, and one year in philosophy together with some acquaintance with logic should be sufficient preparation.

The work is in three parts. The first is an introductory section in which the aims, methods, and vicissitudes of Western metaphysics are briefly set forth. This part is included to give students a grasp of what metaphysical thinking is, and more confidence that they know where they are and where they can expect to be going. I hope it will reduce the bewilderment which philosophy so easily engenders in those who approach it. This section is swift and summary. It is not an impartial review, but a broad-stroke sketch of how one man sees the subject. I make no effort to conceal my own opinions here or elsewhere, for in my estimation a bland neutrality serves only to mask the interest, conviction, and even passion in the real life of metaphysics. Those with different views will be able to take steps to correct my exaggerations, misrepresentations, and omissions.

In part II, one branch of cosmology, the philosophy of matter, is treated through a study of atomism as a specimen of theories based on concrete particulars. My approach is quasi-historical; the career of atomism from Newton's time to its contemporary demise is used to illustrate the variety of ways in which cosmologies are vulnerable and resilient. This example provides opportunities for discussion of the relations between science and metaphysics, problems of reduction, and doctrines of primary and secondary qualities. The alternative cosmologies of Spinoza, Leibniz, and Boscovich are introduced by way of contrast. Although there is no attempt at a scholarly treatment, this section does aim to provide some understanding, which every educated person ought to have, of the development of one set of ideas crucial in modern thought.

Part III concerns ontology and is contemporary in theme. It deals with the problems of establishing an inventory of categories of being—in the sense in which concrete particulars constitute one category, and events, sets, or universals are other candidates. Quine's doctrines of canonical notation and ontic commitment are expounded and are then used in a discussion of various candidate categories which introduces the work of Davidson, Goodman, Putnam, and D.C. Williams. I have endeavored to make this abstract material sufficiently comprehensible to allow its inclusion in undergraduate courses at an earlier stage than is at present possible. In the final chapter I try to stimulate further investigation of Williams' doctrine of tropes, or property instances, as a basic category.

Parts II and III are substantially independent, each containing material for a course of about thirty lectures or their equivalent. Although the ontology of part III comes earlier in the order of reason and is more nearly a first philosophy, I recommend that where both parts are being treated, they be tackled in the order in which they are printed. Part II is less formidably abstract and, being concerned with the character of the material world, lies closer to people's natural concerns and curiosities.

For a course in which part II is given the chief place, the works of Spinoza, Leibniz, and Boscovich, all available in paperback, offer suitable further reading. R. Harré's *Matter and Method* handles some of the same themes, and for a course with more emphasis on philosophy of science, J.J.C. Smart's *Between Science and Philosophy* or *Philosophy and Scientific Realism* would be a suitable companion. Work centered on part III calls for study of Quine's *Word and Object* or *Ways of Paradox*. The Bibliography furnishes further suggestions and information. Metaphysics abounds, to the confusion of the beginner, in technical terms and jargon titles for doctrines. In keeping with the book's purpose as a text, a Glossary has been appended, giving explanations of all such expressions used.

Metaphysics has a rich and many-stranded history, and no one book in this field can hope to be comprehensive. Of the several traditions in formulating and addressing metaphysical issues, this text stays most closely with that branch of empiricism which takes metaphysical problems to rise from, and stand under the judgment of, the more concrete knowledge of the sciences. And within this manner of approach, there are further limitations. The reader is warned that he will find no attempt at even superficial treatment of the philosophy of necessity, or of mind, or of philosophical theology. Nor is there any attack on the metaphysical problems generated by epistemology—the character of sense data, for example—or on those which arise in moral philosophy, such as the reality of free will or the ontological status of values.

In a work of exposition it is, as William Temple said, idle to specify obligations. But on a more personal level I gratefully acknowledge the advice and encouragement of my colleagues Professor D.M. Armstrong and Professor D.C. Stove, and the patience and cooperation over successive drafts of Mrs. P. Trifonoff and Mrs. J. Walter, typists and secretaries.

Contents

Preface   *iii*

PART I
METAPHYSICS
ITS PROGRAM AND PROBLEMS

Chapter 1:	*A Sketch of the Background*	1
	The Classic Tradition	1
	Appearance and Reality	2
	The Response to the Problem of Appearance	5
	Metaphysics in Crisis: Hume's Fork	7
	Kant's Modest Proposal	9
Chapter 2:	*Metaphysics in Recent Years*	13
	Logical Empiricism: The Crisis Deepens	14
	The Decline of Logical Empiricism	16
	Metaphysics Restored	17
	The New Challenge to Metaphysics	19
	The Division of the Subject Matter	21

PART II

ONE BRANCH OF COSMOLOGY THE PHILOSOPHY OF MATTER

Chapter 3:	*The Framework of Concrete Particularism*	25
	The Philosophy of Matter	25
	Preliminary Assumptions	26
	Concrete Particulars	27
	Basic Particulars	29
	The Causal Role of Particulars in the Philosophy of Matter	31
	Temporal Parts	32
	The Cosmology of Events	33
	The Problem of Change	35
	The Perduration of Basic Particulars	36
	Basic and Derivative Particulars	37
	The Explicative and Theory-Founding Features of Basic Particulars	38
	Reduction Programs	40
Chapter 4:	*Classical Atomism*	44
	The First Modern Revolution in Physics	44
	Locke's List of Primary Qualities	48
	Newtonian Primaries	51
	The Atomist Reduction Program	52
	Patterns of Reduction	53
	The Initial Philosophical Assault on Classical Atomism	55
	Other Lines of Attack on Atomism	57
Chapter 5:	*Primary and Secondary Qualities*	59
	The Problem of Secondary Qualities	59
	Locke's Ontic Criteria	61
	The Interaction Pattern Criterion	63
	The "Magic" Difficulty for the Interaction Pattern Criterion	65
	Basic and Derivative Primaries	68
	The Complexity of Primary Quality Predication	69
	The Essence of Matter	71
	Secondary Qualities	72
Chapter 6:	*Alternative Particularist Systems*	75
	Spinoza's Cosmology	75
	Spinoza's System and Atomism	78
	Identifying and Nonidentifying Properties	79

	Leibniz: The System of Monads	81
	The Reasoning Behind Leibniz's Cosmology	83
	The Lessons of Leibniz's Cosmology	85
	Boscovich	86
	The Merits of the Theory: (i) Elegance	88
	Mechanical Martians and Ghosts	90
	The Merits of the Theory: (ii) Flexibility	92
	A Difficulty in Boscovich's Theory	93
Chapter 7:	*Atomism and Modern Physics*	95
	Dalton's Atomic Chemistry	95
	Electricity and Magnetism	96
	Atomic Physics	98
	Quantum Physics: Atoms Dissolved	98
	Boscovich Turned Inside Out	99
	Mass-Energy Transformations: The Final End of Atomism	100
	Russell's Cosmology	101
	General Relativity: The Return of Spinoza	103
	Summary and Unfinished Business	104

PART III
A FIRST SURVEY OF ONTOLOGY

Chapter 8:	*The Tasks of Ontology*	107
	Categories	107
	Method in Ontology: The Connection with Logic	108
	Subject-Predicate Sentences	108
	Ontological Principles of the Subject-Predicate Form	111
	Problems with the Subject-Predicate Form	112
	The Overpopulated World	119
	Other Problems in Natural Language	120
	Canonical Notations	122
Chapter 9:	*Quine's Canonical Notation*	125
	Vocabulary	125
	Formation Rules	126
	The Semantics of the Canonical Notation	130
	The Reasons for Choosing This Canonical Notation	135
Chapter 10:	*Regimentation or Paraphrase*	137
	The Language to Be Paraphrased	138
	Paraphrases	138

Chapter 11:	*Constructions Which Have No Paraphrase*	162
	Opaque Constructions	162
	Modal Constructions	163
	Propositional Attitudes	165
	The Strong Conditional	166
	The Adequacy of the Canonical Language	173
Chapter 12:	*Ontic Commitment and Reduction to a Minimum Domain*	174
	Ontic Commitment	174
	Problems with the Rule for Ontic Commitment	177
	The Resolution of These Difficulties	180
	Ontic Commitment and Straightforward Paraphrases	181
	Reduction Programs	184
	Quine's Minimum Domain	184
	Ordinary Things	186
	Naturalism and Facile Materialism	188
	Measures	189
	Geometrical Objects	191
Chapter 13:	*Events and Sets*	194
	Events	194
	Adverbial Expressions	195
	Quantification over Events	198
	Sets or Classes	200
Chapter 14:	*Universals and Tropes*	206
	The Problem of One over Many	206
	Quine's Position: Quasi-Nominalism	207
	Putnam's Argument	209
	Why Not Accept the Existence of Properties?	210
	Abstract Particulars or Tropes	212
	Tropes and Concrete Particulars	213
	The Problem of Individuals	214
	Tropes and Universals	216
	Tropes and the Other Categories	217
	Quantifying over Tropes	218
	Tropes in Cosmology	218
	The Ontology of Logic	219
Glossary		220
Bibliography		235
Index		243

I
METAPHYSICS: ITS PROGRAM AND PROBLEMS

1 A Sketch of the Background

THE CLASSIC TRADITION

Ever since the human race has been able to reflect and think in general terms, we have been facing the great problems: What manner of creature is man? What kind of world does he inhabit? With whom does he share it?

These problems, which are clearly of the first importance, lie at the base of metaphysics and so at the heart of philosophy. They give philosophy both its direction and its drive. The elaborate intellectual systems developed during the history of Western thought furnish comprehensive answers to these simple yet profound questions. Metaphysics is concerned with the overall framework of reality. It asks the character of matter, life, mind, and God; of space, time, and numbers; of cause, freedom, and fate; of objects and events. Details, by contrast, tend to be left aside. You will not find, in a book of metaphysics, any account of the difference between one sort of spider and another.

An interest in man's situation and destiny is not, of course, a monopoly of the philosophers—every reflective or curious person wonders about such things, and every religion gives its own answers. What sets metaphysics apart is not the peculiarity of its basic questions, but its distinctive method of approach. Metaphysics is the attempt to answer our simple, central questions thoroughly and systematically, and to answer them using only natural human faculties, of which reason is the chief. This is what makes philosophy the rival of revealed religion; religion offers for the problems of our origin, nature, and fate, solutions deriving from tradition, or from a divine revelation claimed by a visionary. But the rule in philosophy is to accept and adopt only those doctrines which can be substantiated by the use of man's natural powers for finding things out.

The impulse to metaphysics is the desire to know, and to know in general terms, which it shares with the sciences. (Indeed, the difference between metaphysics and science is itself a philosophical problem of some importance, as we shall shortly see.) This impulse has given us the great philosophies of time and eternity, of matter and spirit, of atoms and ideas, which adorn our intellectual history. These philosophies are rival answers, each claiming the endorsement of reason, to the great conundrums of man and nature—the problems, in Kant's epitome, of God, freedom, and immortality. But they are not just rivals. They form a tradition, for they grow out of one another by development and reaction. The history of metaphysics is the history of a sustained attempt, often lost or diverted, often renewed, to find out the general nature of the cosmos, and to determine man's place in it.

Our Western tradition in metaphysics is classic in both senses; it derives from the Greek civilization of classical times, and, like the traditions in portraiture or the novel, it forms a connected achievement in terms of which new departures are defined and understood. Its program, to determine the general structure of all being, clearly engaged Descartes and Spinoza in the seventeenth century no less than Plato and Aristotle in antiquity or Aquinas in the Middle Ages. And beneath the confusion into which modern philosophy has fallen, that program is with us still.

APPEARANCE AND REALITY

Metaphysics aspires to provide a correct, profound, and comprehensive account of the true character of everything there is; it is clearly a most ambitious enterprise. Anyone with a properly modest conception of human capacities might well wonder whether the task metaphysics sets itself does not overtax us as much as we think it overtaxes other living creatures. So the classic tradition has never been without its skeptical critics aiming shafts of argument or derision at the pretensions of metaphysical philosophy. In modern times this skepticism captured philosophy and precipitated a crisis in metaphysics whose origin and progress we must now consider.

To work out a general theory of the world with only our senses and our wits to go on is hard enough. Especially as we do not know in advance how much, or what, may be imperceptible, or too far away, or somehow "outside" space altogether. And it is made immeasurably more difficult by human fallibility. Our race early discovered, as each of us rediscovers, the cardinal if discouraging truth that things are not always what they seem.

We can err in perception, mistaking strangers for friends, sticks for snakes, or swifts for swallows, especially if the light is poor or the objects far off. Even in good conditions, spearing fish from above the water can be a frustrating business.

We can err in conception, too, classing seals with sharks, or taking dreams to be travels in a magic land. Sometimes we are lucky enough to learn of our mistake, and if this makes us more canny our chances of survival improve. But just think how much more difficult the metaphysicians' program now appears. For the philosophical mind will quite naturally wonder how many *undetected* errors there are, how much even the best perception is misleading, and how often new, revised, "correct" opinions will in turn be revealed as less than adequate to the facts. This questioning mood is reinforced by contact with other peoples whose philosophy and science differ greatly from our own, and by the spectacle of scientific theories constantly modified, subverted, and replaced. The beginning of wisdom is a lively sense of how much our opinion may be no good guide to reality.

This sense springs not only from catching ourselves in error occasionally; positive reasons support it. Darwin's account of our origin encourages us to expect perceptual information to have survival value at the expense, perhaps, of metaphysical accuracy. Marx's account of the formation of opinion in society, tracing it to social structure rather than the natures of things, furnishes fresh grounds for diffidence. Freud's portrait of our mental processes scarcely gives us new confidence in the rationality of man. But these modern developments only continue and confirm a loss of innocence that is as old as philosophy itself. It can be summed up thus:

Ordinary ways of coming to know are fallible, and so ordinary belief is at best partial and provisional. The chances are that a fair proportion of historical, scientific, and common sense belief is false.

In metaphysics, the upshot of the loss of innocence was a distinction between appearance (how the world seems) and reality (how it actually is). The painful truth is, then, that appearance and reality may, or may not, coincide.

The metaphysician, whose aim is to discern reality, thus finds one more hurdle in his path, a hurdle of unknown but clearly considerable height.

Appearance is not to be confused with illusion. Illusory beliefs are exactly those with no basis whatever in reality. They are unmitigated falsehoods; they cannot serve as a guide or basis in any way. But appearances are not so forlorn. They concern how the world seems, and do depend on the realities of the matter. Thus, for example, my dream belief that I am fixed to one spot belongs to illusion, and my waking account of the world need not accommodate any fact of fixedness. But my belief that the sun traverses the sky belongs to appearance. If I am to deny this, my theory must point to some fact—the spin of the earth, perhaps—which explains the sun's apparent motion. Folk who see the sun sinking slowly in the west are not having hallucinations. They are not dreaming. Even if not adequate, their belief has a claim to consideration. It rests upon and derives from some real fact. A sound philosophy must account for the sun's apparent motion, but not for my being apparently (in my dreams) fixed to one spot. In that case, the only thing to be accounted for is my mistake that I am fixed.

When Democritus claimed that in reality there were atoms and the void, while all else, such as colors, existed only "by convention," he did not mean that a blind or colorblind man was no worse off than a normal person in exploring the world. He meant that, for example, the real difference between a green and a golden apricot, the difference in the objects, underlying and explaining their difference in appearance, was not an ultimate and basic difference in color, but a difference in the shapes, sizes, arrangements, and motions of the imperceptible atoms. There *is* a difference between green and golden apricots. This difference, apparently one in color, is really one in atomic constitution. Color vision is a guide to reality, but not a direct one. Colors belong to appearance, not illusion, in the theory of Democritus.

The distinction Democritus makes between appearance and reality is crucial to science no less than philosophy. The philosophers have just used the idea more widely and more radically. Berkeley, for example, claimed that in reality there were only minds, divine or created, and no material bodies. He held that what we call bodies were collections of "ideas," mental things such as looks, tastes, and feels. He did not mean that there was no difference between a madman having visions of Armageddon and a sober gentleman, in command of his faculties, inspecting his estate and assessing the crops. He meant that the difference was not, as commonly thought, between what was really there to be seen and what wasn't. The difference was, rather, between consistent and reliable patterns of ideas in the experience of the sober gentleman, and detached, fragmentary, unintelligible sequences of ideas in the other.

The distinction between appearance and reality is not necessarily between what is *perceptible* and something else; rather it is between what is claimed in a superficial or unreflective theory of the world and what goes closer to the heart of things. The theory (appearance) which is to be surpassed, in some philosopher's thought, need not be one closely tied to perception. For example, when Russell argued that atoms, being imperceptible, should be considered as "logical constructions" out of perceptible items, he was relegating atoms to the world of appearance. He was not dismissing atomic theory as illusory; he agreed as cordially as anyone that the world behaves *as if* there are atoms. He was recommending that we think of atoms as we think, for example, of trends. Consider the trend of population from the country to the city. Everyone knows there is *really* no such thing as a trend. To go looking for it, in the country, or the city, or even on the roads and railways leading from one to the other, would be ridiculous. This trend is a logical construction out of people's changing their places of residence. To say there is such a trend is to say changes from country to city outnumber changes in the other direction. Such a trend is no illusion. We would be under an illusion if we thought the trend was the other way; no real facts underlie the reverse trend. But a trend is not a reality either. We can express this situation by saying that a trend must be reduced to a relationship—in our example, a relationship among changes of residence. And Russell was recommending that atoms should be reduced to elements and relationships among what can be directly perceived. The problems involved in reduction will engage our attention later. In general, though, appearance is to be reduced to reality, and illusion is to be detected and then ignored.

Any metaphysical project takes shape about the threefold distinction among reality (what truly is), appearance (what merely seems to be, yet has its foundation in real facts), and illusion (what merely seems to be, and lacks foundation). The metaphysician's task is (just!) to determine the constitution of reality, to account for appearance on that basis, and to set illusion aside.

THE RESPONSE TO THE PROBLEM OF APPEARANCE

The recognition of human fallibility poses for metaphysics a severe problem. It opens up the possibility that all ordinary methods of discovery yield appearance only. All ordinary knowing is provisional and subject to revision. It may all prove on deeper analysis to give no specification of reality but remain wholly within the domain of appearance. Yet the very task metaphysics sets itself is to pierce the veil of appearance, to pass beyond how things seem, to reach to the basic, inner, and perhaps hidden heart of the world.

Philosophers responded to this dilemma by seeking a special method for metaphysics. They sought some way of proceeding which would not be fallible, but which could offer a guarantee of surmounting the hurdle of appearance, which could win through to certitude and thus reality.

So Plato devised the method of dialectical ascent, in which, by analysis of common opinion and reflection upon it, we may rise to abstract thought. We attain a new, higher vantage point of thought from which the necessary structure of reality is visible to the "mind's eye." We come to comprehend the adequate reasons which guarantee our beliefs, and so reach knowledge of reality.

Out of this approach grew the practice of analyzing the concepts we employ in describing the world, sifting from among them certain essential basic elements, categories, which must underpin any knowledge whatever. It was the claim of Aristotle and the Scholastics who came under his influence that these ideas, such as substance, cause, and change, are quite indispensable to thinking. They must therefore be given a place in any metaphysic. Observation and hypothesis, the methods of science, are fallible and concern details. But reflection and analysis, the methods of metaphysics, working on knowledge rather than on the world directly, uncover the necessary and general structure of fact.

Descartes's response to the problem of appearance was to reject everything provisional and uncertain. He claimed that only the immediate, rational apprehension of "clear and distinct ideas" could provide any basis for a knowledge of reality. Logic and the intuition of some few indubitable truths, such as that Descartes is a thinking being, would enable him to pass beyond the hazard and confusion of that fun fair, appearance, to the limpid security of reality.

The requirement of a superior method for metaphysics combined with an enthusiasm for the new, mathematically formulated rational science of the seventeenth century to produce, in Descartes and still more explicitly in Hobbes and Spinoza, a commitment to mathematical method. Euclidean geometry furnished the model, with its axioms evident to logical insight, its proofs so rigorous as to exclude error, and its theorems so unexpected, so enlightening, and so incontrovertible. First principles manifest to the natural light of reason and arguments of deductive strength were to yield a solid edifice of metaphysical truth. This metaphysics would incorporate the new physics of Galileo and Newton as appearance but pass beyond it to an account of the real nature of time, cause, and matter and extend to a doctrine of God and of man.

In its most austere form, the mathematical method required that every component doctrine in a metaphysical system be guaranteed by the principle of noncontradiction. That is, every component must have a negation which is a self-contradiction. Since a self-contradiction cannot possibly be true, *its* negation (the original doctrine) cannot possibly be false. A metaphysics composed in this way would thus treat of what must be. Its subject matter would be reality itself. This austere reliance on nothing but the principle of noncontradiction was explicit in Spinoza from the first. Leibniz had two principles, noncontradiction and sufficient reason, the latter requiring of a doctrine that it be demonstrated from necessary premises. Subsequent commentators hold, for the most part, that the sufficient reason principle amounts to a reformulation of noncontradiction rather than a genuinely new rule.

With the adoption of the mathematical, rationalistic method, a beguiling prospect opens before us. The new method will yield us propositions of a higher order than the vague, confused, and changing deliverances of perception or tradition. The mutual connection of these propositions will guarantee their truth. We surmount the barrier of appearance and can hope to make out at least the main features of reality. No wonder many an author in the seventeenth century wrote a treatise on the "right conduct of the understanding" in which the mathematical method was recommended and exemplified. Metaphysical knowledge will be doubly excellent, at once most sublime in content and highest in certitude.

There was, however, a hitch. The recommended method for metaphysics was clear: imitate formalized mathematics, of which Euclidean geometry provided the most shining example. The result of employing this method should match the result in mathematics. We should arrive at a compact body of doctrine, assented to on all sides by all who take the trouble to understand it. But nothing of the sort happened. Rather, dispute and disagreement flourished as never before. Consider the systems of the four most notable practitioners of mathematizing philosophy. Descartes's world contains a single, spread-out material cosmos or space (with an internal complexity which accounted for the appearance of many distinct bodies), a divine mind, and sundry finite minds (people) associated with portions of matter. His philosophy is theistic, dualist in kinds of substance, and admits a plurality of minds.

Hobbes's system is atheistic (though he didn't say so) and recognizes just one kind of substance, matter.

With Spinoza we find a strictly monistic system; there is just one substance, God-or-Nature, of which bodies commonly considered, atoms or particles of a scientific kind and finite minds like ourselves, are all aspects or "modes"—all appearances. As reality's properties are all eternally necessary, time and change must also be in some sense mere appearance, but space (God's extension) is real. Spinoza is a pantheist, and his God is both material and mental in character.

Finally in Leibniz's portrayal of reality we encounter infinitely many minds, most of them very elementary, called "monads," plus God, a special monad distinct from the others. Space and matter belong to appearance; everything real is a living experiencing being. The system is a theistic idealism.

A SKETCH OF THE BACKGROUND 7

What a bewildering array of doctrines! Think of the scandal such confusion of teaching would occasion in mathematics. The failure to arrive at agreed results by the method which seemed to promise them was serious enough on its own. And this failure carried a special sting because of the faith the method places in the principle of noncontradiction. For in every case of disagreement, at least one party must be denying a metaphysical truth. So if metaphysics is governed by the principle of noncontradiction, at least one party must be asserting a self-contradiction. It followed that some of the finest minds in Europe could not spot a contradiction when it was directly before them. This certainly couldn't be explained away by saying they were not paying attention. Yet the ability to detect contradiction was supposed to be part of the basic logical endowment with which all nonidiot humans are equipped for the trials of life.

In this situation a judicious observer would suspect that something had gone badly awry. But what? It was that skeptical Scot, David Hume, who furnished a diagnosis. When the implications of his diagnosis were fully appreciated, metaphysics was plunged into a crisis of unprecedented severity.

METAPHYSICS IN CRISIS: HUME'S FORK

In Hume's opinion, metaphysics was a fatally and irredeemably misconceived enterprise. In the celebrated passage with which he ends his *Inquiry Concerning the Human Understanding*, we read:

> If we take in our hand any volume, of divinity or school metaphysics, for instance; let us ask, Does it contain any abstract reasoning concerning quantity or number? No. Does it contain any experimental reasoning concerning matter of fact and existence? No. Commit it then to the flames; for it can contain nothing but sophistry and illusion.

Why is it impossible for metaphysics to be anything but sophistry and illusion? Because it is designed to be superior in two different ways from common science or history: it claims to pass beyond appearance to reality, and it claims the certitude of necessity. Hume undertook to show that these excellences, so far from reinforcing one another, were incompatible and mutually destructive. He argued his position with subtlety and at length in classic works which you must surely read.

Let us use a more modern jargon to express Hume's point. We can classify truths in many different ways; three pairs of contrasts are these:
1. Some truths are *necessary* and some are *contingent*. That is, some express what *must* be so, while others express what is so, as it happens, but could have been otherwise. Black swans must be black, but they just happen to be, say, indigenous to Western Australia.
2. Some truths are *a priori* and some are *a posteriori*. That is, some can be known in a way quite independent of observation, experiment, or other laborious method of discovery. They are known by a faculty of mind which

grasps the truth with no assistance from perception or guesswork. That there are prime numbers greater than one million, for example, counts as a priori, for it is provable (an a priori procedure) from simple arithmetical truths to which we assent as soon as we grasp their meaning. That in Queensland some fish have lungs, on the other hand, is a truth discovered a posteriori, by exploring with our senses and our wits about us.

3. Some truths are *analytic* and some are *synthetic*. A truth is analytic if the property ascribed by the predicate is already affirmed, explicitly or implicitly, in the term by which the subject is named. Thus, if I say "All legless lizards are legless," the predicate merely echoes a part of the subject. Likewise if I say "Venomous snakes have a poisonous bite," but in this case the repetition is implicit and only emerges when a definition is supplied in the place of "venomous." Much the same applies in a negative sense, too. "No fresh water crocodiles live in salt water" is analytic.

A synthetic truth, by contrast, has a predicate which passes outside the circle of ideas introduced by the subject term. "No legless lizards are venomous" is an example, and so is "All penguins can swim."

Hume's argument now proceeds: Every synthetic truth introduces a new idea not present in the subject term. This newly ascribed property may or may not belong to the subject. So every synthetic truth is contingent. Furthermore, if a truth is contingent, it can only be known by a laborious discovery procedure. No immediate grasp of its truth, when once it is understood, is possible. So every contingent truth, if known at all, is known a posteriori. Consequently, although we have three sets of distinctions, they all divide truths into exactly the same two classes: those that are contingent, a posteriori, and synthetic on the one hand, and those which are necessary, a priori, and analytic on the other. This twofold division of truth is Hume's fork.

How can analytic truths be known a priori? Because we need only compare the ideas in subject and predicate to see whether they include or exclude each other. To tell whether legless lizards are legless, or black swans black, no investigation of lizards or swans is required. Analytic truths are necessary for a similar reason; since they affirm only relations among ideas, they can remain true no matter what we find when we turn from ideas to the world itself. But there is a heavy price to be paid for the necessity and certainty of analytic truth. Precisely because analytic truths run no risk of falsification by the concrete nature of the world, they can make no substantial contribution to our knowledge of that world. Analytic truths record only which of our ideas are contained in or excluded from each other. They do not advance our knowledge of the world which we describe by means of those ideas. Only synthetic, a posteriori, contingent truths can do that.

This philosophy wreaks havoc with the rationalist metaphysics of the classic tradition. Knowledge, in Hume's account, comprises "abstract reasoning concerning quantity and number" (logic and mathematics), which is analytic and necessary, and "experimental reasoning concerning matter of fact and existence" (science, history, common sense), which is synthetic and contingent.

But metaphysics as proposed by Plato, Aquinas, or Spinoza belongs to neither category. It aspires to be "abstract reasoning concerning matter of fact and existence." The being of God and the nature of the world are not matters of "quantity and number."

Hume's diagnosis portrays metaphysics as claiming to be simultaneously substantial and necessary. And he claims that no truths can be both. His argument has two parts. First, all necessary truths are analytic. Second, no analytic truth is substantial. So no truths are both necessary and substantial, as classical metaphysics requires. No wonder he dismissed the entire corpus of school metaphysics as sophistry and illusion.

The comprehensive ruin of metaphysics which Hume proclaimed requires one more step. A defender of the traditional program could concede that analytic truths are unable to map out the basic framework of reality. Yet he could insist that some special way of knowing, some spiritual intuition or divine illumination, some inner light or gift of discernment is available. Further, he could claim that by proper use of this special faculty we may come to substantial synthetic truths, which will not be necessary in the way that truths of logic are, but will nevertheless be superior to the findings of geographers or chemists in profundity and certitude. These truths, the fruit of special insight, specify reality.

Hume's empiricism blocks this defense. Empiricism is the doctrine that in the last analysis, all we have to go on in the discovery of synthetic truth is the testimony of our senses. All inner intuition and supernatural assistance are denied. But the testimony of the senses is testimony to appearance only. The route out of appearance into reality is barred. Metaphysics is a forlorn endeavor, a waste of time, a misbegotten enterprise born of miscalculation about the scope and depth of human capacities.

KANT'S MODEST PROPOSAL

Hume's criticism of the traditional practice of metaphysics gained in power and effectiveness the more widely it was understood. Kant acknowledged that it aroused him from his "dogmatic slumbers" as an inheritor of Leibniz and Wolff in Germany.

Thoroughly awakened to the unsatisfactory nature of rationalist, "mathematical" metaphysics with its fatal reliance on the principle of noncontradiction alone, Kant set about a salvage operation. In his classic *Critique of Pure Reason*—another book you must surely read—he assessed the situation thus:

a. Hume is right that analytic truths cannot yield substantial knowledge of the kind a real philosophy requires.

b. Hume is right, further, that we lack any faculty of mind which can pass beyond what appears in perception and reveal to us the character of reality. In Kant's terminology, appearance is the "phenomenal world" while reality is "noumenal." We have no intuition of noumena, he concedes.

c. But, perplexingly, Hume is wrong to affirm we have no synthetic a priori knowledge. Kant made a reappraisal of this question, reaching the conclusion that we are in possession of synthetic a priori knowledge in mathematics, both arithmetic and geometry, and on certain metaphysical questions, for example:

> Space is three-dimensional; time has one dimension.
>
> Everything perceived has a location in space.
>
> Every event has a cause.
>
> The phenomenal world (appearance) is made up of stable, enduring, reidentifiable things.

Kant's theory to account for this otherwise inexplicable fact was boldly radical; we have knowledge not of reality, but of the necessary form which appearance must take. Mathematics and metaphysics, contrary to all previous hopes, contain truths valid for appearance only. The modesty of his proposal now emerges. For we account for the a priori and necessary character of these special synthetic truths by a desperate expedient; the content of experience is a subjective succession of ideas. These ideas, generated we know not how by we know not what realities, are put into an intelligible form and order by the active, structure-imposing mind of the perceiver. The examples given above of claims concerning space, time, and cause express this form and order which are impressed on experience by the receiving mind. These truths are synthetic, for they express a substantial fact of order which might, abstractly, have been different (though we could not imagine experience in which they failed).

They are necessary in the sense that no sequence of experience, conforming by hypothesis to these orderings, can refute truths in which that order is expressed.

They are a priori, for no rummaging among perceptions is required to discover their truth. Reflection upon any sequence of experience confirms them beyond the danger of revision.

Kant's modest proposal is therefore to abandon the high aspiration of unlocking the universe's secret, and to rest content with a revised program for metaphysics which hopes only to delineate the inevitable structure of the sequence of perceptions in experience. Mankind's knowledge is confined within the limits of appearance. We can never attain to knowledge of the real world.

In Kant's philosophy, as in Hume's, appearance is peculiarly confining. It extends only to the mental experiencing involved in perception. It does not include even the familiar material world, independent of mental experience, which in common life we claim to know something about. We do not see birds and trees, or crash into doors and tables, as these matters are ordinarily understood. We enjoy perception, of a mental character, *as of* birds, trees, doors, or tables, and dignify properly behaved patterns of these mental perceptions with the honorifics 'bird', 'tree', or whatever. A knowledge of appearance is, for these idealist philosophers, knowledge of a subjective inner world of experience. We cannot claim even a half-reliable grasp of real things beyond our own minds. Kant consoles us in our ignorance with knowledge of certain orderly patterns into which our experience must of necessity fall.

In my opinion, Kant's modest proposal should not be accepted. Kant claimed that all scientific observation must surely confirm certain laws, but the most important of these have been repudiated: in general relativity, space does not conform to Euclid's theorems; in special relativity, motion does not obey Newton's laws; in quantum theory, the strict principle of causal determinism does not apply. Kant backed some losers, and so we would be better off with Hume's cautious "wait-and-see" attitude to scientific theories (theories concerning, in these idealist philosophies, the patterns of perceptual experience, not the behavior of independent things).

But it is not just that Kant was unfortunate in his choice of synthetic necessary laws. Rather, seeking for, or even finding, necessary patterns in experience is no substitute for a science and a metaphysics which attempt to discern the nature of the real world. And to call the new search for patterns in subjective experience by the old name "metaphysics" is just whistling in the cosmic dark. If we do decide subjective appearance is the limit of knowledge, we do better to express our decision in a frankly skeptical way, like Hume, and abandon any pretense of metaphysics at all.

Yet really to abandon metaphysics of the traditional kind is far from easy. Kant himself encountered this difficulty. Apart from God, in whom he believed for reasons deriving from moral philosophy, we are told that the real or noumenal world contains 'things-as-they-are-in-themselves' (that is, not-as-experienced-by-us) whose nature is unknown and unknowable *except* that they are not in space, not in time, not subject to causal law, and yet they somehow manage to give rise to successive, spatially ordered perceptual experiences in us, and we ourselves are in turn mysterious noumenal objects. This is, for all its negative tone, a doctrine of the nature of reality, a metaphysics. And, we may add, an extremely incredible one.

Kant cannot do without it, however, without allowing that perhaps birds, trees, doors, and tables cause our perceptions. These objects, having a reality of their own independent of the mind which perceives them, would not have to conform themselves to the mind's structural principles. So Kant would be left without any explanation of how some synthetic truths can be necessary. His defense of "metaphysics" as setting out the sure frame for all our experience would fail.[1]

So philosophy was in a dilemma. On the one hand, metaphysics seemed inevitable. On the other, empiricist criticism made it seem impossible. To sum up that empiricist criticism, human powers of attaining truth are not adequate for the aspirations of classical metaphysics to transcend appearance and apprehend

---

1. This is a very brief review of the thought of a great philosopher. The ultimate interpretation of Kant is still a subject of controversy, and some commentators deny that he is committed to the doctrines which make his position, in my opinion, unacceptable.

reality. We can know nothing beyond the circle of appearance. For we can know only that which can be authenticated in perception, and since perception is fallible, it cannot take us beyond appearance.

A stalemate prevailed throughout the nineteenth century, with some philosophers, such as John Stuart Mill, continuing in the skeptical tradition of Hume, and others following Hegel in clinging to the view that pure reason—using a more powerful dialectical logic, perhaps—can surpass the limitations of perception, exploration, and experiment.

2 *Metaphysics in Recent Years*

With the new century, Russell and Wittgenstein led a return to the Aristotelian strategy in metaphysics. Their procedure was to make a careful analysis of assertions in which we describe the world. This analysis, properly performed, will reveal the elements which any well-formed assertion must have. And corresponding to them will be necessary structural elements of the world which the assertion describes.

There are two steps to the procedure. First, sentences in common speech and even in the sciences often hide their true logical form and must be recast to show their form clearly. This may require some surprising revisions. For example, sentences containing ordinary proper names such as 'Plato' or 'Pegasus' or definite descriptions such as 'the richest man in Scotland' give rise to logical anomalies in those cases where there is no object corresponding to the name or description; so Russell proposed to recast them all in such a way that proper names and descriptions no longer appear.

Second, once sentences are cast in proper logical form, we must determine their truth conditions, that is, settle what the world must be like in order for them to be literally true. Included in these truth conditions will be formal, structural elements which will make up the metaphysics.

This procedure is similar to Aristotle's, but the logic used in recasting ordinary sentences is symbolic or mathematical logic, which had recently been developed by Frege and Russell himself,[1] among others, and which supersedes the traditional logic descending from Aristotle. When we use this method, with mathematical logic as the basis, the result is the philosophy of logical atomism.

---

1. Frege was a German mathematician and philosopher whose *Begriffschrift* was his most important logical work. Whitehead and Russell's *Principia Mathematica* is the English classic.

According to logical atomism, the world is a structure compounded from absolutely simple facts. The simple facts correspond to the atomic, or simple, logical sentences. And the familiar, complex facts of experience are built up from them in ways which parallel the combinations of logic.

It was not metaphysics on this Aristotelian pattern, but mathematical rationalism, which was the primary target of Hume's critique. But the empiricist challenge is one that all forms of metaphysics, including logical atomism, have to meet. In this case what needs to be shown is that careful, reflective dissection of truths cast in proper logical form, although not a method relying on the use of the senses, can yield substantial information, and not just the empty "relations among ideas" which we find in the standard examples of analytic truth. I think that this can be shown; to avoid Hume's criticism, however, we will have to abandon the idea that this method will give us knowledge guaranteed necessarily correct by the principle of noncontradiction. But this way of meeting the empiricist challenge never was explicitly worked out. So the status of metaphysical doctrine remained in doubt.

LOGICAL EMPIRICISM: THE CRISIS DEEPENS

In the years following the First World War, an influential band of philosophers known as the Vienna Circle, and their followers, worked to make the empiricist critique of metaphysics deeper and sharper. These men, of whom Carnap is the most representative, developed a philosophy known as logical empiricism or logical positivism. It is called *logical* empiricism because it is based not so much on an epistemology (an account of the limits of human knowledge) as on a semantics (a doctrine of the meanings of terms and of the sentences they form).

The basis of this philosophy, implicit in much earlier empiricist thought but now brought to the surface and moved to the center of the stage, is the principle of verification.[2] This principle is concerned with contingent truths and has two strands:

a. A concept is legitimate only if rules can be given for its application within experience.

b. A proposition's meaning is given by specifying which experiences verify and which falsify it.

For empiricists, experience is always perceptual experience.

You will readily appreciate that metaphysics does not fare well under this principle. It emerges as either impossible or unnecessary. On the one hand, if the great metaphysical concepts such as God, substance, being, or cause can be

---

[2] See A.J. Ayer, *Language, Truth and Logic*, for a general exposition of this principle.

found no place within perceptual experience, then metaphysics is impossible. The history of metaphysics becomes a tale told by a succession of idiots, full of sound and occasional fury, signifying nothing. This was the favorite stance of the iconoclastic positivists.

On the other hand, if the great concepts and doctrines can be reinterpreted in such a way that, after all, they make no reference except to the world of appearance, then metaphysics is unnecessary. For on this alternative, metaphysical truths merely use a high-falutin' verbiage to express truths of experience, and a homespun vocabulary would be less misleading.

If the verification principle is correct, we are cut off from speaking or thinking in words of any world but that of perceptual appearance. What cuts us off is the incapacity of human language to make any significant claim about any other world. A doctrine transcending appearance is not merely one we cannot know; it is no genuine doctrine at all. For despite its misleadingly normal form, the sentence used to express it is meaningless. The attempt either to prove or to refute metaphysical pseudodoctrines does not commend itself to people of good sense.

But if the verification principle is correct, and metaphysics is meaningless pseudodoctrine, what had the great philosphers actually been doing when they wrongheadedly attempted the impossible and proposed a description of the world's true character? Various accounts were offered. Carnap considered that some doctrines were misleading expressions of a recommendation to cast all genuine, verifiable knowledge in one form rather than another. A metaphysic of substances, for example, was actually a recommendation to use the traditional subject/predicate form of sentence. A preference for subjective idealism or objective realism was actually a preference for the vocabulary of sensation or the vocabulary of ordinary things in our descriptions.[3] Wittgenstein, by this time uncompromisingly hostile to traditional metaphysics, regarded it as the mere product of confusion over the conditions governing the significant use of terms. When these conditions are violated, metaphysics, a body of dogma with no value, is the result.[4]

John Wisdom was kinder; he held that the ordinary use of terms often involves incompatible conditions in tension with one another. A metaphysician is a person who selects in a one-sided way just some of the incompatible rules and presses them to the limit. In this way he produces doctrines astonishingly at variance with common sense, such as the unreality of time, or the dependence of everything upon everything else, or the nonexistence of matter.[5]

Morris Lazerowitz takes a different tack. He holds that the logically pathological formulas which make up traditional metaphysics are expressions of deep psychic conditions, generally conditions of conflict, in the philosopher's mind. They appeal by reverberating in the conflict-torn psyche of the reader.

---

3. R. Carnap, "Empiricism, Semantics, and Ontology."
4. L. Wittgenstein, *Philosophical Investigations.*
5. J. Wisdom, *Philosophy and Psychoanalysis.*

The clue to metaphysics is psychoanalysis; a metaphysical treatise can illuminate the state of a thinker's mind, but as a doctrine of the world it purports to describe, it is worthless.[6]

THE DECLINE OF LOGICAL EMPIRICISM

Fortunately for the reputation of metaphysics, the verification principle proved a great deal too drastic for its own good. First, there was the problem that the principle itself consisted of statements which could not be validated by a direct appeal to perceptual experience. The principle did not conform to the very rules that it itself laid down. Was it then meaningless? Why then should we adopt it—or rather what was there to adopt? (In a similar way, since Hume's *Inquiry* contains neither abstract reasoning concerning quantity or number, nor experimental reasoning concerning matter of fact, it should perhaps be committed to the flames, as the *Inquiry* itself recommends.)

Second, the verification principle made a clean sweep of traditional religion and required a radical moral philosophy in which statements of right and wrong, or good and evil, are reinterpreted as making no objective statement of any kind whatever.

These were difficulties enough to give outsiders pause, although they were not sufficiently crucial to persuade adherents of the principle to abandon it. The crunch came when it was fully realized what havoc the principle wreaks in the sciences themselves, for logical empiricism was fundamentally an attempt to account for the superiority of the sciences over superstition, prejudice, religion, and metaphysics.

It emerged that science and history are full of statements about what cannot be experienced because it is past, or too far away, or too small, or too quick, or because humans are not sensitive to that sort of thing at all.

Attempts were made to reinterpret such statements in terms of perception alone. For example, it was suggested that statements about the past mean something about the *future* discovery of visible traces of the past, and statements about electrons mean something about instrument readings and deposits on electrolytic plates, and statements about electromagnetic waves mean something about the behavior of television and radar sets. But it became clear that these reinterpretations result in such a severe impoverishment of scientific theory that, so far from being a celebration of science, logical empiricism turns out to be an assault upon it. Furthermore, this assault rests on nothing more solid than the verification principle, which is a restrictive account of what concepts and propositions can mean. Yet there is no guarantee that this restrictive account is correct. The principal support for the verification principle is that we do not have any clear account of how a less restrictive range of meanings is possible. Such negative support is insufficient. The verification principle reveals itself as a

---

6. M. Lazerowitz, *The Structure of Metaphysics.*

dogma, subversive of all that is best in human discovery, namely theoretical science. It deserves to be rejected. With this rejection we open up again at least the possibility of a reputable metaphysics.[7]

METAPHYSICS RESTORED

The attempt to set metaphysics apart from other inquiries has been the root cause of the crises in its history. The picture often drawn has shown science and common sense together on one side, as fallible, changeable, dependent on perception, revealing only an apparent world, and so comparing unfavorably with metaphysics, which is portrayed as certain, based in reason, and able to sit in judgment on science and history from its elevated contact with reality. This picture positively invites the charge that the pretensions of metaphysics outstrip any likely performance.

To my mind, a juster view of the relation of metaphysics to science is one of collaboration, not contrast. Our understanding of both science and philosophy must change. W.V. Quine has been the most prominent of those advocating the needed changes during the last twenty years or so.[8]

On the side of science, it is crucial to realize how much physical or chemical or psychological theory is often attempting. The sciences are not restricted, as is sometimes thought, to bringing order into perceptual knowledge. Often, scientific theory is not merely an extension or refinement of perceptual data, nor just a revelation of regularities in the pattern of phenomena, nor just the introduction of quantitative measure. Theories often pass beyond the phenomena altogether and postulate an unseen world whose detailed workings explain and unite diverse phenomenal effects. The wave theory of light, the atomic theory of valency, the subconscious mental theory of anxiety are typical examples.

So the sciences themselves are operating with a distinction between appearance and reality. Like metaphysics, they are embarked upon the search for the true character of the world, underlying how it seems. Within the sciences one theory gives way to another which promises a deeper penetration of the world's mysteries.

Metaphysical inquiry is distinguished from science, on this point of view, only by attempting a more comprehensive and more systematic basic theory.

And on the side of metaphysics, a *rapprochement* is to be made. Metaphysicians must abandon the hope of finding a theory of the world which can be guaranteed certain. We cannot expect to arrive at any knowledge more surely founded than the self-corrective yet still provisional theories which scientific method yields. Metaphysical truths are synthetic. And they are not necessary in any tough logical sense. They cannot be guaranteed by the principle of noncontradiction. How then are they to be validated? The short answer is that they

---

[7]. Here, as with Kant, I am being blunt and short with a comprehensive, important, and in many ways still influential philosophy.

[8]. See his *Ways of Paradox* for more introductory essays on this theme.

stand at the bar of experience as do all opinions of common life or recondite science. To expand that a little:

The basic complaint of the empiricist critique was that metaphysical truths are immune from refutation in experience. If this is correct, then even if they are synthetic and make claims about the world, they are still pathological. For in that case they could never make good any claim to be believed. That claim can be made good only through having consequences which turn out to be confirmed. Any theory can be immune from refutation only if it has no consequences which, by turning out correct, could establish it.

The immunity from refutation which metaphysical doctrines seem to have is, however, an illusion which springs from too simple a notion of refutation. The problem is that there is no single, specifiable run of perceptions which would prove or disprove "Everything is material" or "Space is not real" or "The world depends on God" or "The link between cause and effect is a necessary one." So the empiricist demand for a specification of the experiences which would prove or disprove such a claim cannot be met in a tolerably brief and straightforward way. And in consequence, these claims become suspect. But on closer inspection it turns out that precisely the same is true of any theoretical statement in science, such as "Gases are clouds of molecules" or "Atomic particles are composed of quarks" or "Radio stars recede rapidly." In all these cases there is ample room to reconcile the theory with an apparently conflicting experimental result. This is done by introducing subsidiary hypotheses explaining why the expected result is not obtained. *Ad hoc* hypotheses can protect any theoretical statement from refutation.

The relations between theory and data are more complex than the idea of refutation by a specifiable run of perception would allow. A theory is accepted and retained so long as it remains an integral part of the best overall explanatory account of the phenomena we encounter. And precisely the same is true of responsible metaphysics. Space, time, God, events, casual determinism, spiritual minds, properties, classes, numbers, substances all have a title to a place in our metaphysic to the extent that they belong in the best total theory. The best total theory is only the best, not the only possible one, and only the best for the time being.

It is, or course, possible to insulate any metaphysical belief from the risk of refutation. This is done by always explaining away every consideration which seems to refute it. But this is not something special about metaphysics. It is equally possible to insulate any belief whatever, whether a favorite scientific theory or some particular claim as to matter of fact, in just the same way. Macbeth can hold onto "There is a dagger before me" so long as he chooses, without self-contradiction, by introducing theories about intangible daggers, violations of laws of gravity, hallucinations of seizing nothing when actually a dagger is in his hand, the unreliability of metal detectors, and so on and so on.

This process of insulating favorite beliefs is familiar enough. It is dogmatism and is an enemy of reason wherever it appears. Metaphysical doctrines are rather more prone to this pathological loyalty than others, because their vast importance gives people a strong emotional commitment to them. But metaphysical questions are not themselves illegitimate just because they can be treated in a dogmatic way.

A clearer conception of the nature of science, together with a chastened program for metaphysics, thus leads us to view metaphysics as continuous with science, sharing both its risks and its dignity. Metaphysics is the attempt to interpret all experience, including science, so as to form one coherent and systematic view of the world and man's place in it. In this way it tackles those simple yet profound questions from which we began. As we shall find, the great philosophers of the past can be seen as engaged in this great enterprise, even if that is not how they themselves would have described it.

In this view metaphysics is in no privileged position from which it can lay down the law for knowledge of other kinds. It is in no position to insist, for example, that every science must be deterministic. Metaphysics stands subject to correction in the light of the development of science no less than the other way about. As Quine would put it, there is no first philosophy which can give the law to science and pontificate, for example, as to the reality of atoms. Rather, atomic theory and metaphysics both must be validated in the light of one another and the continuing test furnished by the unfolding data of experiment and discovery.

In the words of D.C. Williams:

> Philosophy is not higher and suprascientific. It is the lowest and grubbiest inquiry round the roots of things, and when it answers real questions about the world, it is and can only be an inductive science.[9]

THE NEW CHALLENGE TO METAPHYSICS

The paths of true philosophy never do run smooth. The restoration of metaphysics to an honorable if not supreme place in human thought had scarcely occurred before a new challenge arose. This new challenge comes from a new approach in the philosophy of science.

Hitherto, it had been taken for granted that scientific progress really was progress. That is, when one theory displaced an earlier one or, more spectacularly, took the place of an unorganized collection of facts, problems, and suppositions at the "birth" of a new science, it was assumed in philosophy that the new beliefs were better than the old. And they were better in being more likely to be true, more penetrating, closer to the real truth of the case.

Only on this assumption can the interdependence of metaphysics and science provide a means for validating metaphysical theory. For all contingent truths have a claim to our adherence only if they are rationally superior (more likely to be closer to the truth) than any of the available alternatives.

Now the new approach in the philosophy of science is much more strongly

---

9. D.C. Williams, *Principles of Empirical Realism*, p. 147. Williams means by an inductive science one of the same logical character as physics.

historical than its predecessors. It has a lively awareness of scientific opinion as constantly changing, either in detail or globally, as one great central theory, like Newton's in physics, gives way to a new one, like Einstein's. And detailed study of the historical record uncovers reasons and motives in the change of scientific belief which are much more haphazard, much less rational, than philosophers have thought to be the case.

We have been accustomed to see scientific change as an orderly march from one theory to another which is more exact, more general, more adequate, and better connected with other theories—in short, a rational advance. But in the work of Thomas Kuhn, for example, we get a picture rather of scientific change as a lurching, directionless course from one poorly based, hazily conceived, and woefully incomplete position to another. Education, fashion, habit, prejudice, and accident seem to determine change as much as anything rationally compelling.[10] The implication is skeptical; what reason have we for supposing that in such circumstances we can approach more nearly to the truth? And in that case, what of a metaphysics which alters, as we saw in the previous section, to accommodate current orthodoxy in the sciences?

Worse follows. Both with Kuhn and with Paul K. Feyerabend, the other most notable radical in contemporary philosophy of science, the standard view of how a theory gets validated is severly handled.[11] It is a mistake, the argument runs, to think of data, the results of observation and experiment, as existing independently of theory. Data do not exist in some objective and unarguable fashion as a firm rock of fact against which to test a theory. Rather, the very lines of inquiry we select, the terms in which we express our results, the frame of reference within which we assess their significance, are all dependent on, among other matters, the very theory for which the data are supposed to provide a test. To put it bluntly, the game is rigged in favor of the theory. The theory leads us to ignore many findings which could prove embarrassing, and as to those we do have to take into account, the theory provides ways of interpretation and adaptation, where results don't quite fit or are 'anomalous', which enable us to cling to the theory despite its *prima facie* refutation by experimental results. When, for whatever reason, we switch to a new theory, then once again the validation game is rigged, but this time in favor of the new theory.

If this is an accurate account of the logic of scientific theory and scientific change, on what grounds could we hold that a metaphysics working in collaboration with developing science is a progressive approach to the reality which underlies appearance?

There is yet a third aspect to the skeptical, antimetaphysical cast of recent philosophizing about science. It is the problem of the validity of the criteria we use in judging a scientific theory. These tests include the precision and simplicity with which the theory accounts for the phenomena, the extent to which the theory is confirmed by new facts beyond those it was invented to explain, and

---

10. T.S. Kuhn, *The Structure of Scientific Revolutions*.
11. P.K. Feyerabend, "Problems of Empiricism," for example.

how naturally it fits into the general view of the world which we favor. Now these criteria did not drop from heaven engraven on tablets of gold. The tendency to use them is not, so far as we can tell, an inevitable and innate feature of the human mind. On the contrary, their authority developed gradually and painfully in the course of the development of science itself. It is not so long, after all, since conformity with Holy Writ, or conformity with the works of Aristotle, was a recognized criterion for the acceptability of both metaphysical and scientific theories.

But what guarantee could there be that the criteria we now use will select theories which are always getting closer to the truth? Suppose the world is arbitrarily, wildly complex. Suppose different causes are at work each time a similar effect is produced. Those theories which pass our present tests for scientific excellence will in that case misdescribe the world, and the better they are as science the further they will be from touching reality. The skeptical worry here is that perhaps we are demanding the wrong characteristics in our scientific theories.

The problems raised by the new philosophy of science are not spurious. If the traditional view of science as a rational approach to reality is to be vindicated, this new challenge must be met. To do this it must be shown first that despite the vagaries of the actual course of science, later theories are rationally superior to earlier ones; second that despite the links between theories and the data they account for, theories can be objectively tested by comparing their consequences with the actual run of affairs; and third that there is no vicious question-begging involved in the development of a self-critical standard of judgment for theory within the scientific tradition.

It is not yet known whether these three things can be done. Work is still in progress, and it is not clear what the outcome will be. Yet the vindication of metaphysics depends on it. For we have argued that metaphysics, the attempt to approach reality, can be pursued only with and through the attempt of science in the same direction. If science cannot really make any advance of this kind, metaphysics is a lost cause.

For my part, I am confident that this latest challenge can and will be met. But in the long run the only permanently convincing vindication of metaphysics is to be found in the results it can achieve. To a consideration of some of these the remainder of the book is devoted.

THE DIVISION OF THE SUBJECT MATTER

Metaphysics divides into two rather different branches, which D.C. Williams dubs *analytic ontology* and *speculative cosmology*.

In analytic ontology we ask questions about the categories we need for understanding any facts, for example: Are there properties as well as objects? Are there such things as events, or only objects which change? Are there such things as sets or numbers apart from things in sets or things counted? Are there facts or propositions? What is a disposition? What is a cause? How does a theory make commitments as to the existence of things?

In speculative cosmology we are not so formidably abstract. We seek a general account of the main features of the world and ask, for example: Are there spirits as well as bodies? Are there gods or angels? What of space and time? What sorts of causes are at work in determining events?

Analytic ontology is more general, and in an orderly exposition of a metaphysical system it would be laid out first, to set the ground frame of sorts of items (such as objects, properties, events, causes) within which a cosmology can be developed by introducing specific examples of such items (such as God, materiality, vibration, natural selection). But everybody is interested in cosmology before they come to study philosophy, and the point of questions in ontology is often hard to see unless we have cosmological consequences in mind. So in this book we will proceed directly to a discussion of the cosmological problem of concrete particulars, with special attention to the philosophy of matter, and then raise abstract ontological problems concerning the categories of being in the third part.

II
ONE BRANCH
OF COSMOLOGY:
THE PHILOSOPHY
OF MATTER

3 The Framework of Concrete Particularism

THE PHILOSOPHY OF MATTER

The ambitious task of cosmology is to provide a systematic description of the general features of the cosmos. It undertakes to identify the chief kinds of being to be found in it, their nature, and their relations to one another. The classic schedule of Western speculation has included among the principal realms of the whole universe, God, mind, life, and matter. Philosophical theology, the philosophy of mind, and the philosophy of matter have, accordingly, grown up as branches of cosmology.

In this part of the book we tackle the philosophy of matter, where the problem is to give an account of the nature of spatiotemporal being. Or at least, to give an account of its nature insofar as it is "merely" material or spatiotemporal. Living things, and beings with minds, may be partly (or entirely) material in character. We leave that question aside. To make the business plainer, we concentrate on inanimate spatiotemporal reality.

Among the various ways of thinking about matter, the most natural takes familiar material objects, such as knives and forks, as the basic type of spatiotemporal being. Familiar material objects are, in the jargon of philosophy, *concrete particulars*. Our strategy in tackling the philosophy of matter will be first, to set out the general character of any kind of concrete particularism; then second to describe atomism, which is the most fully worked out variety of concrete particularist cosmology; and finally third to consider the ways in which atomism is vulnerable to criticism, and what alternatives might be superior to it.

PRELIMINARY ASSUMPTIONS

Since, in the philosophy of matter, we are embarked on the business of giving an account of the nature of spatiotemporal being, our first question should be, Is there really any spatiotemporal world at all? Everyone takes an affirmative answer to this question for granted in all normal circumstances, and so asking it can strike us as being like asking whether two and two are really four. Still, it is part of the business of philosophy to call in question that which is ordinarily and universally taken for granted. The reality of any world outside of the experiencing subject, independent of the subject's consciousness, has indeed been challenged. Ingenious men can make that assumption appear doubtful or even false. And to challenge the assumption is to introduce one of the classic problems of philosophy, the problem of the external world—the problem, that is, of demonstrating that there is good reason to affirm the reality of an external world.

Using the language of part I above, the problem is to show that there is not just a conscious subject and a world of appearance which consists of his experiences, but other realities too.

In this book, we are going to assume a positive solution to the problem of the external world. In my opinion the affirmative side has by far the best of the argument,[1] and we have neither space nor time to study the matter properly. There is another reason for setting this problem to one side: to deny the reality of any external world is a *desperation option* in our metaphysical inquiries. Another desperation option is, for example, that the world began five minutes ago, complete with fake memories and pseudofossils. I call these doctrines desperation options because their truth would invalidate and descredit most of the methods for finding things out that mankind has developed—in these cases, methods concerning what goes on when we are not looking or how long natural processes take.

It is reasonable to accept such an option only as a last resort, only after every alternative has been clearly refuted, only when it alone promises to provide a coherent account of our situation, only, in short, when our science and philosophy are in a desperate plight. So before denying the reality of an external world we need to know, for example, whether or not a coherent philosophy of matter can be worked out. Which requires a study of the philosophy of matter. Let us proceed.

Even if we assume the existence of an external world, it does not follow that the external world or any part of it is spatiotemporal. For in this context "external" means "other than the self" and not necessarily "outside the self." But there does *seem* to be a spatiotemporal world. That is what gives the philosophy of matter its subject matter.

We will take as a starting point the common, public world of more or less solid objects in motion or at rest in space, coming into being, enduring a while, and then passing away. This is the world of cultural artifacts—chairs, tables

---

1. D.C. Williams, "Realism as an Inductive Hypothesis."

THE FRAMEWORK OF CONCRETE PARTICULARISM   27

machinery, art objects—and of natural objects—stones, trees, ice, and fire. It is the world, in Austin's phrase, of "medium sized specimens of dry goods."[2] Our assumption is that the objective world includes something which is, apparently, a world of material objects in space and time. Thinking of the world in this familiar, inevitable way is to think in terms of what Sellars dubs the *manifest world image*.[3]

The common public world of this image is the subject matter of a philosophy of matter. Notice that although we assume that appearance includes a space-time world, we do *not* assume that reality is material or spatiotemporal. *That* is for the philosophy of matter to find out. We must leave the way open to an *eliminative* philosophy of matter, such as Leibniz's. Leibniz did not assume, but rather came to the conclusion, that space, time, and matter belong to appearance only, and not also to reality. His philosophy eliminates them. For him the external world is not material. To leave that course open, we must not beg the question by assuming that they do belong to reality.

We just put to one side, for separate consideration (beyond this book), the other great branches of cosmology, the philosophy of God (natural theology), and the philosophy of mind. Gods, angels, souls, and spirits fall outside the scope of the philosophy of matter. They are not outside the scope of *materialism*, of course. Materialism is a general thesis. It affirms that the philosophy of matter is philosophy enough, that it completes the positive side of cosmology. The philosophy of matter itself makes no such claim.

CONCRETE PARTICULARS

We can survive in our environment because, among other reasons, it contains solid, compact, things with definite surfaces, like rocks, knives, cars, chairs, and tables. The things which cohere firmly together and are therefore strong, are dispersed in a medium, the atmosphere, which has none of these features to any extent. We ourselves hang together, and we can act on our environment because we and our tools can move through it and then have an effect on it. The manifest world is one of cohesion *within* bodies and discontinuity *between* them. In such a situation it is natural, and probably inevitable, for us to think of ourselves, our tools, and the familiar landmarks of our world as *unities*. We think of them as individual, separate objects, largely independent of all others, each existing in its own right, each its own particular self. Call such things *concrete particulars*. A book, a pen, a pipe, a house, a yacht are all concrete material particulars—and material particulars are our concern here. Any definite material thing is a concrete particular.

How can we distinguish concrete particulars from other sorts of thing? A first rough test is this: common nouns which apply in the space-time world and take the indefinite article generally name a kind of concrete particular. 'Water' does

---

2. J.L. Austin, *Sense and Sensibilia*.
3. W. Sellars, *Science, Perception, and Reality*.

not do this, for 'a water' is unacceptable, but 'pool of water' does. 'A pool of water' is quite standard speech, and pools of water are concrete particulars. As we find in this example, the range of concrete particulars tends to broaden from the original central cases. The central cases are of rather rigid bodies with relatively definite and permanent surfaces. But definite locations and unity are what count. For a concrete material particular we must be able to specify which portion of the cosmos contains it, and we must be able to show that everything inside that region deserves for some reason to be treated as a unity—unity of composition, as with pools of water; or of use, as with knives and doors; or of mobility, as with dogs and cats; or of all three, as with nails.

On this broader basis, we can identify as concrete particulars some objects which from the initial point of view would not be included. The atmosphere, for example, will count. Its exact net location is constantly changing, of course, as other concrete particulars move through it. But at any given time it does have one definite location. The ocean is in just the same condition.

The whole spatio-temporal cosmos will also count, for although we cannot say where it is (except everywhere), we can specify which fragment of the cosmos is involved, and it has the unity of comprising whatever is spatial.

We can also countenance scattered particulars, such as the territory of Indonesia or all the gold in the world, which are not continuous but have some parts detached from others. Here we clearly pass beyond the *common noun which takes the indefinite article* test.

A cloud is a concrete particular, although it is not rigid or possessed of a stable and definite surface. It is also, if we look closely, scattered in that the water drops which comprise it do not all touch each other.

Location and unity, the conditions for a concrete particular, carry (relative) stability along with them. If the properties of some part of the world are changing rapidly, without discernible pattern or steadiness, we are not likely to think of that part as occupied by one thing. So, for example, a region through which a bird flies is filled with air, invaded by bird, vacated by bird, filled with air again. It lacks material unity and so is not a concrete material particular. It is, of course, a region of space, and 'region of space' is a noun phrase taking the indefinite article. Are regions of space concrete particulars? This is a question that calls for decision (we can make up our own minds how we wish to use the expression "concrete particular"). What is not a matter of decision, but of scientific and philosophic discovery, is whether all regions of space possess some appropriate unity *beyond* their unity of location, and if so, what this is. So far as the manifest world is concerned, a region of space is at any rate not a *material* particular. For a material particular we require location and unity, and as we now see, that unity must spring somehow from the way the region of space is filled. It must spring, in other words, from properties of the region other than the purely spatial ones.

Concrete particulars dominate the manifest world. This is a contingent fact—the world might have exhibited neither the local unity nor the discontinuity from one region to another which makes it a world of concrete particulars. But it *is* a fact, and one which gives us a starting point for a philosophy of matter. We now want to know, for example: Are all concrete particulars in space-time concrete *material* particulars? (Apart from regions, as noted above.) Is a river a material particular? Is a waterfall? Is the spray of the waterfall? Is the rainbow formed in the spray? Is a flash of lightning or a clap of thunder a material particular? What about a wave? What about the crest of a wave? What about the gleam on the crest of a wave? What about the crashing of the wave on the sand? What about the light radiated by the sun?

As this short set of samples shows, we think of the manifest world in terms not only of things (paradigm cases of concrete particulars) but also of their parts, collections of them, properties of things, and events involving things. One of our tasks is to sort out the relationships among all these diverse aspects of being. The examples of rainbow and lightning flash also suggest that for genuinely material particulars, the unity they need must derive from some special kinds of ways in which the region they occupy is filled, from some special kind of unifying property. Since concrete particulars dominate the manifest world, a natural and rational first proposal in the philosophy of matter is to place them in the center of our account and claim that the world is a world of material particulars. Everything that is, in the material world, is itself a material particular or is an aspect or activity of one. Everything is or depends upon material particulars. An inventory of the material particulars of the world, with an account of their nature and their doings, would cover the entire reality of the spatiotemporal world. Everything in the manifest world is to be understood in terms of that world's concrete material particulars.

If the plain man has a philosophy of matter at the moment, I would guess that this would be a great part of it. It was also a great part of Aristotle's philosophy of the spatiotemporal world, and so it's perfectly respectable, if somewhat old fashioned.[4] Call it material concrete particularism.

BASIC PARTICULARS

We will examine in part III the possibility of organizing a cosmology about some conception other than that of the concrete particular. Here, we proceed to a development of concrete particularism.

The first complication to deal with is that of *complexity*. Many objects have parts which are themselves concrete particulars. A car has a carburetor, wheels, tires, pistons, bearings, and so forth. Every rock has parts which, though undetached, are themselves rocks. The solar system consists of sun, planets, moons, comets, and other concrete particulars.

Clearly, if in our account of the world we include the car *and* its carburetor, or the solar system *and* the planets, we will be counting many things many times over. This is undesirable in itself, and besides, it prevents us from attaining a clear view of the world's structure and relations.

Equally clearly, the source of trouble is that some particulars are compounds,

---

4. Aristotle, *Metaphysica*, books Z and H.

made up of other particulars, and so are derivative rather than fundamental denizens of the cosmos. We need to single out, among particulars, those which are basic and distinguish them from those which are not. A first step in this direction is to recognize parts and wholes and to insist that basic particulars are those with no parts which are in turn concrete particulars. Call such parts *simple*, and rule that basic particulars must be simple.

But this first step must be made with care. When we think of the parts of a car, we think of those pieces from which we can assemble a car. The parts exist independently of the car, and if they are brought together in a particular way, a car is the result. But consider a river. We might say the river is composed of eddies, swirls, and tumblings. Yet it would not be possible to assemble a river out of eddies, swirls, and tumblings. For there could not *be* any eddies, swirls, and tumblings unless there were *already* a river whose eddies, swirls, and tumblings they are. Eddies, swirls, and tumblings are parts of a river quite different from the pistons, wheels, and spark plugs of a car.

The difference is one of dependence in existence. A's depend on Bs if there could be Bs but no A's (spark plugs but no cars). Where the whole depends on the parts as cars on spark plugs, we can call the parts *true parts*. Sometimes the relationship of dependence is symmetrical, as with the inside and the outside of a box. No insides without outsides, and vice versa. Similarly, no plank without ends, and no plank-ends without planks.

The dependence which concerns us is dependence in *existence*, not dependence in description. We have many pairs of correlative terms, such as 'husband' and 'wife', 'parent' and 'child', whose use introduces dependence in description. That is, no one can be a husband unless there is somebody who is his wife. In *that* sense, the sense that he couldn't be *described* as a husband but for the wife, the husband is dependent on the wife and vice versa. But the man who is the husband can exist in an unmarried state. His existence does not require the existence of any wife. And conversely for her. They are dependent on one another *only* in description. Each needs there to be something describable by one correlative term in order to qualify for description by the other correlative term.

The same holds for father and child. Yet this example introduces a further complication, namely the *casual* dependence of child on parent. As a contingent fact about how living things come into being, without the existence of the parent at a particular time, the child would have no being at all. This remains true even though the child can continue to exist even when the parent does no longer.

We are not at this stage interested in causal dependence in existence, but logical dependence. That the child does not vanish when the parent ceases to exist shows that the child is not logically dependent in existence upon the parent. Contrast the car and its parts. When the parts cease to be, the car must also cease to be. There is no time at which I can remove (and not replace) all the car's parts without thereby destroying the car. That is the kind of dependence which here concerns us.

We can say that A's are *more fundamental* than Bs if Bs depend upon A's but not vice versa. And A's are *fundamental* if there are no other particulars upon

THE FRAMEWORK OF CONCRETE PARTICULARISM   31

which they depend. Basic particulars must be fundamental in this sense. This is the idea behind *simplicity*. Simples are fundamental with respect to the part-whole relation. They can be parts of complex things but cannot themselves have true parts (that is, parts which are in turn particulars), for these parts would be more fundamental than they.

Yet the simplicity of partlessness, while necessary, is not sufficient for a basic particular. Basic particulars must be simple, that is, not dependent on parts or on things they are parts of, but also independent of one another. The test of genuinely fundamental status is: Could this simple particular be the only thing in the universe? If so, it is a basic particular. If not, not.

Something is basic provided it is independent of every other thing. Thus for example, suppose there cannot be *the thing at place* P *at time* T *with volume* V unless there is "also" *the thing at place* P *at time* T *with shape* S. This does not show that neither of these things is basic. Even though they seem to depend on each other, like the north pole and the south pole of a magnet, they may well be the very same thing described two ways. In that case, all we have shown is that the thing is dependent upon itself—which is another way of saying it is independent.

The idea of what is basic thus involves three interconnected notions: basic particulars are simple, fundamental, and independent. To be simple is to be independent of true parts. To be fundamental is to be independent not only of parts but of every other thing.

Must there be any objects in the world which satisfy these conditions? Is it necessary, that is to say, that if there are any concrete particulars at all, there must be basic particulars among them? I do not think so. We are considering spatial things here, and if space is infinitely divisible, then any extended thing, no matter how small, has even smaller portions which make it up. And it could be that every portion, no matter how small, was itself a concrete particular. In that case everything would have true parts (even though we could not separate them), and nothing would be simple.

Atomic theories of matter, of course, insist that beyond a certain point, further division of material things will not yield concrete particulars. That point is when we get down to atoms. But if this is true, it is true only as a matter of fact. It is not necessary that there should be anything at all which is simple. So at least it seems to me. But the question is controversial. Some philosophers—the most notable of them Leibniz—believe there just *must* be simple particulars.

THE CAUSAL ROLE OF PARTICULARS IN
THE PHILOSOPHY OF MATTER

A philosophy of matter endeavors to give a correct and profound account of the space-time world. If it is a system of particulars, it will develop, as we have seen, a doctrine of basic particulars, which will be simple and independent. Now a difficulty arises. What about, for example, the number seven? It has no parts (or no spatial ones, anyhow—or, at least, no spatial parts according to many of the best authors). And it does not seem to be produced by more ordinary things. Is the number seven, then one of our basic particulars?

No, we want to say. Certainly, a total metaphysic owes us some account of what numbers are, but they do not belong to the philosophy of matter. Numbers, like classes, propositions, and functions, are often called *abstractions* to signal this idea. It turns out to be a rather tricky business saying exactly what it is about numbers or propositions which allows us to ignore them in pursuing the philosophy of matter. Our first impulse, to disqualify abstractions on the ground that they are not spatiotemporal, is unacceptable. In the first place, that begs questions that should be left open, about such things as propositions and numbers. In the second place, not being spatiotemporal does *not* disqualify an entity from a place in the philosophy of matter. If the material world is a created world, that fact is of cardinal importance as a fact about matter. If must figure in our philosophy of matter. So a philosophy of matter as created involves God, and he is (at least according to many of the best authors) not spatiotemporal. Moreover, many important philosophies of matter resolve the entire space-time world into the appearance of a reality whose basic particulars are *not* in space and time at all. Berkeley and Leibniz both did this. Our first impulse, to set abstractions aside because they are not in space and time, would beg the question of the reality of spatiotemporal being. And question begging is not sound philosophy.

A better notion is this: the philosophy of matter extends to include whatever has an effect in the space-time world or in what the space-time world is resolved into. This is the basis on which God, for example, figures in some accounts.

Causality is thus an intimate part of the conception of a basic particular in the philosophy of matter. A causal role is an entity's passport into the philosophy of matter, and within that sphere, all qualities and relations rest on qualities and relations of basic particulars. In any event or process in our space-time world, the real participants, both those producing the change and those which are affected in it, are basic particulars. So we will thoroughly understand no event or process in nature unless we discover and explore her basic particulars.

If there are no true basic particulars, we must be content with the increase of understanding which comes from uncovering the successively more nearly basic objects which enter into causal transactions. Even here, the causal role of objects is crucial to their place in a developed doctrine of matter.

TEMPORAL PARTS

So far, we have drawn our examples of concrete particulars from the manifest world of everyday life. Cars, rivers, and magnets are familiar spatiotemporal objects. Having both a size and a duration, they are extended in both space and time. Like everything else of comfortably human scale, they all have spatial parts which are themselves particulars.

Do they, and other things which perhaps have no true spatial parts, have temporal parts? It seems so. Modern physics assimilates spatial and temporal dimen-

THE FRAMEWORK OF CONCRETE PARTICULARISM 33

sions, discouraging us from treating one differently from the others. And there is another, much simpler argument to the same conclusion. Consider a knife. Suppose it lasts for twenty years. Consider another knife which endures for only ten years. This second knife is still a knife, and just as much a knife as the first. If a ten-year knife is a whole knife, what about the first ten years of the twenty-year knife? Why isn't *it* a knife? Why discriminate against it solely on the ground that after ten years it was not destroyed but continued?

If continuing cannot make the first ten years something less than a knife, then knives do have temporal parts. True, these parts of knives are themselves knives. But this is only slightly unusual, not scandalous. After all, parts of rocks are themselves rocks, parts of clouds are clouds, and the spatial part of a knife which consists of all but one millimeter at the end of the handle is also a knife.

Yet the philosophy of concrete particulars does not recognize temporal parts. Let us develop the reasons for this. If the first ten years of a knife is a knife, then so presumably are one year, one day, and one minute in the life of a knife. There is no reason to stop in this process of division. But what about a knife that endured for but a microsecond? Is it a knife, though quite as useless as the mere shadow of a knife, which is not really a knife at all? And why stop at a microsecond? Many modern theories of time hold it to be continuous, so that any interval of time, however small, embraces other intervals still briefer.[5] If once we admit temporal parts, how can we avoid admitting endless division? And endless division will dissolve our familiar knife into an infinite succession of infinitely evanescent knives.

Perhaps this is the course we should take. We would have to abandon our familiar conviction that we can cut a rope with one knife. Instead, we would have to think of an infinite succession of (exceedingly similar) knives which take one another's place in the infinite succession of things we call our hand during the cutting. And the rope being cut would no longer count as one thing. But this does not seem to be an impossible way to envisage the situation. If familiar convictions rest on not thinking things through thoroughly, philosophers should not flinch at giving them up.

THE COSMOLOGY OF EVENTS

If we follow the idea that concrete particulars have temporal parts which are complete particulars in their own right, we soon travel out of the territory of concrete particulars altogether. A cosmology based on *things* gives way to one based on *events*. In a system of concrete particulars, or *substances* as they are sometimes called, the universe consists of objects. Things happen to these objects; they grow or shrink, get hot, gain weight, go musty. These happenings, or events, occur to and in objects. Events are not independent entities; they can occur only because there are objects to which they occur. They have a secondary

---

5. An exception is Whitehead's. See *Process and Reality*. Perhaps time occurs in minimum 'drops' of finite extent.

and derivative reality, being happenings or changes in objects, which are the genuine realities.

Since many happenings, the ones we call processes, take some time to be completed, they can be divided into indefinitely many subprocesses because of time's infinite divisibility. But any temporal chunk of an *object* less than its whole life is not considered to be a genuine concrete particular. It is an item manufactured by the mind, not a proper individual which goes into the composition of what it is a part of, the way the front wheels contribute to a car.

If things are thought of as subjected to a real temporal division into parts, however, the whole picture changes. There are no temporal atoms—or so most theories suppose—and so the division can continue without limit. And the resulting items are *instantaneous conditions* of regions of space. The presence of a condition such as heat, rust, hardness, or acidity, at a particular place at a particular time furnish the fundamental elements of our system. If we divide processes and subprocesses in the same way without limit, we arrive at these same instantaneous conditions, which are dubbed 'events'.

The familiar things of the manifest world image now appear as special collections of such events, collections which are stable and continuous. The cluster of instantaneous conditions at one place and time—the place where, for example, we say there is a knife—passes away into successors very close in position and quality to those that came before. When we try to describe the situation where in familiar language, a hand holds a knife and cuts a rope, we should not speak as we did above in terms of a succession of evanescent knives and hands. We should try to do without the vocabulary of knives and hands altogether. So we should say, rather, that sharpness, shininess, solidity, steeliness, and so on are instantaneously present, close to warm, soft skin character. And in regions close by one another, these events give way to others very like them, while the whole collection passes through a region of successive ropey events.

In what we call rest and stillness the successive events are so similar to one another we cannot detect change. In chaos and rapid change there is also succession, but later events differ more or less markedly from earlier ones. Stability is rather illusory, for it does not involve the very same items enduring. Stability is no more than similarity among the events in a succession. No fundamental entity endures for any time whatever. No *things* are basic in a cosmology of events, not even what we have been calling basic particulars. Basic particulars have no true *spatial* parts. But all things have indefinitely many temporal parts which are not themselves things but these special instantaneous 'events'.

The gritty, reliable, material stuff of the world is thus dissolved away into a mere flux of transient occurrences. This grates on our accustomed ways of thinking, but prejudice is no guide in philosophy. The cosmology of events takes seriously the analogy between space and time which modern physics claims. And it is well placed to deal with the revelations of particle physics about the insubstantial and unthinglike behavior of the smallest chunks of matter.[6]

---

6. See below, Chapters 7 and 14.

THE FRAMEWORK OF CONCRETE PARTICULARISM

Yet philosophers have not persevered with a cosmology of concrete particulars just out of stubbornness. They have adhered to a system of *things* principally because of the problem of change.

THE PROBLEM OF CHANGE

When the world is different from one moment to the next, we say a change has occurred. Changes in position are motions (velocities or accelerations); changes in other properties can be given another general name, such as 'alterations'. The particular complex of causes (if any) which bring about any particular change or sort of change are for special scientific investigation to discover. We look to physics, not philosophy, for a specific account of eclipses, to physiology for details of changes in our own bodies, and so on. All these special problems have different solutions, so what do philosophers mean by *the* problem of change, as if there were only one such problem?

They have meant, traditionally, how is any change, of whatever kind, possible at all? What structural features must be present in any and every instance of a change? And the answer they have given has included the requirement that *something* underlying or involved in the change remains or *perdures* through the change. Thus, if an arrow flies from bow to target (changes place), what arrives at the target is the very same arrow as the one which left the bow, (though changed in place). If a yellow door is painted green, the green object is the very same door (though changed in color) as the yellow object with which we began. In more radical changes, like making a desk out of a tree, we retain not the same tree but the same timber. When we grind wheat into flour we deal throughout with the same molecules. When a log is burnt to ash, smoke, and gas, the atoms involved remain the same throughout. Even in nuclear reactions in which atoms are destroyed, a conservation of energy principle is employed.

In all our accounts of change there is both continuity and transformation. Some perduring element in the situation provides the basis; processes which involve this basis but do not destroy its identity account for the alteration which we are explaining.

Why is this the invariable pattern of our understanding of change? Consider the alternative. Suppose that absolutely nothing perdures throughout a given change. Then what has happened is not that some object A has changed from state x to state y. Rather, situation S has been not changed into but *replaced by* state S'. And because nothing is preserved, there is no underlying mechanism or process in terms of which we can understand the alteration. One situation has ceased to exist, and another has taken its place. Why or how this has happened we will never grasp, for there is no lasting basis in terms of which to account for it.

We cannot even appeal outside nature to God's will, for example, for that would be to make God the continuing basis underlying the change. And our hypothetical example is one in which there is *nothing* as a continuing basis. So to sum up, change is intelligible only when there is both continuity and transformation. Pure replacement, in which nothing is preserved, must remain a brute fact, an impenetrable mystery.

Now philosophers have had the bad habit of concluding that what is not intelligible and explainable cannot occur. This inference is fallacious. We have no guarantee that the world is intelligible and no grounds for holding that brute facts never occur. Yet a system which does make room for understanding is for that reason to be preferred—provided it works, of course—and the theory of concrete particulars is on this score notably superior to a pure cosmology of instantaneous events. The event cosmology is one in which every alteration is a sheer replacement. There is annihilation of one situation and creation of another, and yet nothing endures to do the annihilating and creating. It is to avoid this result that in the philosophy of concrete particulars we do not find them dissolved into infinitely many infinitely brief temporal parts.

THE PERDURATION OF BASIC PARTICULARS

Concrete particulars are just the right sort of thing to provide the continuing element in change situations. The objects we describe as changing in position, or size, or shape, or texture, or composition, or smell, or whatever, are typically familiar concrete particulars. Wheels turn, sirens howl, torches flash, and aircraft land. In all these changes, the concrete particulars perdure. That is, they retain their identity, as the very same wheel or siren or whatever, throughout the change.

But all these familiar concrete particulars also enter into changes through which they do *not* perdure. Wheels collapse and aircraft crash. All our typical concrete particulars come into being and pass away, and clearly they cannot perdure in the processes of their own creation and destruction. They perdure in some, but only some, situations.

So, quite naturally, in all theories of concrete particulars a search is begun for special particulars which perdure through *all* the changes in which they are involved. These will be basic particulars. For they will have such an extraordinary measure of perduration only if they are independent and partless. We will find our basic particulars if we can find a set of things which cannot be made by any set of operations involving other things, and cannot be destroyed by any process. Any process in which something is brought into being or passes away reveals some *other* perduring structure as the true bedrock of the cosmos.

What perdures in some changes, but not all, is a derivative thing. It is dependent upon the cohesion of its parts or the continuation of its sustaining cause. What does not perdure at all is not a thing at all. It is a quality, perhaps. The color of a door, for example, does not perdure through any change in which the color of the door is involved. Or it could be an event or process, any change in which is a replacement of one state of affairs by another. What is of maximal perduration, retaining its identity through all the changes into which it enters, is a basic particular.

THE FRAMEWORK OF CONCRETE PARTICULARISM

BASIC AND DERIVATIVE PARTICULARS

In the ways touched on above, a theory of concrete particulars becomes elaborated into a theory distinguishing special, absolutely independent, absolutely perduring basic particulars from other derivative, dependent particulars which are either assemblages or products of the basic particulars.

In a theory like atomism (of which much more anon), all derivative particulars consist of assemblages of basic particulars. In a monistic theory such as Spinoza's, the derivative particulars among which we live and move and have our being are passing aspects or phases of the one true underlying reality. To put it crudely, in atomistic theories many basic particulars "add up" to a derivative particular, while in theories of the Spinozistic stamp all derivative particulars "add up" to a basic particular. But whatever the details of the way in which the derivative particulars depend on the basic, the *basic* particulars are, in the last resort, the real bearers of all qualities, the real terms of all relations, and that in which all else consists.

Thus if we wish to express ourselves with strict metaphysical accuracy, we must transform, for example, "This suitcase weighs forty-five kilograms" into another sentence which speaks only of the basic particulars upon which the suitcase depends. In atomism it will be something like "The atoms which make up this suitcase and its contents each have weights which, when combined together, form a total of forty-five kilograms." This is a particularly simple example. Again, for "Bricks are rougher than window panes" a metaphysical purist would wish to substitute "The atoms making up bricks are so arranged that the angles formed between contiguous atoms of a brick's surface are on average more acute than those between the corresponding atoms in a window pane." Derivative particulars have the properties they do have, and stand in the relations they do stand in, totally and solely because the basic particulars involved have certain properties and stand in certain relations. If God, in contemplating the universe, thought only of the properties and relations of basic particulars, he would have left out nothing. For the properties and relations of basic particulars embrace and include *all* realities, whether basic or derivative. Of course this is not always readily apparent, and it is the task of science and philosophy to show in what way the characteristics of the basic particulars present themselves as features of what is derivative.

Basic particulars are thus *exhaustive*. Everything that is, when we get to the bottom of things, when we reach through all appearance and touch reality, is a basic particular. A complete account of the world, in its most penetrating form, involves only basic particulars, their qualities, and their relations.

An important exception to the view that basic particulars are exhaustive has been the orthodox Christian position which accords to spatiotemporal things a dependent reality. Whatever should prove to be basic within the natural order—suppose it were atoms, for the sake of argument—depends not just at its creation but throughout its time of being on the sustaining activity of God. The natural order is a created order, and so incapable of independent existence. God himself is the only strictly independent and so strictly basic particular. Yet Christians are not pantheist; not every property of anything is in reality some feature of God. God is the only strictly basic particular, and yet he is not exhaustive.

Orthodox Christianity is unusual in being a system of dependent and independent particulars in which the dependent are not always *constituted out of* the independent.

Church influence on classical systems of concrete particulars is seen in a rather awkward double scheme of dependence. In the background we have the natural world dependent on (that is, created by but not constituted out of) God. In the foreground we find, among natural particulars, some dependent on (that is, made up from) other more basic ones. The systems of Descartes and Leibniz are both like this.

THE EXPLICATIVE AND THEORY FOUNDING FEATURES OF BASIC PARTICULARS

Theories of concrete particulars, then, single out a special class of objects, the basic particulars. Individually, these are simple, independent, and maximally perduring. Collectively, at least within the natural sphere, they are exhaustive. That is, whatever is, is one or many basic particulars, and all that happens, happens to basic particulars. These are their explicative features, that is, the features which we mention in explaining what a basic particular is. These features are agreed to by all who admit basic particulars, no matter how different their competing philosophies may be. But explicative features are not the whole story. Basic particulars must have features other than these. We have not yet been told which things are actually basic; we are not in a position to identify basic particulars should we encounter them. We need to know what special characteristic gives particulars the basic status which we have spelled out. Until we know more about the basic particulars, our knowledge of the world is merely formal.

This is where different theories come in. Different accounts of the basic particulars yield different philosophies of matter. Atomism is one alternative. Pantheism is another. These theories differ not over the explicative features of basic particulars, but over what kinds of object satisfy the requirements set by the explicative features. Atomists say they must be tiny, solid, massy, and in perpetual motion. Pantheists say they must be spiritual and worshipworthy.

There is nothing peculiar to metaphysics about this distinction between explicative and theory-founding features. It is to be found whenever there is a clash of theory. For example, you and I differ about the yeti, or abominable snowman. We agree over certain explicative features of yeti—let us say, that they are approximately bear-sized animals inhabiting the high Himalayas. If we did not agree over this, it would not be the *yeti* that we were in dispute over, but something else. Now you claim it is an otherwise unknown variety of giant panda, which explains how it can be a bear-sized Himalayan-living animal, while I maintain it is a tall Sherpa with a sense of humor, which also explains the explicative features from which we began. We develop our different theories by adding different additional, explanatory features to the agreed list of the yeti's explicative features.

Again, suppose you and I differ over cancer. We agree on the symptoms, the progress, and the termination of the disease. These form the explicative features, which we would use in explaining the subject of the dispute to medical students. But you hold that it is caused by a viral infection, while I say a mutation in cell proteins is to blame. We each build our theory of cancer on a new feature, no part of the explicative set, which is to account for the explicative features and, we hope, much more besides which research will uncover about cancer.

Again, two detectives working on a case may agree over who is killed, where, and when, yet differ in their theory of the cause of death, with the consequence that one suspects Nick the Knife and the other Harry the Harpoon.

Disagreement in theory occurs whenever there are different theory-founding features conjoined with a common set of explicative features. In the philosophy of matter, this situation arises with basic particulars. It arises, in fact, with something of a vengeance. There is no shortage of philosophies of matter, mutually incompatible, in competition with one another, each favoring a different choice of theory-founding features, and each in consequence building a different systematic world-picture, or metaphysic. Atomism, with its impenetrable corpuscles in perpetual collision, is one of these. Here are some other examples:

According to Leibniz,[7] nothing can be basic which is not *truly simple*. This requires that basic particulars have no parts whatever. Since everything in space is extended, and so has spatial parts, no spatial thing can be basic. Space is a mere appearance, and reality consists in simple (not material but) mindlike things, monads, all dimly conscious of one another. All monads, including ourselves, are set in a nonspatial order which they are conscious of as the spatial order. The world consists of infinitely many completely independent minds and protominds. Close similarities of consciousness among colonies of monads present themselves to *our* consciousness in the form of the cohesive material objects of everyday life. For Leibniz, the theory-founding feature is simplicity, and the consequent theory is the system of monads.

Spinoza[8] chose *radical independence* as his theory-founding feature. A basic particular, or substance, must be *causa sui*. That is, it must contain within itself the total reason for its own existence and nature. A full conception of a substance involves no reference of any kind to any other thing. What is truly independent in this way can be shown to be single, perduring, and exhaustive. Spinoza's system, built on this foundation, recognizes just one single, total, all-embracing substance which is eternal, unique, and divine. He called it *Deus-sive-Natura*, God-or-Nature; another suitable name is Everything-There-Is.

---

7. G.W. Leibniz, *Monadology*, § 1.
8. B. Spinoza, *Ethics*, Part 1, Def. 3.

The complete disparity between Leibniz's world of infinitely many separate particulars and Spinoza's world of complete interconnection within a single substance rests on the different choices of theory-founding feature in their philosophies of matter. We will return in chapter 6 to a closer look at these alternatives to atomism.

To take another example, Berkeley held that the only way in which causal interactions can be made intelligible is by basing them on the spontaneous self-generated changes of which a will is capable. Anything capable of self-initiated change is *active*, and to be active was Berkeley's requirement for a genuine basic particular. Matter was in his time notoriously passive; it changed its condition only under the influence of externally applied forces. So Berkeley's metaphysics can admit no material objects—or objects with a spatial nature, for that matter—as basic particulars. His system is idealist; that is, it recognizes as substances only minds—the infinite divine mind which creates patterned successions of ideas, and many finite created minds, such as ourselves, which receive these orderly sequences of ideas and misinterpret them as experience of a material world in space.[9]

As a final illustration, consider Minkowski's work on Einstein's Special Theory of Relativity.[10] Although not presented in this way, his treatment of the special theory belongs to the tradition of seeking the best theory-founding feature for basic particulars. Einstein's special theory deals with astonishing changes in the size, shape, mass, and velocity of material objects, and changes in their relative position in the order of events, under changes in the reference frame from which these quantities are measured. Minkowski pointed out that by insisting that the basic particulars are not familiar three-dimensional objects (atoms or whatever) but four-dimensional space-time worms not moving through but existing in an unchanging four-dimensional world, the paradoxes of special relativity disappear. When we are emancipated from the accidental standpoint of some special reference frame, we attain an orderly and coherent vision of the material cosmos. To be independent of an accidental standpoint for measurement, our basic particulars must be four dimensional objects whose "changes" are differences in quality along their length in the time dimension. Einstein accepted the four-dimensional interpretation of his theory. The natural philosophers of this century are often to be found in physics departments, but they belong to the central metaphysical tradition.

REDUCTION PROGRAMS

Every cosmology has its own reduction program. That is, in every system which identifies some special objects as basic particulars, there must also be an account of how everything *else*, everything which is not a basic particular, turns out to be, or boils down to, or can be shown to consist in or derive from, basic par-

---

9. G. Berkeley, *Of The Principles of Human Knowledge*, Part 1.
10. A. Einstein, *Relativity . . . A Popular Exposition*.

ticulars. This account is a reduction program. Clearly, different basic particulars call for different reduction programs. To reduce *A*'s to *B*s involves showing how statements about *B*s, and *B*s alone, can be substituted for all statements about *A*'s that we really must affirm.

Suppose you are an atomist and think that tables really are (nothing but) swarms of tiny corpuscles. To establish this, you must show how everything that we ordinarily and correctly say about this table—in sentences with "this table" as their subject—can be equally correctly but more accurately said in sentences about this swarm of corpuscles.

So, "This table is in the corner" is replaced simply by "This swarm of corpuscles is in the corner." "This table is wooden" gives way to "These corpuscles are of such kinds and in such arrangements as to make wood"—trusting to discover as science advances what these kinds and arrangements actually are. "This table is old" goes over into "This swarm of corpuscles has retained its cohesion and overall arrangement for a considerable period." I am sure you will be able to see how to deal with the table's being varnished, supporting the crockery, being three feet wide, and worth two dollars, even though none of the corpuscles, individually considered, is varnished, supports crockery, is three feet wide, or is worth two dollars.

In all these cases, the reduction program is dealing with reality (corpuscles) and appearance (tables). Not all sentences about tables, however, can be given this treatment. "The table is one thing" and "All parts of the table are at rest," although acceptable enough in everyday thought, are rejected as false in atomism. They are consigned to illusion, the metaphysician's third category, to be accounted for not in terms of what tables are really like, but in terms of how men come to make mistakes about the world they live in. "The table is dark brown" is a controversial example, some philosophers consigning it to reality, some to appearance, and some to illusion.

Now suppose you are not an atomist but a phenomenalist, a thinker in the tradition of Hume, Mill, Russell, and Ayer. Then your basic particulars will be some variety of *sense data*, that is, perceptions, experiences of the world as looking (feeling, sounding, . . .) thus and so. And in consequence, your reduction program for tables will take a quite different form. A table is now not a collection of corpuscles but a patterned collection of looks (touches, sounds, . . .). "This table is in the corner" can no longer have a simple reduction. It must go over into something which begins "There is a regular and reliable set of looks in which a table look is to be found close to a corner look. . . ." "This table is wooden" is reduced to "The look, touch, sound, smell, . . . of this tablish part of these regular and reliable sense data are of the type *wooden*, and so are the sense data concerning how things appear in saw-cutting and fire-lighting situations." "The table is dark brown," on the other hand, gets direct treatment: "The tablish parts of this ordered collection of visual sense data are dark brown." And "No parts of the table are in motion" emerges as a truth, which is given a normal reduction from appearance to reality.

Each cosmology has its own reduction program, distinct from others both in where it terminates and in the patterns of reduction which it uses on the familiar sentences of common life which express the manifest world image.

So far, I have spoken glibly of reduction as finding sentences about basic particulars which express the same truths as sentences about derivative particulars, but express these truths better, that is, with more metaphysical depth. But there is a philosophical problem of the first magnitude hidden in the idea of "the same truth." We can call it the problem of the reduction relation. Let p be a true sentence about tables, say, which is to be reduced, and let q be the reducing sentence, say about atoms. The problem then is, What is the logical relationship between p and q?

The sentences must at least be material equivalents; that is, they must have the same truth value. For any program which reduces truths to falsehoods or vice versa is disqualified. No falsehood can express underlying reality behind a truth, nor vice versa.

But material equivalence is much too weak a relation. It links far too many pairs of sentences. Thus if p^1 is any other truth about tables and q^1 any other truth about atoms, then p and p^1 are material equivalents, and so are p and q^1, but these pairs do *not* stand in the reduction relation to each other. They may not even be about the same part of the world.

Is the relationship, then, one of *necessary* equivalence? That is, is it not merely a fact which is so, but a fact which must be so, that p and q are equivalent? No. It is not necessary that if the table is square then some corpuscles are arranged symmetrically. For the world might have been made of Leibniz's monads. Or the basic particular might be Spinoza's God-or-Nature. In either case, although it would be a truth of appearance that the table is square, there would be no corpuscles to be in symmetric arrangement. It follows that the reduction relation cannot be necessary equivalence.

There is another argument showing this. Even supposing that atomism is the true cosmology, and even supposing that q is a full statement about corpuscles which everyone agrees is the appropriate one for reducing p, p and q may *still* not necessarily be equivalent. For q may deal with, say, the motions of corpuscles. Then q could be true even in a world in which there are no humans, and so no human purposes and no objects made or used for these purposes. But in such a world there are no *tables*, only things which might be tables in *our* world. In a world without tables, p is false, for it says something about tables. So there is a possible world in which q is true although p is false. Therefore, p and q are not necessarily equivalent, for necessary equivalents have the same truth value as one another in all possible worlds.

More generally, there can be a reduction only where there is what Quine calls a *proxy function* by means of which we can move from the original statement which is reduced to the outcome which is its reduction.[11] A proxy function for reducing the manifest world to an atomist cosmology is neither a statement in the manifest world image nor a piece of atomic theory but a statement relating those two bodies of discourse.

---

11. W.V. Quine, "Ontological Reduction and the World of Numbers."

THE FRAMEWORK OF CONCRETE PARTICULARISM 43

The need for a proxy function shows that the reduction relation is not an absolute one, a relation in which two sentences stand just because they are the sentences they are. Strictly logical relations, like contradiction, or mutual entailment, are absolute in this sense. But the reduction relation is not. It is something made by a specific theory. We should say, not just that p and q stand in the reduction relation, but that *in theory T*, they stand in this relation. For q reduces p in theory T, but not elsewhere. For example, sentences about corpuscles reduce sentences about tables in atomism, but in phenomenalism and some allied philosophies of science it is the other way round. And q, rather than q^1, reduces p in theory T if it is from q, not q^1, together with T and other contingent information, that we can infer p. The relationships between p and q are logical, but in this complex and theory-bound way. From p and others like it we reason or grope towards q and its fellows as their explanation. From q and its fellows we deduce p and others like it which serve as q's confirmation. Reality is most basic in how things are, but appearance is more fundamental in finding things out.

Now q, q^1, and so on are of course themselves part of the theory T in terms of which they are reducing sentences. And much of T may be involved in connecting q with p. So strictly, we should not say of individual sentences that they stand in a reduction relation. Rather, the whole body of sentences which make up a cosmology—atomism, say, or Berkeley's doctrine of spirits with ideas—are offered as reduction for appearance. But we can be excused for retaining the particular way of putting the matter—"p is reduced to q in theory T"—by the central and crucial place which q, a particular proposition and not a generalization like the main part of the theory T, plays in the derivation of p. I do not think anyone knows how to specify this central place with formal precision.

In discussing the reduction relation we seem to have moved some distance, from "expresses the same truth" to "holds a central place in a derivation within a theory." Why were truth and sameness of truth brought into reduction in the first place? The idea, again an intuitive rather than formally expressible idea, is this. The sentence q involving basic particulars sets out what are, if the theory is correct, the actual concrete conditions under which p is true. q specifies truth conditions for p, not in the semantical way of setting forth those circumstances which, in view of the linguistic structure of p, must hold if p is to be true, but in a metaphysical way, setting forth those particular real conditions of the world under which appearance p obtains. q, then, gives the real but obscure content of p. In this sense p and q express the same truth. To use the language of facts, the truth of both p and q rests on the same facts, but what those facts are is best set forth by q.

Reduction programs, then, are part and parcel of any theory which distinguishes basic from dependent particulars (that is, any interesting theory of concrete particulars). Each cosmology has its own reduction program, and each reduction program must deal with all the relevant phenomena as convincingly as it can, relating appearance to reality, and consigning the irreducible to illusion. It is by the success or failure of its reduction program that a philosophy of matter, and any more comprehensive complete cosmology, stands or falls.

4 Classical Atomism

THE FIRST MODERN REVOLUTION IN PHYSICS

As you should all know, a revolution in physics occurred at, and helps to mark, the onset of modern times. It began in astronomy, where the ancient, earth-centered theories of the solar system deriving from Aristotle and Ptolemy had been supreme for centuries. The essentials of the modern sun-centered view were set out by Copernicus, advanced by Kepler, and made popular and convincing by Galileo. This change, the Copernican revolution, displaced the earth, and hence man, from the center of the world, and so (perhaps) from a central place in the purposes of God. It also required a vastly enlarged universe, because no parallax differences could be observed in the apparent positions of the fixed stars throughout the earth's annual orbit of the sun. Men could now feel lost in space, which was vastly unsettling and full of consequences for mankind's vision of himself, his nature, and his destiny.

But the Copernican revolution did not, of itself, carry deep implications for cosmological theories of the nature of material things. True, the new account of the solar system did abolish the old distinction between a sublunary world of change, of generation and decay and all imperfection, and a superlunary world of serenity, eternity, and perfection. The new account opened the door to the idea that the constitution and behavior of matter "up there" was essentially no different from that which we can observe on earth. And new precision in charting the courses of comets, in which Tycho Brahe played a large part, destroyed the idea that planets and stars were set in special, invisible crystalline spheres whose rotations within one another carried the heavenly bodies on their rounds.

Some implications in the theory of matter were thus set aside. But the new astronomy did not bear directly on the crucial central problem: what is the character of matter, of rocks and rivers, shoes and ships, and lumps of sealing wax? Here men of learning continued to flounder with the four elements—air, earth, fire, and water—with moist and dry, hot and cold, with form imposed on bare matter, with essences, quiddities, and ignorance. Gassendi was attempting to reanimate the atomism of ancient Greece, the atomism of Democritus and Epicurus, which had been popularized by the Latin poet Lucretius, but labored under the crushing burden of Aristotle's repudiation.

So matters stood early in the seventeenth century when Galileo, with telescope and dialectic, was establishing the supremacy of heliocentric astronomy. Now although the new astronomy did not throw any light directly on the theory of matter, or the nature of space and time, it did set developments in train from which results in this field followed. It happened in this way:

The new astronomy, like the old, merely described the motions of sun, moon, planets, earth, stars. The old Ptolemaic system sent them along bewilderingly elegant courses built up from several circular motions: orbit, epicycle; eccentric, and so on. The heliocentric system favored ellipses. Both systems produced as consequence a description of the heavenly array which matched well enough what could be observed. Neither, since Tycho's errant comet had smashed the crystalline spheres, furnished any tolerable account of what forces, acting in what way, maintained the heavenly bodies on their paths. Why did the planets not stop? Why did they not fall to earth? What kept them so regular and predictable in their motion? What moved the earth itself? This called for more physics than just a general account of what the motions of the heavenly bodies actually were.

In the seventeenth century, more physics was provided. First Galileo went to work on discovering the relationships among distance, time, velocity, and acceleration by study of balls rolling down grooves in inclined planks. With pertinacity and genius he managed to work out the relation that nowadays we express in the equations for motion (of any body whatever): using s for distance, t for time, u for initial velocity, v for final velocity, and a for acceleration; these are:

$$v = u + at$$
$$s = ut + \tfrac{1}{2}at^2$$
$$v^2 - u^2 = 2as$$

These equations stand at the heart of *kinematics,* which is still descriptive of motion, but which embraces not just stellar motions but all motions of all bodies. Most important, a kinematics enables us to compute, for the planets as a special case, for example, what accelerations they undergo, given their distances, times, or changes in velocity.

We still lacked a credible account of what keeps the solar system in motion and what keeps it stable. We lacked any doctrine of the forces at work in the solar system producing the observed results. A crucial start on this problem was made by Galileo. He recognized that forces acting in different directions on the same body each produce their effect unobstructed by the other. And in his work on the composition and resolution of forces by the parallelogram method, he showed how to determine the resultant of many forces, or how to fix the magnitude of individual forces where only their combined effect could be observed.

It was the incomparable Mr. Newton who solved the dynamical problem of the solar system—the problem of discerning the forces at work in maintaining its motion. His dynamics, that is, general doctrine of the manner in which forces affect the motions of bodies, is based on the celebrated three laws of motion. (They could be better named, in my opinion, since they concern not just change of position over time. Newton's laws specify the effect of forces upon motions.) Let us see how they work in solving the dynamical problem of the solar system.

The first law is that of rectilinear inertia, the doctrine that bodies remain at rest or in uniform motion in a straight line, unless an outside force operates upon them. This law determines whether or not any force is acting, and of course it differs dramatically from the Aristotelian rule according to which every motion requires a force to sustain it. On Newton's scheme, not mere change of position but only change in speed or direction, that is, in velocity, requires a force to produce it. One haunting problem in astronomy—how the planets keep going *at all*—disappears in Newton's scheme. It is, in Newton's scheme, a pseudoproblem generated by failure to grasp the character of inertial motion.

The second law, that the magnitude of a force is directly proportional to the mass of the body it accelerates and the magnitude of the acceleration produced, is a law determining the size of forces. It imposes a measure of force.

The dynamical problem of the solar system is now to determine what forces, acting in which directions and at what strengths, are required to produce the effect? The effect is a stable system in which bodies orbit along elliptical paths (or, more generally, along conic sections), varying in rate as Kepler had discovered, moving faster when closer to the sun and more slowly when more distant. Newton was able to show that inertial motions (along straight lines at uniform velocity) would be transformed into just such elliptical motions under the operation of a central force, that is, a force operating along the line from the planet to the sun. He was also able to show that this force varied from planet to planet in a regular way, conforming to the most justly celebrated law of gravitation, which asserts that this central force is proportional in strength to the masses of both sun and planet (or earth and moon) and inversely proportional to the square of the distance between them:

$$F \alpha \frac{m_1 m_2}{d^2}$$

The triumph was complete. The result was stunning in its beauty and conviction. It inspired in men a new hope that they might truly understand the nature and workings of matter, because it dealt with the way matter worked on matter, and it offered a new approach to the problem of matter's inner constitution. It generated a new philosophy of matter, and no wonder. That new philosophy was *corpuscularianism,* or *classical atomism.*

Newtonian physics was a dramatic advance over its predecessors in several respects. It was more general, for it unified the earthly and celestial regions, claiming to apply to all material interactions, large and small, near or far, here on earth or beyond the moon. It was more exact, for in its kinematic and dynamical equations were set down the mathematically expressible effects of precisely quantified causes. It was more parsimonious, for the principle of rectilinear inertia removed the need to postulate forces operating merely to keep things moving. Even more important in this connection, the new physics reintroduced the idea that there is only a small number of basic ways in which matter acts on matter, that is, only a very limited variety of interactions.

The theory of matter which the new physics almost irresistibly suggested was one of the basic material objects, moving in accordance with the kinematic equations, changing motions in conformity with Newton's laws when forces were impressed, and—the third element needed to complete the picture—actually exerting forces on one another in two ways, by impact (collision) and by gravitation.[1]

Now if the common phenomena of everyday life are to be accounted for on this sort of basis, the primitive bodies in the theory must be very small. For example, try explaining the permeability of earthenware crocks, or the fact that when sugar is put in tea the level rises and then slowly descends as the sugar dissolves, except on the hypothesis that water, earthenware, tea, and sugar are made up of imperceptibly small parts with imperceptible gaps between them. So the theory of matter as composed of imperceptibly small corpuscles, which had had some currency among the Greeks, returned to the center of the stage. These corpuscles were indivisible Newtonian bodies, the smallest naturally occurring objects. They behaved in accordance with Newton's laws, interacting by impact and gravitation. This theory becomes a philosophy of matter in the hands of philosophers who are *scientific realists,* that is, people who hold that the best available scientific theory is the literal truth, the whole truth, and nothing but the truth about the space-time cosmos.

We have described the theory with some idealization. It suggests a rigor and severity beyond what most corpuscularians would have agreed to. Newton, for example, worried about whether light and magnetism could be brought into the mechanical account of matter and in his *Optics* he suggests fermentation as a further basic interaction of a chemical type. Even Lomonosov, the eighteenth century Russian who was perhaps the most complete corpuscularian, had his doubts about the material constitution of heat. But we are concerned here with the central pattern of the philosophy.

---

1. Many a scientist, Newton included, hoped that one day gravitation would be shown to be (that is, reduced to) a complicated set of collisions, on the ground that action at a distance was impossible. In retrospect, the ground seems bizarre and the hope chimerical. So let us say that two, rather than one and a half, sorts of interaction were recognized.

That central pattern was set forth by Locke at the end of his *Elements of Natural Philosophy:*

> We have hitherto considered the great and visible parts of the universe, . . . it may be now fit to consider what these sensible bodies are made of, and that is, of unconceivably small bodies, or atoms, out of whose various combinations bigger moleculae are made: and so by a greater and greater composition, bigger bodies; and out of these the whole material world is constituted.
>
> By the figure, bulk, texture, and motion, of these small and insensible corpuscles, all the phaenomena of bodies may be explained.

Corpuscularianism, then, is a philosophy of matter grounded in physical theory. That philosophy of matter is denied by idealists, phenomenalists, and monists who accept the scientific theory as a respectable and convenient intellectual structure for certain restricted purposes (such as prediction or environmental control) but do not accept it as literal, final truth.

Let us keep company with scientific realism and explore corpuscularianism more fully as a philosophy of matter.[2]

Its basic particulars are minimal Newtonian bodies. These have the explicative characters of basic particulars noted above, and to ensure their simplicity and perduration they must be indivisible, impenetrable, incompressible. They are thus of infinite hardness and infinite rigidity. They are the only bodies which present an absolutely uncompromising and inviolable surface to the world. Beyond this, when we come to their theoretical features, they have all and only those properties required for Newtonian behavior. To conform to the Newtonian physics, bodies must be capable of motion and acceleration, and they must be able to affect other bodies by impact and gravitation. So all bodies, and a fortiori those minimal bodies, the atoms, must each severally possess certain qualities enumerated by, among others, John Locke.

LOCKE'S LIST OF PRIMARY QUALITIES

John Locke, in the *Essay Concerning Human Understanding*, claimed that, for several reasons which we will go into later, all bodies are possessed of five crucial features:

    extension   (size)

    figure   (shape)

---

[2]. "Corpuscularianism" is a cumbersome term, and "corpusculism" is not English, thank goodness. Henceforward, the theory is denominated "atomism," but it must always be remembered that this is *classical* (Newtonian) atomism, in which atoms really are the smallest material things, and *not* objects composed in their turn of sundry subatomic particles.

solidity   (bulk)
motion or rest   (mobility)
number   (individual unity, collective countability).

One reason Locke did not give, although I suspect it was at the back of his mind in his self-appointed role as underlaborer to the incomparable Mr. Newton, is that without these features, matter cannot possibly behave in Newtonian fashion.

Let us see how. The material cosmos is held to be a swarm of atoms, colliding and gravitating. Collision and gravitation, and even swarming, clearly require *mobility*. Motion or rest itself requires, what Locke sometimes takes for granted, that each body stand in definite (although changing) position relative to each other body at all times. Newton assigned every body a position in an absolute space and time, which was certainly sufficient to allow mobility; many later natural philosophers have thought that something less, namely relative position, is all that is necessary. If we introduce absolute space and absolute time, as Newton did, then we are not strict atomists—we don't say, "There is nothing but atoms," but rather, "There are space and time, which are not bodies, and in them all bodies are, or are composed of, atoms." This second form counts as a version of atomism for all but the fanatically pedantic.

Now the path actually followed by any body, including any atom, depends on the collisions and gravitations it encounters. For a collision to take place, *both* objects must have a surface at which the other is (more or less resolutely) excluded. No surfaces, no collisions. Points or lines cannot collide with themselves or anything else. They pass through things. Surfaces require *size* and *shape*. The size of the atoms was unknown, except that it must be very small. Their shape was an equally dark matter. But contrary to the atomism of ancient times, Newtonian atomism favored the sphere as the only atomic shape. Spheres produce the same effects at collision no matter what their orientation, and this alone promised any manageable account of collision phenomena in precise, mathematical, quantitative general terms.

Surface is not by itself, however, sufficient for collision phenomena. Some surfaces are purely visual, for example the sky, rainbows, or the black area you see on looking into the front of a camera with the lens removed. Nothing can collide with such surfaces, for nothing encounters any resistance to its motion in traveling up to and through such a surface. Resistance to penetration is a required feature of anything which qualifies for the description 'body', and it has come to be called *solidity*, although shared by liquids and gases as well as solids in the more common sense. To say a body is *solid* in the context of atomism is to say that it excludes all other bodies, absolutely, from the space which it itself occupies. Liquids and gases do have this feature. They are more easily displaced than rigid bodies, and they get pushed aside to give way at the approach of rigid bodies, but they never strictly share place with any other body. When we say, roughly, that the stone has fallen into the water, the real situation is that the stone now fills a place recently filled by, and still surrounded by, the water. Arrows, likewise, only travel through the air in this displacing way. At no time does any place contain both arrow and air, or stone and water.

The *mutual exclusion* of bodies, what Locke sometimes calls their *bulk*, shows itself in bouncing-off behavior among rigid solids and in deflecting or slowing or heating in the case of fluids. In atomism, of course, the basic phenomenon is held to be the rebound of absolutely rigid corpuscles. The variety of effects observable on the human scale is to be accounted for by variety in the way corpuscles cluster, move, and relate to one another.

Collisions, then, require the meeting of surfaces which are surfaces of mutual exclusion. Size, shape, and solidity are required in bodies which collide.

Locke's list of primary qualities ends with *number*. This is a rather mystifying addition, for number is surely a feature of collections of bodies, not of bodies considered individually. When we say "Bodies are solid," we imply that each body is solid, but when we say "Bodies are numerous," we do not wish to claim that each body is numerous. What Locke meant, in my opinion, was that bodies need definite boundaries of such a kind that it is clear where they begin, where they leave off, and where another body of the same kind begins. Bodies have unity considered individually—they are *one* hammer, chisel, tree, rock, pool, or cloud—and countability taken together—we can count any collection of hammers, trees, or pools, and because of their distinct, bounded unity as individual bodies, we can come to a definite total in counting.

Now no one has shown that nature cannot be composed of swirling, melting, indefinite things which shade into one another, divide, separate, and reform in a flux which defies any attempt to accord unity to individuals or definite number to collections.[3] But in atomism the opposite line is taken. The basic particulars are absolutely single, as they cannot be destroyed or divided by any natural process. They have absolutely definite, geometrically precise surfaces, so that where one atom ceases and another begins is absolutely definite. Space is in one or other of exactly two states, absolutely full and absolutely empty. Where there is an atom, space is absolutely full, completely jampacked solid with matter. Where there is no atom there is nothing but space, mere void. The boundaries of these two regions are absolutely sharp. There is no graduation whatever in the presence of matter in space; it is there in maximum form or not there at all.

In this picture every basic particular is a strict unity, and every derivative particular comprises a definite number of atoms. The behavior of definite numbers of definite, perduring atoms is capable of mathematical treatment for which the new physics formed the basis.

Some definition of unity and boundaries is required for the very conception of a *thing* from which concrete particularism takes its rise. In atomism these matters become absolutely definite. By including number among the primary characteristics of all things Locke was showing, although not explicitly, his allegiance to an atomistic philosophy of matter.

---

3. As Russell put it, Is the universe a bowl of molasses or a bucket of sand?

NEWTONIAN PRIMARIES

Locke's list of primary qualities thus includes features of bodies necessary for a Newtonian atomism in which all phenomena are held to consist in Newtonian interactions, of impact or gravitation, among tiny corpuscles. But the list is not complete. Newtonian behavior requires position, which Locke recognized but did not put on the official list (perhaps because that is implied in motion).

More importantly, Newtonian behavior requires that the bodies involved possess *mass*. Indeed two species of mass are required, inertial and gravitational. Inertial mass is the inertia, the reluctance to be accelerated under an impressed force, which characterizes matter. Without inertial mass, any force whatever would induce an infinite acceleration. The same force would produce the same effect on two cannonballs, one twice as big as the other. Newton's second law affirms that the acceleration any force induces is inversely proportional to the (inertial) mass of the body involved. An orderly dynamics requires some such rule to fence us against chaos. Yet Locke's list of primary qualities includes nothing of the kind.

How did he come, in setting forth the basic features "common to all material bodies whatsoever," to overlook this? Solidity, which Locke does mention, suggests some kind of massy resistance to acceleration. Still more does *bulk*, one of Locke's alternative expressions. But we can be more exact. Solidity is what objects have which exclude other bodies at their surface. This is a feature quite distinct from inertial mass. A ping pong ball, for example, is much "more" solid than it is massive. Think of an absolute ping pong ball, always deflected, never penetrated, yet weightless (hence massless) and so subject to infinite accelerations. Such an imaginary object shows that solidity, in the sense of exclusive power, and mass, that is, resistance to acceleration, are distinct ideas. *Bulk* is a confusion of these ideas. We might say our imaginary absolute ping pong ball is without bulk (that is, without material stuff requiring a force to accelerate it). Or we might say it has bulk (that is, a volume from which it excludes other things). Let us avoid such ambiguous terms and insist that Newtonian behavior requires both solidity and inertial mass.

Bodies also require, in classical atomism, *gravitational* mass. To have gravitational mass is not to resist acceleration, but to induce it in other bodies. It is perfectly conceivable that bodies could resist acceleration yet not induce it. Or that they should have one sort of mass in different degree from the other. But they do not. In Newton's physics, the inertial and the gravitational masses of bodies are in a strict, constant relation. (With a suitable choice of units, they are equal.) This is a contingent, indeed mystifying fact. Einstein was inspired to develop the General Theory of Relativity to explain what is, in classical terms, an inexplicable cosmic coincidence.

The very fact that Einstein tried to explain this correspondence shows that gravitational mass is a different conception from inertial mass. It is clear that the theory of collision and gravitation requires that the corpuscles have both features.

The structure of classical atomism as a philosophy of matter is now set out. It is a variant of concrete particularism in which the explanatory feature of the basic particulars (corpuscles) is that they are minimal Newtonian bodies. It follows that they are possessed of Locke's primary qualities—size, shape, solidity, motion, and number—plus position, and inertial and gravitational mass. This cosmology is sometimes called the *closed billiard table* model of the universe, or *the dance of the atoms*, an image of a world as a restless, swarming confusion of tiny, massy, hard balls forever bouncing, jostling, gravitating, themselves everlasting and unchanging (except in position and velocity). All being and all becoming and passing away consist in rearrangements of atoms. The material world is at bottom colorless, lifeless, and purposeless. Although Newton, Boyle, Locke, and most of their immediate followers in the Newtonian school were Christians, it is not surprising that many felt atomism to be a cheerless, even chilling doctrine, under a suspicion of impiety. It certainly contains no flattery for vain mankind.

THE ATOMIST REDUCTION PROGRAM

As with all cosmologies, classical atomism had its own reduction program. Because atomism rested on a new physics of unprecedented clarity and precision, the reduction program was particularly clear and stark in its demands. For every genuine material property of every material body must be shown to arise from the position, motion, impact, and gravitation of its constituent corpuscles.

And ideally this demonstration must be quantitative, explaining, for example, not just why ice melts, but why it melts at just that temperature. The quantitative studies were much the harder, and hinged upon fixing quantities for the size, mass, average velocity, and average number per unit volume of corpuscles in various substances, which was all research material of great difficulty.

But in a general, qualitative way, the reduction program got off to a good start. The three states of matter—solid, liquid, and gas—through which many bodies can pass and be recovered to all appearance unaltered, lend themselves readily to an atomic account in terms of tiny bodies which are more diffused, and differently clustered, in liquids and gases (let's for the moment overlook ice and typemetal, which expand upon freezing).

That hotter and colder represented more and less rapid motions of constituent particles was an opinion already circulating which atomism naturally adopted. Thermal expansion gets a ready accommodation in the same picture (more rapidly agitated particles collide more often, keeping a wider space clear in which they themselves move).

Variations in density, as between wood and iron, for example, otherwise so arbitrary and problematical, appear readily intelligible as the more or less sparse distribution of atoms through the body. Atoms themselves, of course, all have the same nature—for example, all the same (maximal) density. This is the common nature all material things share *as material*.

Variations in texture—rough or smooth, velvety or polished, satin or chalk

CLASSICAL ATOMISM

—can be reduced, so the program would maintain, to variations in the microscopic shape of the surface involved, the positions of surface atoms with respect to their neighbors, and perhaps the pattern of grouping of atoms in the approximate plane of the surface.

The diffusion of fluoride through the water in a reservoir, the existence of apparently solid but permeable bodies, the fact that no body—solid, liquid, or gas—can be compressed into zero volume are all (at any rate apparent) successes for the reduction program.

But perhaps the most notable triumph in this endeavor was the kinetic theory of gases, which took a couple of centuries to achieve. Very early on, in Newton's time, Boyle had studied gases under compression, arriving at Boyle's law that the pressure and volume of a given body of gas are inversely proportional. And Gay-Lussac refined this result by showing how changes in temperature affected values of pressure and volume, so that (over middling ranges of the values)

$$\frac{p_1 v_1}{t_1} = \frac{p_2 v_2}{t_2}$$

Now this result can be derived mathematically from the hypothesis that a body of gas is a swarm of tiny bodies, separated by relatively large distances, in rapid motion, and affecting one another and the walls of the containing vessel by elastic (Newtonian) collision. The derivation was achieved in the Maxwell-Boltzmann theory of the nineteenth century.

The gas laws can be shown to be consequences of the atomic theory of matter. Reductions do not come any more convincing than this.

A reduction program is also, especially when the philosophy involved takes its inspiration from scientific theory, a program for research. The search for a reduction in atomist terms furnished a pattern for tackling all sorts of problems. How does the wind exert a force? How does a centrifugal separator separate? What accounts for the different strengths of different materials? (This last has no satisfactory answer within classical atomism, as it depends on interactions other than impact and gravitation, or so we now believe.) In each of these cases the answer required now has a definite form, for example: How does a swarm of agitated atoms (the wind) exert pressure on another swarm making up the sail of a windmill? Answer, in general terms: By impact. The direction of research is set and the conditions of satisfactory explanation are clear.

PATTERNS OF REDUCTION

In every atomistic reduction, some characteristic of a derivative particular, such as a table, is displayed as consisting in the possession of some characteristic(s) by the basic particulars, the atoms, which make it up. Although not all derivative particulars are comfortably human in scale (molecules, cells, and particles of talcum, for example, are not), let us for convenience's sake label the features of derivative particulars *macroproperties*, and those of basic particulars (the Newtonian primaries) *microproperties*.

Reductions then account for macroproperties in terms of microproperties. A reduction shows that inasmuch as basic particulars have certain microproperties, derivative particulars will display the macroproperty in question. In the reduction program of classical atomism there can be several different relationships between the macro- and microproperties, or several different patterns of reduction:

1. The macroproperty may also be possessed by the atoms, and the reduction consist in a straight transfer. Velocity of translation is a good example. The earth orbits the sun; this reduces to the constituent atoms of the earth themselves orbiting the sun.
2. The macroproperty may also belong to the atoms, yet the reduction fasten on different microproperties. Thus atoms have shape, but the shape of a table does not reduce to the shape of its atoms, but rather to their array, that is, their relative positions, their distances and directions with respect to one another. Similarly, atoms may be spinning, but the spin of the earth does not reduce to the spin of its atoms, but rather to an orderly pattern in the relative velocities of the atoms along circular paths (except for those atoms which actually lie along the earth's axis).
3. The macroproperty may not belong to the atoms at all. In these cases, of course, the reduction is from a macroproperty to some different property at the micro level, and these are the most interesting and controversial cases. A famous instance is that of temperature, a macrofeature which consists, according to atomist reduction, in the mean kinetic energy (a complex involving mass and velocity) of the constituent particles.[4] Atoms, considered individually, have no temperature whatever. Temperature proves to be best understood in such a way that it is defined only for collections of corpuscles. Other cases of this reduction pattern abound. Macrobodies can be compressible, malleable, ductile, acidic, rusty, and inflammable, but atoms have none of these properties. Here, as with temperature, reduction must appeal to Newtonian primaries and complex properties whose elements are Newtonian.
4. There is a fourth possible reduction pattern which classical atomism does not use. The macroproperty could be reduced to microfeatures which do not occur as properties of macrobodies at all. In classical atomism, the properties of basic particulars (the Newtonian primaries and their complex derivatives) are all themselves properties of many, if not all, macrobodies. All these microproperties are also, when present in sufficient magnitude, more or less directly open to perception and everyday experience. This gave classical atomism a reassuringly commonsensical air.

The theory did indeed involve some assault on common sense. It inherited

---

4. The velocity in question is a velocity of agitation and oscillation. It does not include velocities of translation. The velocity is measured in a reference frame in which the macrobody is at rest.

the shocking elements of the new physics, for example, that not all bodies come to a halt when they are no longer pushed, that not all unsupported bodies fall to the earth, that some rapid motions can be quite unnoticeable. The theory also alleged that all objects, no matter how apparently serene, were in reality swarming with internal motions, and no matter how apparently solid, really contained empty spaces.

Nevertheless, classical atomism credited atoms only with imperceptibly small degrees of familiar properties certifiably present in the manifest world. When the further, bolder step is taken, of introducing as microproperties features unknown among macrobodies, this fourth and most radical pattern of reduction is made possible. Leibniz did this in describing his monads, Boscovich with his material points, modern physicists with their fundamental particles and quarks.

The microproperties in these cosmologies are not merely imperceptible, but strange; they are not merely too fine for perceptual discrimination, but altogether different from perceptible properties. This has the often mentioned consequence that we "cannot form a picture" of these worlds and clearly gives rise to serious epistemic problems about how any such theory could be properly understood, let alone justified as a rational hypothesis. These problems are still very much alive, but they belong to epistemology, which is not our main concern, and that gives us an excuse to bypass them.

THE INITIAL PHILOSOPHICAL ASSAULT ON CLASSICAL ATOMISM

The corpuscularian philosophy—classical atomism—was a scientific realism based on the new physics of Galileo and Newton. It inspired the opposition both of those who rejected any form of scientific realism, and of those who clung to the older, Aristotelian tradition in physics. Both sorts of opponents tried to strangle atomism at birth, before it had the chance to show its paces. Of those who resisted scientific realism, who declined to accord to developing science the honor of telling the whole literal truth about the material world, we will speak later.

Here let us turn our attention to two doctrines which belonged in earlier physics: the categorial distinction between quality and quantity, and the impossibility of the void.[5] If either of these doctrines is true, then atomism is a mistake not just in detail but in principle, a totally confused and impossible account of materiality and change in space-time. Both doctrines are general, a priori, and so "philosophical" in flavor, and both drew argumentative replies of a rather philosophical kind from defenders of atomism.

First, then, quality and quantity. The problem concerns the relation between a "difference in kind" (a matter of quality) and a "difference in degree" (quantity). According to the atomists, corpuscles do not change at all "in themselves";

---

5. For a fuller account of these questions, see R. Harré, *Matter and Method*.

all alterations, of whatever kind, are in reality changes in atomic positions and motions. That is, all changes can be expressed in terms of a change in the numerical values of relevant distances, directions, velocities, and accelerations of atoms. With the exception of shape, the Newtonian primaries are all quantities. That is, they are all subject to measure, and changes in them are all quantitative changes. So far as shape is concerned, atoms of course never change. Changes in the shape of macrobodies reduce to changes in the measurable *quantities* of direction and distance among atoms.

But according to the old doctrine, quality and quantity are "categorially" (roughly "absolutely and unbridgeably") distinct, and changes of one type can never consist in, or reduce to, changes in the other. After all, we can imagine the argument run, changes in quantity will only give you more or less of the *same* quality. Difference in degree will never amount to a difference in kind. They will never lead to any *different* quality. That requires qualitative change. So classical atomism, which seeks to reduce all change to quantitative change, is barking up the wrong tree entirely.

Robert Boyle, Earl of Orrery, a great experimenter and publicist for classical atomism, attacked this argument by plausible counterexample.[6] Consider an egg. It starts its development with the familiar yolk and white within and finishes with a chicken. Qualitative changes have occurred. On the plausible assumption that nothing chickenish has entered the egg from outside the shell, and that qualities of white and yolk have not departed through the shell to reveal a pre-existing chickenishness which they previously disguised, what can have happened *except* that the material inside the shell has been rearranged?

Quite a number of things *may* have happened, or course, but the strength of Boyle's position lies in this: until some convincing alternative account of the development of chickens is produced, we have no right to deny that rearrangement (quantitative change) has given rise to qualitative change. And if that can happen in an egg, why not elsewhere in nature? Boyle does not even need to show *how* quantitative change can give rise to qualitative; it is sufficient to establish that it (probably) does, and the a priori denial of such processes is discredited. Indeed, looking back from the twentieth century, it is rather hard to understand why people were so confident of the a priori principle in the first place.

The second philosphical challenge to atomism concerned the void. Void is empty space, and the atomist's world was a void in which atoms moved. All space was either absolutely full (a plenum), where an atom was, or absolutely empty, where there was no atom. Yet the void was something of a scandal. It was too much like nothing-at-all for comfort. People do not in general think nothingness exists. Descartes, for example, argued that to say there is a void between two atoms is to say there is nothing between them. But if there is nothing between them they must be touching, and so no two things can be separated by a void.[7] This argument begs the question at issue, for to say there is

---

6. R. Boyle, *Origin of Forms and Qualities.*
7. R. Descartes, *Principles of Philosophy,* part 2, § 18.

a void between two atoms is to say, not that there is nothing between them, but that there is *nothing but space* between them. Then the real question emerges clearly: Can there be nothing but space anywhere?

Gassendi tackled the void problem on behalf of atomism.[8] The argument he dealt with was Aristotelian in inspiration and ran as follows. Everything that exists is either a substance (a concrete particular) or an accident (a property of a concrete particular). So space is either a substance or an accident. If it is a substance, then wherever there is space there is a thing. If it is an accident, an accident can only exist where the substance of which it is an accident exists, and so again wherever there is space there is a thing. But a void is a place where there is nothing, so there is no void.

Gassendi replied that what this argument shows is *not* that the void is impossible, but rather, that not everything is either substance or accident. The argument shows, he claimed, that space has some special third status, neither substance nor accident, and on this basis a void is possible after all.

This is one possible line of reply. Newton in effect took another line. He affirmed (though not in these terms) that space was a substance. Wherever there is space there is indeed a thing, and so where there is only space there is not nothing at all, but nothing but space, that is, a void. This interpretation of a void forms part of Newton's *absolute* theory of space, according to which space is an infinitely extended, sempiternal, uniform Euclidean entity (a void no less) in which atoms (and all other material things) live and move and have their being.

So a Newtonian version of classical atomism is more accurately described as space-plus-atomism. A pure atomism, according to which there is strictly nothing spatiotemporal except atoms, needs some reductive account of space which analyzes it in terms of relations among objects and denies that it is a thing in its own right. Such relational theories, which derive principally from Leibniz,[9] are very much live options in the philosophy of space and space-time. But this is a highly complex field, and we must postpone entering it.

OTHER LINES OF ATTACK ON ATOMISM

As well as the attempts to destroy atomism in its cradle, two of which we have just discussed, the theory was subject to several quite different and more serious lines of attack. The complaint that it was soulless and impious because it left out gods and angels, hearts and souls, need not detain us. Atomism was a philosophy of matter. It did not in itself claim to deal with all existence; that is characteristic of *materialism*, which is a total cosmology. In fact almost all atomists from the seventeenth century through to the nineteenth were Christians, or at least believers in worlds beyond the spatiotemporal. By curious accident the few materialists there were, such as Hobbes in England and Holbach in France, tended not to be atomists in their philosophy of matter.

---

8. P. Gassendi, *Syntagmata*.

9. See the Leibniz-Clarke correspondence, particularly Leibniz's third, fourth and fifth papers.

THE PHILOSOPHY OF MATTER

But there were three lines of criticism which we will follow up, for besides casting light on the credentials of atomism, they show by example the ways in which a cosmology is vulnerable to critique and replacement. It was charged that:

1. Atomism is defective because its reduction program fails to account for a special set of qualities, the 'secondaries' (color, taste, smell, and the like—qualities apparently more aesthetic than scientific in character).
2. Atomism is defective because it makes a totally wrong identification of the basic particulars. Its reduction program is misdirected. It strives to reduce appearance to the wrong reality. This was the view of (among others) Spinoza, Leibniz, Boscovich, and Berkeley, each of whom had his own alternative to urge in atomism's place.
3. Atomism is defective because it cannot accommodate within its reduction program qualities and connections uncovered in subsequent scientific investigation. Atomism, in this view, was a heroically bold and successful general framework-hypothesis for physical science. It gave direction and purpose to investigations into all sorts of phenomena. In so doing, however, it prepared its own ruin, for under the auspices of atomism, scientific research took the form of seeking in the microscopically tiny the key to the understanding of the large and familiar. But the microworld proved uncooperative; phenomena on the microscopic scale proved resistant to reduction within the terms of classical atomism. According to this third criticism, atomism is vulnerable to empirical refutation, as are all serious cosmological theories. The difference between atomism and more typical scientific theories is that atomism is so general its downfall requires a whole new cosmological vision; the change involved counts as a revolution in our view of the world, not just an adjustment.

Here are three charges against atomism. Let us consider them in turn.

5 Primary and Secondary Qualities

THE PROBLEM OF SECONDARY QUALITIES

The world about us seems to contain objects with color, smell, taste, and sound. The *manifest image* of the world is rich with an interest, life, and variety for which these qualities are chiefly responsible. It is these qualities, more than others, which give our environment beauty and ugliness. It is these qualities, more than others, which inspire and are used in the arts, which fire and sustain the passions, which attract and repel us and so influence our actions.

Yet in the *scientific image* of classical atomism they seem to have no place. The atoms dance their jig of collision and gravitation, but red and green, bitter and sweet, shrill and dulcet are no part of the description given them. This cosmology provides a bleak landscape: bare, cold, forbidding, inhospitable, without variety, and without interest. Classical atomism, like many other cosmologies, offered no reduction for the very qualities most prominent in the manifest image. Part of the romantic reaction of the nineteenth century was a protest at this uncongenial, ascetic world picture.

Because it offered no reduction of these prominent features of the manifest world, atomism seemed to be seriously incomplete. But it could be saved, as a complete account of physical, spatiotemporal reality, if these embarrassing irreducible qualities could be reassigned to a distinct, subjective, even mental, and in short *secondary* status. In that case color, warmth, and felt texture would not be true, first-grade properties of physical objects. They would belong to appearance rather than physical reality. To reduce them to qualities of collections of atoms would not be necessary. Indeed, it would not even be possible. So the lack of reduction would not be an embarrassment to atomism any longer.

Dividing qualities into two groups, the primary and the secondary, was the strategy of Locke, and indeed of many a philosopher seeking to defend the completeness of the physicists' account of the space-time world. Democritus, a philosopher of ancient Greece, for example, is reported to have said that "by convention there is sweet and sour . . . in reality there are Atoms and the void." And in our own day J.J.C. Smart has continued the same tradition.[1]

What any doctrine of secondary qualities must do is provide a convincing explanation of why there is no reduction of those secondary qualities to characters of atoms (or whatever the basic particulars are in our cosmology). This explanation must not just *assert*, but *show*, that the secondary qualities are not, directly and straightforwardly, qualities of physical things. Unlike the favored primary qualities, secondaries must in some way depend for their existence on the presence and contribution of the observer who experiences them.

So it will not do to baldly claim that size, shape, and motion, for example, are primary and exist independently of any perceiving experience of them, while colors, sounds, smells, and the like are secondaries which owe their existence to the presence of a perceiver endowed with color vision, hearing, and sense of smell. We must be given some reason to believe this claim, or it amounts to begging the question of the completeness of the atomist theory of physical nature.

Nor will it do to point out that perception of color, sound, taste, and smell involves *sensations*, which are psychological phenomena (and hence may be subjective and no proper guide to impersonal physical reality), while the perception of position, size, or shape seems to involve no comparable specific sensual experience. For on ships, trains, lifts, and roller coasters we can "enjoy" vivid sensations of motion, and yet motion is claimed as a primary. Similarly, perception of heat and cold involves sensations, and yet the reduction of temperature in classical atomism is claimed as one of its triumphs, a triumph establishing the complete physical reality, independent of observers, of heat and cold. Yet again, the textures rough, smooth, slippery, sticky, and so on furnish sensations to the sense of touch, and yet textures of surfaces are primary. And solidity, the most primary primary of all, can be felt and thus yield sensations.

A more sophisticated version of this "sensation" doctrine might hold that the perception of primaries may or may not involve sensations, but that in the perception of secondaries there always is a sensation, and *that is all there is* in the secondary case. Locke held that colors and tastes were properties of perceptions which sprang from 'powers' of the object perceived. These powers were powers to produce certain types of perception, of course, and they were dependent on the primary qualities (the qualities on Locke's famous list) of the minute particles of bodies.[2] Now this might be true. But the crucial question here is, what reason can there be for thinking so? Why should we think there is anything especially subjective about colors or tastes? Unless we are given a reason, this is just another way of *assuming* that atomism is a complete account of matter.

---

1. J.J.C. Smart, *Philosophy and Scientific Realism*, chapter 4.
2. Locke sometimes called these powers in bodies 'secondary qualities'. They are a special type of physical property, with nothing subjective about them. We might call them 'secondary qualities in bodies'. See footnote 5, p. 62 below.

One attempt to give such a reason is to point out that secondaries are sense specific, accessible to one sense only, while primaries are accessible, in appropriate cases, to many senses. This does seem to be the fact of the matter; we can see and feel size, shape, and motion, but we can only see colors and only hear sounds. But this does not show that physical things do not have colors and tastes in just the same objective, impersonal way that they have position and solidity. For suppose human beings were endowed with an additional sense by which they could detect magnetism. Suppose we could tell by a special sensation in the diaphragm, the direction and strength of the magnetic field where we are. This would be sense-specific perceptual information. But the fact that it is sense specific would have no tendency whatever to show that magnetism is in some way subjective, perceiver dependent, and ontically second rate. And in general, the fact that some quality is sense specific does not show it is secondary.

Another reason for thinking that some qualities in our perceptions arise from quite different powers in bodies is this: when we explain our perception of, for example, shape, we must make reference to the real, physical shape of the thing perceived, while in explaining perception of color we do not refer to color itself in objects, but patterns of wave-length distribution in the light leaving the colored surface. But this difference in our explanations of the perception of various qualities only arises once we have *already* decided that color, for example, is secondary. Once we have decided that color is not part of the physicists' account of physical reality, and that the physicists' account is complete, we set about finding an explanation of color vision which makes no mention of the independent physical existence of color in objects. Unfortunately, this procedure begs the question at issue here. For the question is whether or not the physicists' account *is* complete. So we must not assume that objects are not, in themselves, colored in the same way that they have shape and are solid.

What we need is a criterion for marking off primary from secondary qualities which provides a rationale for the view that secondary qualities differ from primaries in their standing as features of the real world, and differ in such a way as to justify the view that secondaries belong not so much to the physical world as such, but rather to the peculiarly human perspective on that world which our particular sensory endowment gives us.[3]

LOCKE'S ONTIC CRITERIA

Locke made two attempts to provide just such a criterion.[4]

First, universality. Some qualities are truly universal; that is, any and every material object, no matter what its size or complexity, has these qualities. Locke

---

3. The labels 'primary' and 'secondary' have also been used to mark *epistemic* distinctions, distinctions in the kind and value of knowledge gained in perception of the various qualities. This has resulted in a good deal of confusion in the philosophy of primary and secondary qualities. See my "Primary and Secondary Qualities."

4. J. Locke, *An Essay Concerning Human Understanding*, book 2, chapter 8.

thought size, shape, and solidity were among these. In modern particle physics this claim appears at best doubtful, but let us admit position, for the sake of argument, as universal. Locke suggests that all and only universal qualities are primary. Universality indeed seems *sufficient* for primacy, for a quality belonging to all bodies, including imperceptible ones, can scarcely be an artifact of the peculiarities of the distinctly human perceptual system. But universality can hardly be a *necessary* condition for primacy. Not all objects are magnetic, or elastic, or radioactive. These are not directly perceptible qualities, so cannot be secondary.[5] Their objective reality can be called into question only in a philosophy which calls into question everything imperceptible. If we allow that there may be real qualities for which we have no direct detecting sense, then magnetism and radioactivity, although not universal, have a perfect title to primary status.

Furthermore, as mentioned above, not even shape and solidity, which are perceptible and yet primary on all accounts, can be claimed to be universal in the light of modern developments in physics. So the universality test fails as a criterion of primacy.

Locke's second criterion is essentiality. Some qualities have, in this view, a very special status: they belong to the *essence* of matter. That is, we cannot think of a material thing without thinking of it as having these special characteristics, just as we cannot think of a cat, for example, without thinking of an animal. In Locke's words, the mind finds these qualities (he meant his famous list: size, shape, solidity, motion, and number) "inseparable from its thought of any material thing whatever."

This criterion is even stronger than universality; qualities which belong to the essence of matter would have to be universal not merely as a matter of fact, but of necessity. Just which qualities, if any, are essential to matter is a hard question, and it is discussed further below. Here we need only point out that being essential to matter is at best a sufficient, and cannot be a necessary, condition for primary status. The examples of magnetism and radioactivity used above in discussing universality show this. They are primary but not essential.

More generally, matter may in fact exist in several ultimately different forms; suppose there are just two forms, types A and B. Then the qualities which *distinguish* type A matter from type B matter will be primary, but not universal (since type B matter does not have them). Still less will they be essential, for type

---

5. In ibid., § 26, Locke suggests that some characteristics of bodies, whereby they produce effects in other things, may be called 'secondary qualities mediately perceivable'. Such characteristics alter primary qualities of other bodies so that these other bodies look different to us. And it might be suggested that magnetism and radioactivity were like this, acting on instruments through which we detect them. But what Locke calls secondary qualities, mediately perceivable, are by his own description fully effective physical features which exist quite independent of perception. So there can be no excuse for not being able to reduce them to combinations of features of atoms. *They* must figure in any complete account of physical reality. So as we are using the terms, they cannot count as secondary. Secondary qualities, mediately perceivable, are one variety of secondary quality in bodies.

PRIMARY AND SECONDARY QUALITIES

B matter is *matter*, but not matter with these qualities. So essentiality also fails as a criterion for the primary status of qualities.

In passing, we should note that in a world so various as ours it would be rather surprising if primary qualities were either essential or universal. Only if we get hypnotized by Locke's list of rather *basic* qualities—size, shape, motion, and so on—and forget all the explosive, corrosive, adhesive, or electrical features which some bodies have and others lack, could we be tempted to propose such strong criteria. The distinction between fundamental and derivative *primary* qualities, which must not be confused with the distinction between primary and secondary qualities, is discussed below.

THE INTERACTION PATTERN CRITERION

We are still without a general principle distinguishing the so-called secondary qualities from primaries in such a way as to show that there need be no reduction of the secondaries. How would we expect an objective, observer-independent quality to differ from one arising out of the commerce of the world with a particular type of perceiver? One reasonable answer is that a quality P existing independently of perception and knowledge would make a difference *within* the inanimate world. That is, in having P, an object would have a pattern of actions and reactions with objects in its environment.

For example, cubes don't differ from spheres just in perception. They don't just look and feel different. Cubes behave differently on inclined planes, sliding instead of rolling. The effect of a push on a cube at rest is not the same as the effect of the same push on a sphere. Cubes roll differently, bounce differently, stack differently. A cube differs from a sphere in whether twisting it a little will make a difference as to whether it will pass through a given hole. Cubes and spheres of the same volume need different quantities of paint to cover them. And so forth indefinitely.

To summarize, cubes differ from spheres not only perceptually, but also in each having its distinctive pattern of interaction with other objects. These distinctive patterns belong to the qualities *being cubical* and *being spherical.*

In like manner, things that are strong or weak, magnetic or nonmagnetic, electrically conductive or insulative, acid or alkaline, explosive, solid, two centimeters long, rusty, malleable, boiling, and so on all have their distinctive ways of acting on and being affected by their surroundings. These patterns of interaction are special and peculiar to the particular quality they belong with; all and only spheres, for example, have exactly *that* pattern of interaction which is characteristic of spheres. Furthermore, we can specify these interaction patterns without any mention, at any point, of how things seem to perceivers, human and otherwise.[6]

---

6. We would not of course *know about* these interaction patterns unless we could perceive. But what we do know about is something other than perception, just as when an astronomer talks about Jupiter he speaks of a planet, not of the image in his telescope without which he would not know what he does about Jupiter.

Now if there are any perceptible qualities *without* one of these distinctive and observer-independent interaction patterns, these will be secondary. Here we have what we seek, a feature which sets some qualities apart in such a way as to show that they are not fully a part of the objective world independent of man's experience. Such qualities cannot be expected to have a reduction within atomism or any closely related cosmology. To possess an interaction pattern is to be primary. To lack such a pattern is to be ineffective except in respect of observers.[7]

Whether a quality P is primary or not is a matter for empirical investigation, that is, the search for an objective pattern of interactions. This pattern may be a very subtle one, as in the case of sounds. But this investigation does not require us to assume in advance any particular general cosmological theory. We do not beg the question for or against atomism in our search for interaction patterns. With atomism, as with any other cosmology, if there is any quality P which proves to be primary, but which is neither a basic character in the cosmology nor capable of reduction in it, then the existence of P refutes the cosmology, at least as a *complete* theory. And if there should prove to be qualities (colors, tastes, smells, or sounds, perhaps) which figure prominently in our apprehension of the world but make no discernible difference to how that world itself runs, then this very fact about them gives us reason to think that an account of *physical* reality which leaves them out is not for that reason incomplete.

Whether any qualities actually are secondary, whether, that is, they lack an interaction pattern with inanimate nature, is a matter for empirical research. As I understand the situation, all discernible characters of sounds can be linked with peculiarities in the pattern of pressure waves which the source of the sound sets up in the air. Each of these has a subtle interaction pattern of its own; for example, it can be "displayed" on an oscilloscope coupled to a microphone, that is, has peculiar interaction patterns with a specific electronic machine. So if sounds are secondary qualities in bodies, then in this way they prove to be primary. They also prove to have a reduction within atomism through the kinetic theory of gases, and so they are no embarrassment to atomism as a complete philosophy of matter.

With smells, Amoore's work on the three-dimensional shapes of molecules of substances which smell is promising.[8]

Colors, however, are to my mind resisting to the last. The case for the view that color is a secondary quality on the interaction pattern criterion is set out in detail in my "Colours."[9] It can be summed up thus: No special feature in the composition of the light leaving the surface of an object is common and peculiar to each discernible shade under all conditions, but no set of conditions can be

---

7. The idea that primary qualities have a monopoly on the 'executive order of nature' is to be found in G.F. Stout's "Primary and Secondary Qualities" and D.C. Williams's *The Principles of Empirical Realism*, chapter 12.

8. J.E. Amoore, "The Stereo-chemical Theory of Odor."

9. In W. Brown and C.D. Rollins (eds.), *Contemporary Philosophy in Australia*, pp. 132–157.

singled out as those under which alone the real color can be seen. No single physical character is linked with each single color, as single physical characters *are* linked with distinct sounds.

Small wonder, if that be true, that color resists attempts at a reduction to characters basic in the scientific world-image. But if color is secondary, its existence need not precipitate the kind of crisis in the philosophy of matter which was (rightly) provoked by the discovery of, for example, electricity and radioactivity. For these qualities are primary by our criterion, and there is no evading the duty of finding a place for them, as either basic or derivative characteristics, within our physical cosmology.

THE "MAGIC" DIFFICULTY FOR THE INTERACTION PATTERN CRITERION

Every quality for which a detecting instrument can be devised is primary. For the detecting instrument only works because it incorporates in its mechanism the distinctive interaction pattern of the quality with some aspects of the environment.

But this opens the way for an objection to the interaction pattern criterion for primacy. Objects which we see as being different in color clearly have different effects on *us*. All and only purple things affect *us* in such a way as to look purple to us (in the right conditions). Now unless perception works by magic—which no sensible person believes—there must be *some* difference between the state of the visual system of eyes, nerves, and brain when something looks purple to me and my state when something looks turquoise or primrose. Furthermore, all our researches to date on the detailed workings of the nervous system suggest that the laws governing these immensely complex systems are the very laws of inanimate physics and chemistry operating in complicated conditions. Granted these two features of perception—that it is not magical and the organs subserving it conform to normal, natural laws—a human perceiver can be viewed as a complex detecting instrument. It is a detecting instrument which in some cases, the cases we have been describing as secondary, registers sameness or difference where no inanimate system will do so. But that is an accident; it just so happens that the only physical structures on which the so-called secondaries exhibit a distinctive pattern of effects are living human (and perhaps animal) bodies. But they do have distinctive effects on such living bodies, and so they are only different from the other primaries in having a rather restricted part of the world in which to show their working. Secondary qualities turn out, so our objection goes, to be after all just a special subclass of primary qualities.

All qualities of bodies are therefore primary, and all must be given a place within any acceptable physical cosmology. The attempt to separate out a set of secondaries which arise only in human observation *and are therefore not true physical qualities* fails once we take a properly scientific view of the physical processes involved in perception. So runs the objection.

Is there any way in which this objection can be answered? In my opinion, we can make progress by using the distinction, already mentioned in connection with Locke, between secondary qualities in perception and secondary qualities in bodies. On one hand we can think of the quality perceived—say, for example, the lilac color of a blossom—and on the other hand the physical state of affairs which acts on our sense organs and gives rise to our perception. In our example, this would be some state of the atoms near the surface of the flower which acts to modify the light as it falls on the surface and is reflected.

Colors offer the clearest examples of the difference between the perceived quality and what we can call its *objective correlate*. But we can make the same distinction, at least in thinking about the question, in other cases too. For example, the shrillness of a singer's voice is a quality as perceived, and its objective correlate is some peculiarity in the pattern of pressure waves in the air which are produced by the singer. With smells and tastes also, there seems to be a natural distinction between perceived quality and objective correlate.

Objective correlates are all, by definition, objectively real. And they are all, judged on the interaction pattern criterion, primary. For they are all qualities or complexes of qualities which have a distinctive impact, at least on the human bodies which detect them, and often on detecting instruments as well. This is what the objection we are considering insists on, and in this it is correct. So objective correlates belong to the executive order of nature and must have a place in any comprehensive account of it.

Having distinguished, in thought, between the perceived quality and its objective correlate, we can then ask how these are related. With primaries that are not directly perceived, there is no problem. There is no perceived quality at all, so there is nothing to distinguish from the objective correlate. Even in the case of perceivable primaries, quality and correlate are not really distinct. We cannot prize them apart. When we are not under illusion, the objective correlate of perceived solidity is solidity. The objective correlates of perceived shape, size, position, and relative motion are likewise just shape, size, and so on. The quality perceived and its objective correlate are the same.

But when we consider those qualities which have traditionally been classed as secondary, we find at least a *vocabulary* in which to distinguish the perceived quality from its objective correlate. Thus the objective correlate of felt warmth is described in quite different terms as a certain mean molecular energy. The objective correlate of color is a power to affect the composition of light. And the correlates of qualities of sounds as we hear them are patterns in air pressure waves.

Locke said that primary qualities of perceptions have their resemblances in things, while secondaries do not. I believe that what he had in mind was this difference in the relation of a quality to its objective correlate. So his idea is a perfectly sensible one. It does not deserve the derision it is apt to receive. It is not taken seriously because it gets mixed up with the disastrous notion that all perceived qualities are qualities of ideas, not of things. And to make matters worse, it gets connected with the bizarre idea that we could tell just which qualities have this sort of primacy by an introspective examination of our perceivings.

I said above that with the traditionally secondary qualities, we find at least a vocabulary for distinguishing between perceived quality and objective correlate. This was a deliberately cautious remark. Perhaps we have two *terms* (warmth and mean molecular energy, shrillness and a pressure pattern) which in fact refer to the same quality. If that is the case, quality and correlate are only apparently distinct, and if we separate them, we are being misled by a superfluity of terms.

This is the idea of those realists about perceived qualities who *identify* warmth with mean molecular energy of molecules, or smells with particular three-dimensional shapes of molecules which fit into "templates" on the interior surface of the nose. For each variation in heard sound, or felt warmth, or smelled odor, there is a single identifiable variation in air pressure, or molecular energy, or molecular shape (or anyway let us grant that speculation for the sake of argument). What could be more rational, more economical, than declaring that these physical features are what sounds, warmths, odors *turn out to be?* That is the view we adopted when we suggested that these qualities turn out to be primary.

When we come to colors, however, there is no single identifiable objective correlate for every instance of each colour. D.M. Armstrong holds that there is some very complicated and as yet undiscovered unity in the objective correlates for every instance of an object looking, say, turquoise, and proceeds to treat color like sound or, to take another example, felt textures like rough, smooth, and slippery.[10] This approach would make every quality, on our definition, a primary. But note carefully that this does *not* involve any attack on scientific realism—on the thesis that a physical cosmology grounded in a scientific theory of, for instance, Newtonian atoms, can be comprehensive and give a full account of material reality. For although this approach does demand that every perceived quality in the manifest image must be given a place, basic or derivative, within the system, it *also* maintains that such a place is available. For identifying all perceived qualities with their objective correlates provides the very place required.

I am not convinced that this identifying approach to the problem of secondary qualities is satisfactory. The case of color is particularly acute. Even if there *were* some single objective correlate of the colors to be found, I share the stubborn but unargued conviction that the physics of the situation leaves out the greenness of greens, or the yellowness of yellows. That is, the experience we enjoy in color vision seems to be inadequately treated when all we describe is the composition of light. And working back from there, I incline to the view that the characteristics of the manifest image we describe as warmth, slipperiness, sweetness of tone or

---

10. D.M. Armstrong, "The Secondary Qualities." In conversation or correspondence, Professors Brian Medlin and David Lewis have suggested that even if there is *no* unity in turquoise's objective correlates, we can identify turquoise with the *disjunction* of all the different physical circumstances in which an object looks turquoise.

taste are linked with, but not the very same thing as, their objective correlates. The shapes Amoore associates with different odors are not identical with the odors themselves. All these qualities would be secondaries in our definition, and only their objective correlates would be primaries. This has not been argued for; what kind of argument could be used? We must concede that to resist the identification of any so-called secondary quality with its objective correlate leaves us with some unpalatable loose ends in our metaphysics of matter. And it creates crucial problems in materialist theories of the mind. So the identification is tempting—suspiciously tempting in fact. It's just too good to be true—or is it?

Happily, so far as the philosophy of matter is concerned, we do not have to be so inconclusive. Either so-called secondaries can be identified with their objective correlates, in which case they are primary and no embarrassment to an atomist or similar cosmology. Or secondary qualities are distinct in a way which makes them observer dependent, and not unequivocally part of the space-time world of matter. So no place in that world need be found for them. What would give real trouble would be *primaries* with no place in our account of the physical world. That situation will be discussed in chapter 7. The existence of secondary qualities does not invalidate a concrete particularist physical cosmology which draws its inspiration from the scientific image of the world.

I think that there are primary qualities, including the objective correlates of all perceivable qualities, and some secondary qualities as well, that is, qualities in perception which are not identical with their objective correlate, such as colors, tastes, and smells. This view is not vulnerable to the "magic" difficulty for the interaction criterion; it does give to conscious experience in perception a rather special position which, in my opinion, it well deserves.

Let us proceed to a further consideration of these primary and secondary qualities.

BASIC AND DERIVATIVE PRIMARIES

Some qualities, such as solidity in classical atomism, are *basic* primaries. That is, they are qualities of the fundamental concrete particulars of the system. Other qualities, such as temperature, are derivative. They are characteristics not of basic particulars but only of complexes of them. *Being a two-foot square* is likewise a characteristic which only a complex can have. It is important to realize that derivative primaries are just as primary, just as objective, just as real, as basic primaries. What they are *not*, of course, is just as basic. They figure as *what is reduced* rather than *what it is reduced to* in the reduction program of the theory. And this very reduction guarantees their primary status.

Locke's list of primary qualities (or at least size, shape, solidity, and motion) are *basic* primaries for Newtonian atomism. And if we slide into thinking that this is a complete, or nearly complete, list of primary qualities, we can make the mistake of supposing that since the basic qualities of atomism are the only primary qualities, they must be the only genuinely objective ones, and so there is some special guarantee that atomism is the correct cosmology. Such a conclusion is quite groundless and false. The only legitimate use of the primary/secondary distinction is to single out as secondary those qualities which belong to the *manifest* world image only and so do not refute a scientific realism.

Now as theory changes, qualities can lose their basic status and become derivative primaries. In the natural philosophy of Boscovich, for example, the basic particulars are material points without size, shape, or solidity. They repel each other with forces which increase indefinitely with very close approach.[11] The solidity of complex objects is no basic quality but is consequential on the array of material points whose rapidly increasing mutual exclusion at tiny distances gives rise to the impenetrable "surfaces" of solids. Solidity, in this scheme, is derivative but still primary.

We can recognize and understand the situation better if we see that there is a hidden complexity in predicating primary qualities of objects.

THE COMPLEXITY OF PRIMARY QUALITY PREDICATION

Consider solidity. When we say "*X* is solid," we refer in part to the fact that it belongs to a class of objects which resist penetration (more or less), which bounce off one another, which cannot be compressed into zero volume, which exclude one another from a given place, and so forth. This is the interaction pattern characteristic of solids. Do we also mean that *X* is full of matter? When we discover that a 'solid' table, for example, is mostly empty space, do we discover that it is not really solid after all? Eddington and Stebbing had a famous controversy on this question during the 1930s. Eddington maintained that what is mostly empty can't be solid, and it is a scientific discovery that things we thought were solid, like tables for example, are not really so. Stebbing retorted that we know very well, without benefit of science, that tables support what is on them, cannot be walked through, and, in general, display the interaction pattern of solids, and so *are* solid no matter what science says on the matter.

This is a dispute at cross-purposes. For

X is solid

is to be understood as asserting

> *X* has such a nature *N* that it exhibits a characteristic pattern of exclusion, resistance to penetration, resistance to compression, . . . (the 'solidity' pattern) in its interactions with its inanimate environment.

There are two elements in this assertion. The first is a blank—'nature *N*'—which is there to be filled by each particular theory's account of what a body

---

11. Boscovich's theory is discussed more fully below, pp. 86ff.

must be like to exhibit the 'solidity' pattern of interactions which is specified in the second element.

An ancient and "commonsensical" view of what nature N is would be "filled right up with matter"—since solids are already fully occupied they exlude one another in the way they do. This theory is what Eddington was saying modern science has exploded. But Professor Stebbing replied as though Eddington was denying that solids really have the 'solidity' interaction pattern. Rather, Eddington was holding that the interaction pattern arises from a different nature N from what was commonly supposed. Because he did not appreciate the complexity of primary quality predication he expressed this badly by suggesting that such objects as tables and ladders are not "really" solid.

If, as in classical atomism, nature N is held to be 'composed of objects which have solidity', then solidity appears as a basic, unreduced quality in the system.[12] If, as with Boscovich, nature N is 'composed of objects which repel each other with indefinitely increasing force on very close approach', then nature N does not itself involve solidity; solidity emerges as a derivative characteristic. All these theories are theories of *solidity* because they all have in common the account of the interaction pattern which identifies that quality.[13] And in all these theories solidity is a primary.

We get into confusion because sometimes in saying

X is solid

we leave the 'nature N' space blank, meaning only that X exhibits the 'solidity' interaction pattern and has whatever it may be that an object needs to have in order to exhibit that pattern. At other times, when asserting that X is solid we are, in addition, describing it as having that particular nature which we believe accounts for its 'solidity' behavior. But once we recognize the complexity in the use of primary quality terms, we can explicity include or exclude any particular nature N from our claims, and confusion is avoided.

The complexity is there for all primary qualities. In general, to say object O has primary quality P is to say

O has such a nature N that it exhibits the P-type interaction pattern.[14]

---

12. In classical atomism, the atoms are thought of as having the 'solidity' interaction pattern because *they* are filled up with matter. Ordinary things are not filled up with matter but have enough atoms to behave in the 'solidity' way.

13. Here is another example of how agreement on explicative features (the interaction pattern) underlies dispute about the theoretical features of some subject matter. Cf. chapter 3 above.

14. There is no circularity in this. *P-type interaction pattern* is just shorthand for a description of interactions which does not mention P. Thus for solids we talk of mutual exclusion, resistance to compression, etc.; for magnets we talk of attraction and repulsion, spinning compass needles, and so on.

THE ESSENCE OF MATTER

It is clear that the 'nature N' slot can be filled in a variety of ways. Most commonly, the description of nature N will mention not P itself but other qualities of O or of O's constituent parts. Thus in atomism most of O's properties are reduced by specifying in nature N the properties of the atoms comprising O. But sometimes there are no qualities beyond P itself available in the theory, and so the 'nature N' slot must be filled by direct appeal to P. In such cases, where there is no way beyond P in accounting for the P-type interaction pattern, P is a basic or fundamental quality for that theory.

If there were a set of qualities which must be fundamental in any theory whatever, these would constitute a real and rather impressive essence for matter. They would not, of course, be the only primary qualities, but they would be features which the mind finds inseparable from the idea of matter. And this would be no merely nominal essence reflecting how a word ('matter') happens to be used. It would be a set of the features that must belong to material bodies no matter how we use words about the situation.

But the outlook on this score does not seem very bright; the chances of finding any substantial essence seem small. For there seems to be almost no assignable limit to the process of resolving the hitherto fundamental into the consequence of newly introduced bedrock. One might have thought that at least spatial and temporal position would be essential. As evidence for this, we notice that theories which do not accord spatial and temporal position to their fundamental entities—the monads of Leibniz and the infinite and finite spirits of Berkeley are cases of this—are held to be immaterialist theories, denying that matter is part of reality.[15]

There are, however, modern speculations in which *fields*, like magnetic or gravitational fields, are the basic particulars. These unfamiliar entities extend indefinitely in all directions. They can interpenetrate. They have no surfaces and do not move. Our familiar material objects—which are solid, have definite surfaces, and are located at definite places—are the result of the interplay of fields, which gives a particular region different characteristics from its surroundings.

Force fields have no size except that of the whole world, no shape except that of the whole world, no place except everywhere. Yet I suppose that they could be held to be spatiotemporal insofar as they fill and belong to space-time. The essence of matter would thus involve just *some kind of spatiotemporality*.

Some authors hold that matter is also essentially 'blind' and 'mechanical'.[16] What they mean is that whatever exhibits consciousness or purposive activity is to that extent not merely material. Where basic particulars are material, everything that happens must admit of complete explanation without reference to what the basic particulars intended, or wanted, or sought, or strived for. Ex-

---

15. Descartes identified materiality with spatiality, and here too the intimate link between the two suggests we are dealing with what is essential to matter.

16. Berkeley and Leibniz, for example.

planations in terms of purposes are called *teleological* (referring to ends in view which determine what happens now). If the ends are purposes not of God, say, or nature, but of the basic particulars themselves, the teleological explanations are said to be (not transcendent but) *immanent*.

And one traditional mark of matter is the absence of immanent teleology. Teleology's alternative is, in a broad sense of the term, *mechanism*, where events are determined, irrespective of any knowledge or desire, by objective conditions which bring them about willy-nilly. The water turning the waterwheel which turns the mill which grinds the corn is a typical piece of mechanical causation. So is the capture, transmission, and reproduction of a television image by such devices as camera, cable, and tube, although this is not mechanical in the narrow cog-wheels-and-chains meaning of mechanical.

Now the thrust and direction of scientific development ever since the breakthrough in physics achieved by Galileo and Newton has been towards the exclusion of immanent teleology from basic particulars in natural explanation.

In biology, for example, any theory which holds that the basic and irreducible particulars for explanation are organisms, or cells, or even special organic fragments of cells which exhibit an immanent teleology, is a variant of vitalism, and with the (so far) triumphant progress of mechanical biochemistry, vitalism in biology is all but dead.

In psychology, the idea that the bearer of consciousness and purpose is a complex, nonbasic particular, the central nervous system, is well established. But no more than well established. The alternative, according to which the seat of consciousness and purpose is a soul or mind which is fundamental and exhibits immanent teleology, still has, of course, many adherents.

The attempts to account for life processes in chemical terms and to interpret psychic processes as functions of the brain are thought of as materialistic developments. This bears witness that the absence of immanent teleology is thought of as distinctive of *matter*.

For my own part, I endorse the attitude Locke expressed when he said that had He chosen, God could have endowed matter with the capacity to think. It could have turned out, although at the present time this seems unlikely, that the basic particulars of spatiotemporal reality are endowed with consciousness and purpose. And had that been the case, any dispute over whether or not to *call* them material particulars would be an essentially trivial verbal wrangle. The absence of immanent teleology is essential to matter only in an unimportant, 'nominal' sense.

SECONDARY QUALITIES

The attribution of primary qualities is complex and involves two elements, as we saw above. If we understand the attribution of secondary qualities to objects as also being complex, we find in the difference between the second elements another way of setting forth the distinction between primaries and secondaries.

By definition, secondary qualities enter into no distinctive pattern of interaction with inanimate nature. This crucial difference shows up in the complex form of secondary quality descriptions. We will not be able to speak of any interaction pattern, but will need to make reference to how X appears to some observer(s). "X is red" could be used to express just how X looks to me. Then its complex expression is:

> X has such a nature N that it appears to me now as red.

Or it could take a form that singles out some conditions of observation and types of observer as standard. Then

> X is red

has the complex expression, for example

> X has such a nature N that it would appear, in noonday sunshine to normal observers, as red.

In both cases, there is no getting away from reference to how something seems to some perceiver. For secondary qualities are just exactly those which play no part in the course of inanimate, observer-independent nature. The fact that an observer must be brought into the picture is what justifies treating secondary qualities as belonging to appearance rather than physical reality.

When we come to fill in the 'nature N' blank, what goes there is the *objective correlate*, the complex of primary, physical features of X which give rise to its red appearance. This will change from case to case (sometimes selective reflection, sometimes selective scattering, sometimes a special pattern of emission of light) and will change as our overall theory of color alters. In every case, primary qualities will specify the nature N. And if we are right that secondary qualities are different from their objective correlates, then nature N will never mention the perceived quality of color, or taste, or smell, or whatever secondary quality is involved.

Here we can see what lies behind the idea that primary qualities are to be distinguished from secondary qualities according to whether they do, or do not, figure in our explanation of how we come to perceive that quality.[17] Some primary qualities are perceptible, and for them, we have not only the complex expression mentioning interaction patterns, by which they are defined, but also an additional complex expression referring to perception. Thus, for squares of a human scale,

---

17. This difference between primaries and secondaries cannot be used as a definition, as we saw above. But it is a real difference all the same.

X is square

is true if and only if

> X has such a nature N that it appears, to normal observers, in standard conditions, as square.

Now in such a case we can fill in the nature N just with *square* or with what square reduces to in terms of basic primaries. So that we explain why X *looks* square by pointing out that it *is* square. With the secondary qualities, however, this agreeably direct procedure is not available.

An air of circularity hangs over the suggestion that we can more fully express

> X is red

as

> X is of such a nature N that it would appear, to normal observers in standard conditions, as red.

But no real circularity is involved. The more primitive idea, in the complex expression, is *not* 'red' but 'appears as red'. This quality, *looking red*, can be specified directly, by ostension. That is, by pointing out instances of looking red, which we do on the assumption that the learner has color vision like the teacher's. We do not need to refer to how things actually are. In particular, we do not need to refer to whether or not they are 'really red'. And if something does *look red* in the right conditions, then it *is* red.

So in the case of the secondary qualities, things are as they seem. Provided we are in the right conditions, if things look red, then that is enough; they are red. But with primary qualities it is different. Some primaries are not perceptible at all; for example, there is no such thing as looking magnetic, or looking ductile, or looking acidic. With perceptible primaries, the quality a thing *has* is determined by its interaction pattern, not by how it looks. In these cases, something can be quite different from what it seems. How things look is not the final determinant.

There is no such thing as being wrong about a secondary quality—if we're in the right conditions. But this security from error is bought at just the high price we would expect. We can't be wrong about secondary qualities precisely because secondary quality descriptions concern how things seem rather than how they are. They concern appearance and are no direct guide to reality.

The existence of secondary qualities cannot show that an atomist concrete particularism is inadequate. Let us now turn to consider the second charge against atomism, that it completely misidentifies the world's basic particulars.

6 *Alternative Particularist Systems*

Some of the greatest minds of the seventeenth and eighteenth centuries rejected classical atomism as a physical cosmology. Three such were Spinoza and Leibniz, the celebrated seventeenth century philosophers, and Roger Boscovich, a Dalmatian Jesuit with a wide variety of accomplishments in science and the arts, who lived in the eighteenth century. In each case, the alternative system proposed was in its own way a theory of concrete particulars, but for various reasons these philosophers maintained that the basic particulars in which the world consists could not possibly be Newtonian atoms. This is obviously not a book about Spinoza or his rivals—they all deserve many volumes to themselves. And the refutation of classical atomism was, except for Boscovich, almost an incidental side-issue to the central concern of their thought.[1] Yet it is instructive to look briefly at how their philosophies diverge from classical atomism and its modern derivatives, if only to see more clearly the pattern of doctrines, in logic and metaphysics, to which a "scientific" philosophy of matter stands committed.

SPINOZA'S COSMOLOGY

Although Spinoza's cosmology is a form of concrete particularism, it could scarcely be more different from classical atomism. In his system there is only one basic particular or substance, God-or-Nature *(Deus-sive-Natura)*. This substance is self-creating, infinite, eternal, undivided, and complete. These are the divine characteristics, and so the substance which has them is to be named 'God'. But further, this substance is not different from but the same as the whole space-time

---

1. George Berkeley was a fourth great dissenter, and the destruction of classical atomism was an important ingredient in his philosophy. Only keeping to a tolerable length has excluded him from consideration here.

frame and everything in it. For outside of God, claims Spinoza, nothing can either be or be thought of. So the single substance in Spinoza's cosmology is also the natural world considered as a unified whole. It merits the name of 'nature' also. Spinoza's philosophy is pantheist; what there is, the only real substance, is the natural world—but that thing is also divine. Another name for it could be 'Everything-There-Is'.

This one substance has infinitely many attributes, of which extension and thought are the two known to us. All familiar, limited, transient things, including ourselves, are *finite modes* of the one substance. The best way I can think of to explain that is to consider the waves on the ocean. There is a sense in which the waves are things; they are more or less distinct from each other, and they come into being, last for a while, then pass away. While they last, they have their own characteristics, as surfers well know. Yet waves are not truly things in their own right. They exist as elements in the form or configuration of the real thing which is the ocean. When waves come into being or pass away, what has happened is that the enduring reality, the ocean, has taken on first one wave form and then another. Waves are not substances, not basic concrete particulars, but aspects of something else.

For Spinoza, all familiar concrete particulars such as bricks or planets or the ocean itself are, like waves, passing forms which God-or-Nature takes on. They are not individuals in their own right, and it is correct to speak of them as things only so long as this is borne in mind.

How did Spinoza reach such a position? You will remember that among the features of basic particulars or substances is *independence*. A substance must exist as itself, and not as the dependent of something else. Spinoza gives an absolutely rigorous interpretation of this independence condition. He defines *substance* as that which is in itself and is conceived through itself.[2] So that a wave, which does not exist in itself but by way of the ocean, or the Cheshire cat's smile, which needs a cat for it to be the smile of, cannot be a substance. Again, a fullback, or a younger son, can be thought of (conceived) only by reference to something other than itself (a football team or a family). So 'fullback' and 'younger son' are not names of substances either. The independence Spinoza demands is total; a substance must be *causally* independent (owe its existence to no outside being) and *logically* independent (be capable of complete description without mention of any reality external to itself).

From the independence requirement it immediately follows that there can be no creation of substances.[3] For whatever is created is dependent for its existence on something outside itself, namely, its creator.

To reach the other conclusions which Spinoza needs, we must add to the independence requirement a further premise, which he leaves unstated: A thing is the totality of its properties. What does that mean? Well, whenever we try to say what a thing is, we describe it. That is, we list some of its properties. We say, for example, that it is a wooden chair with a woven rush seat, turned legs, a covered

2. B. Spinoza, *Ethics*, part 1, definition 3.
3. Ibid., proposition 6.

back, screwed and glued, varnished and rather knocked about. The more fully we describe it, the more properties we list, the closer we get to saying completely what it is. The premise Spinoza needs claims that a full list of properties would exhaust the reality of this chair. The properties constitute the thing, whether it is an artifact such as a chair or any natural object.[4]

If a thing just is the totality of its properties, we can draw further Spinozistic conclusions. There can be no interaction among substances. For suppose there were two substances x and y which did interact. The interaction would have an effect on x. That is, it would give x properties, and these properties could be fully described only if their cause y were mentioned. Because x just *is* all its properties, if x did not have these properties y gave it, it would not be x but something else. So the thing which is x can only be fully described through mention of y. Thus it cannot be conceived through itself and so would not be a substance after all.[5]

A substance is, in Spinoza's terminology, *causa sui;* that is to say, its essence involves existence.[6] In other words, it cannot be clearly thought of except as existing. And it has this astonishing characteristic because it contains within itself the complete explanation of how it comes to have every property it does have. We can perhaps understand this idea better by thinking of more and more comprehensive systems as our units. Thus if we wish to explain why a species of fruit bat is flourishing in a certain area, we may appeal to the availability of fruit (something external to the bat), which in turn depends on the level of pollination by insects (something external to the fruit). But if we consider the whole forest region as a single ecological system, then the factors which account for a goodly bat population (a feature of the ecological system) are other features of the same system. It is from *within* the ecological system considered as a unit that we account for the features of that very system. Now ordinarily what we think of as an ecological system is not entirely self-contained. It is acted upon from *without* by wind, rain, or fire, for example. But the larger our unit, the more self-contained it will be. And Everything-There-Is just *must* be entirely self-contained. Outside of *that* there are no resources whatever for explaining what occurs. And objects whose features are explained from within in this way have a kind of necessity about them. For it is because *they* are as they are, and not because of any external cause, that they have the features they do have. They are dependent on themselves alone.

Because a substance is so comprehensive, it takes on for Spinoza the divine character of necessity. For that which must be as it is must *be*. Spinoza has three arguments here: Nothing *else* can produce a substance, and so it must produce (or be cause of) itself.[7] Further, because interaction is impossible, nothing outside a substance can destroy it. Further yet, if the infinite did not exist, finite

---

4. The alternative view, made famous (or notorious) by Locke, is that in addition to its properties, a thing requires a propertyless, unknowable, underlying *substratum* to support the properties and bind them together into a single being.
5. Spinoza, *Ethics,* part 1, proposition 10.
6. Ibid., definition 1.
7. Ibid., proposition 7.

things would be more powerful than infinite ones, which is absurd.[8] He does not use an argument which would show more clearly the principles of his philosophy: Every fact has its adequate explanation. Because there is no interaction, every fact about a substance must therefore have its adequate explanation within that substance itself. The existence of a substance is a fact about it, so a substance must be self-creating, and so it must exist.

Furthermore, there can be *only one substance*.[9] Spinoza's argument here is indirect, and we will not follow him. He could proceed directly thus: If there were two or more substances, $x, y, z, \ldots$ say, then one fact about x would be that it is one substance among others. But this is not a fact whose adequate explanation lies wholly within x. This is not an attribute which can be conceived through x alone. So it cannot be a fact about x, or x would not be a substance. It follows at once that there cannot be any reality outside the single substance God-or-nature.[10]

I find it easier to appreciate Spinoza's doctrine by thinking in terms of Everything-There-Is. There can only be one Everything. Nothing can exist outside Everything, and so nothing can create or interact with it. All explanations of what Everything is like must look *within it;* Everything contains sufficient richness to account for what happens. And in every happening, Everything takes on, for the time being, some particular form. There is nothing which could destroy Everything from outside, and (at least provided something exists) Everything must exist. Although he does not put it this way, for Spinoza 'Everything' is the proper name of the only true individual substance. All its parts and aspects are dependent, limited, and incomplete entities, merely modes of substance and not themselves full concrete particulars.

SPINOZA'S SYSTEM AND ATOMISM

I need hardly stress how different God-or-Nature is from the corpuscles of atomism. The corpuscles are finite and bounded. There are many of them. They are neither self-creating nor complete. There are other realities outside them. Not every one of their features is necessary to them. What in atomism is a causal relationship among distinct particulars is in Spinoza's system a give and take *within* a single entity which is subject to no external influences whatever.

Yet although Spinoza's cosmology is so different from classical atomism in its doctrine of what the basic concrete particular is, it is important to realize that he was in no way an enemy of the new science. He was neither an obscurantist nor a conservative clinging to old ideas. He welcomed and accepted the methods and results of the new science but gave them a different interpretation. The separate objects such as books and furniture, fish and fowl are modes of extension, which is one of God-or-Nature's attributes. Modes of extension are distinguishable from

---
8. Ibid., proposition 11.
9. Ibid., proposition 14.
10. Ibid., proposition 15.

ALTERNATIVE PARTICULARIST SYSTEMS 79

one another insofar as each has a self-conserving force within it maintaining its continuing independence *from other modes* and restricting the destructive tendencies of the operation of *other modes* on it. Modes can act on each other in the way we describe as causal, and indeed all changes in nature are connected to others by such causal chains.[11]

Furthermore, in the axioms and lemmata following proposition 13 of part 2, Spinoza spells out very succinctly a theory of simple and composite bodies which is clearly a variant of atomism. The simplest bodies differ only in velocity (not in size, shape, solidity, or any other quality). All other differences among composite bodies spring from their manner of composition. An atomistic physics is acceptable to Spinoza provided it is *not* treated as a metaphysical doctrine, provided, that is, it is always remembered that particular, mutable bodies are *not* substances, are not basic concrete particulars. Their being and their motions, from which all physical phenomena derive, are mere aspects, assumed then surpassed, of the divine attribute extension. It is as though space is perpetually shivering and shrugging. We can describe the shivers and shrugs in the language of the motions of simple bodies *(corpora simplicissima)*. But we must never forget that these simple bodies are not genuine substances.

IDENTIFYING AND NONIDENTIFYING PROPERTIES[12]

Spinoza's system consists in a body of ideas tightly bound together by logical argument. The key to it all is his claim that independence requires that *every one* of a substance's properties be explainable by appeal to features within that substance itself. Once we accept that, I do not see how we can escape the conclusion that only Everything-That-Is can be truly independent. And as we have seen, the key claim about independence rests in part on the plausible notion that what a thing is, is the totality of its properties.

Yet this plausible assumption is quite at variance with another, and equally natural, principle of our thought: that a thing can *change*—at least in some respects—and yet remain the same thing. Let us take a chair for example again. If we sand it down and paint it, it is still the same chair. It can change from varnished to painted, and from red to orange, yet remain the same chair. It cannot of course be smashed up for firewood, still less burned to ash, gas, and smoke, while remaining the same chair. Between these extremes are borderline cases—do we have the same chair if one or more legs are replaced, or the back removed? These questions have no determinate correct answer.

The situation is the same for complex natural objects, such as planets or

---

11. Ibid., proposition 28. Cf. part 2, lemma 3.

12. Often, particularly in this section, we discuss properties. Just exactly what a property is, is one of the hardest questions in philosophy, and it is the crucial issue in the problem of universals. Here we must be content to say that a property, or feature, or characteristic, is a something which we say an object has when we describe it using a general term.

animals. Through some changes, the identity of the thing is preserved. In others, it is destroyed. In yet others, there is no determinate answer to the question, Is it still the same thing?

Basic particulars, on the other hand, are special. According to the theory in which they are basic, the only changes they undergo are changes which do not destroy them or convert them into other objects. That is what makes them basic. In classical atomism, for example, atoms can only change in relative position and absolute motion, which leaves their identity untouched.

Now see how this idea of identity through change conflicts with the idea that a thing is the totality of its properties. For if a thing is the totality of its properties, *any* change in property results in a different thing. With the loss of any property at all, or the gaining of any new one, a different thing arrives. Even the restricted sorts of change that atoms can undergo rule them out as real substances. A real substance must be totally unchangeable. All its properties must be eternal; they can be neither gained nor lost. Hence the impossibility of interaction among substances.

Is there any way to reconcile these two conflicting principles, that a thing is constituted by its properties and yet can change? We stand in need of a distinction between the *identifying* and the *nonidentifying* properties of particulars. Identifying properties, as you will readily guess, are those which make a particular the very object it is. To lose an identifying property is to cease being that object, and to become another object or none at all. For chairs, belonging to a particular continuous track through space, their composition, structure, and perhaps use are identifying, while surface finish, color, and ownership are nonidentifying. For natural objects, composition, structure, and track through space likewise identify.

An object can gain or lose any number of nonidentifying properties any number of times and yet remain the same thing. But a single change in any identifying property is fatal. Or, more strictly, may be fatal. For many objects we think of as things have a cluster of properties, no single one of which is essential provided sufficient of the others are retained. Thus an elephant remains the same elephant although it changes size (within limits), provided it keeps other elephantish features. It could, I dare say, become a carnivore. But becoming a tiger-shaped carnivore is a bit much. In the solar system, orbits could change in some degree. But if planets were to move off at tangents we would not have the same solar system.

It is complex individuals which have identifying characteristics in clusters some sufficient set of which is necessary for the identity of the object in question. With basic particulars the ideal is to find identifying features each one of which is severally necessary and which are jointly sufficient for identity. The atoms of classical atomism must have a specific volume, shape, mass, hardness, and gravitational force. None of these features can be lost by any natural process, and so it cannot lose some while keeping others.

Now when we have the distinction between identifying and nonidentifying properties we can say both that in one sense a thing is the totality of its proper-

ALTERNATIVE PARTICULARIST SYSTEMS 81

ties, and that a thing can change, within limits, yet still be the same thing. For a thing has a core of *identifying* properties, which do not exhaust its reality but do suffice to consitute it the thing it is. And it can change its *nonidentifying* properties while remaining the same thing.

And basic particulars (substances), which perdure through all change, can be affected from without *only* in their nonidentifying properties. They can be neither brought into being nor destroyed by natural processes, but they can act on each other to alter their nonidentifying features.

The independence which they require is not a complete independence, in all respects, in both being and conception. Their independence is sufficiently established if it extends only to the identifying properties. This makes room for at least a limited amount of interaction among independent substances. It makes room for a plurality of substances. It makes room for change (in nonidentifying features). So not all properties of a substance need be eternal. A real time dimension is therefore possible.

It is important to realize that the distinction between identifying and nonidentifying properties only makes these things *possible*. It does not show they are actual, and so Spinoza's conclusions may turn out to be correct, even though his arguments break down when we distinguish identifying and nonidentifying properties. Perhaps substances have no nonidentifying properties; in that case there could be no real interaction.[13] Perhaps as a matter not of necessity but of fact, nothing less than Everything is independent in its identifying properties, and so nothing less than Everything is a substance.[14]

Spinoza's method in philosophy was to seek out self-evident first principles, expressed in definitions and axioms, and from them to deduce in the formal manner of mathematics the great metaphysical propositions of his system. Had the method succeeded, we would be in possession of a cosmology free from uncertainty—necessary, complete, and final. We have seen how the distinction between identifying and nonidentifying properties can cast doubt on his conclusions. It is time now to look at another source of doubt. Leibniz followed the same method in pursuit of the same ideal—necessary, rational truth in metaphysics. Yet his conclusions are utterly different from Spinoza's. So there must be a fault somewhere in the mathematical method of procedure.[15]

LEIBNIZ: THE SYSTEM OF MONADS

Leibniz was a younger contemporary of Spinoza in the seventeenth century and one of the finest polymath minds to have graced European civilization. His cosmology is a system of basic particulars which are primitive minds.[16] These *monads*, as they are called, are permanent and independent of one another.[17]

---

13. See the discussion of Leibniz immediately following.
14. This is suggested by the recent history of physics. See chapter 7 below.
15. This point is raised in part I above.
16. G.W. Leibniz, *Monadology*, § 14, 15.
17. Ibid., § 7.

They are active; that is, they contain within themselves the cause of the changes in inner content through which they pass.[18]

Leibniz's world is thus one of a myriad of minds, each more or less clearly perceiving itself and all the others. As he puts it, each monad mirrors the universe within itself.[19] That is, it mirrors within itself all other monads. The form this mirroring takes is a spatial array, but the objects mirrored are actually minds which are not spatial objects. They have no size or shape.[20] If they have location at all, it is in some metaphysical space, not the physical space of ordinary life and science.

We ourselves, that is, our minds, are monads, and when we "see" the world as spread out in physical space we are subject to confusion. The appearance of space derives from the relationship between monads, of greater or less similarity in content. Those very similar are "close together"; those widely dissimilar are "far apart." Space is a "well-founded appearance,"[21] for it is our way of representing these relations of similarity which obtain among monads.[22]

The order and motion we perceive do not result, as they seem to, from the external action of one substance on another. They spring from the divinely *preestablished harmony* which ensures that the inner development of each monad fits in with the inner development of every other to give a systematic illusion of cause and effect.[23]

The universe is a realm of living things. Every real thing is a living monad but does not seem to be, since these living things are aware of one another, often, as material bodies in space. Bodies are actually clusters of monads whose transformations are systematically linked together, so that they seem to be single extended objects. Men, and other animals to a lesser extent, are such clusters or colonies of monads unified under a dominant monad of superior consciousness, the one we call our *mind*.[24] There are infinitely many independent spiritual substances, all transforming themselves from within in harmony with one another. The entire system is created and given form by the activity of God, on which the whole depends.[25]

So the world is very far from being as it seems. *That* is not in itself an unusual claim to come from a natural philosopher. But how did Leibniz arrive at his astonishing doctrine that the familiar and scientific world of matter in motion is but the appearance, behind which everything is organic, alive, in some measure conscious, and not truly affected by any created thing outside its own unextended and only metaphysically 'located' self?

18. Ibid., § 14, 18.
19. Ibid., § 77.
20. Ibid., § 3.
21. Leibniz, *Correspondence with Clarke*, third letter, § 4.
22. Leibniz, *Monadology*, § 60–62.
23. Ibid., § 51; Leibniz, *Principles of Nature and Grace, Founded on Reason*, § 3; Leibniz, *Exposition and Defence of the New System*, § 18.
24. Leibniz, *Monadology*, § 7; Leibniz, *Principles of Nature and Grace*, § 4.
25. Leibniz, *Monadology*, § 48, 60.

THE REASONING BEHIND LEIBNIZ'S COSMOLOGY

We have already seen how Spinoza's system arises from taking the independence of substances with absolute strictness. Leibniz treats the *simplicity* of single basic substances in a similarly uncompromising fashion.

A basic particular is a simple substance. A simple substance is one without parts.[26] And when Leibniz says without parts, he means it literally and absolutely. A classical atom is without parts in this sense: according to the classical theory it cannot be divided *in fact*, by natural processes, into smaller fragments. But for Leibniz it does have parts. It is extended, and so it has a left side and a right side, a top and a bottom, a front and a back. No matter if we cannot separate these parts from one another. Now whatever has parts cannot be simple, hence atoms cannot be simple and therefore cannot be substances. Furthermore, the front and back halves of an atom would themselves be extended, and so they would in turn have parts and therefore would not be simple either. We will never be able to find true substances among extended objects, for they are not truly simple. Any material object is subject to this criticism; it has structure, and hence diversity.[27]

Leibniz now argues that the real unity which extended things lack is precisely what basic particulars must possess. For it is by analysis into simple unities alone that we can explain complex phenomena. Of all objects in our experience, only minds have unity (they are not compounds of parts) yet at the same time have inner richness in the complexity of their perception and thoughts. So only minds provide resources for explaining complex phenomena properly. Basic substances must accordingly have a mental character.

Furthermore, they must be self-contained. They have no "windows" through which they can affect each other. The reason for this lies in Leibniz's doctrine of the *complete notion* of a thing.[28] My thought of an object is the thought of a being with such-and-such properties: a place, size, constitution, behavior, history, and so forth. These features make it what it is. I can distinguish it from other, very similar things only by indefinitely extending my list of its characteristics. Of course only the infinite God can actually extend the list of characteristics indefinitely; we must get along as best we can with partial individual notions. But it is in its complete individual notion that a thing is captured and fully specified.

In the long run, this means that every truth is necessary. "Fred is a frog," for example, would be analyzed as "The thing which is green, shiny, slimy, amphibian, four-legged, big-mouthed, . . . (and, in short, froggish) is a frog." For ordinary truths of fact only God can grasp the necessity. For only He can complete the analysis, since only He is in possession of the complete notion. But the necessity is there, whether or not we can grasp it.

Where every truth is necessary, everything that happens, happens with some kind of necessity. The reason for this, that a true predicate is already given in the

---
26. Ibid., § 1.
27. Introduction to Leibniz, *Exposition and Defence*.
28. See N. Rescher, *The Philosophy of Leibniz*, chapter 1.

complete notion of the subject, also rules out interaction among substances. For the description of any event in which a substance participates forms part of the complete notion of that substance. Now it must be possible for a substance to be the only thing there is, and so the complete notion of a substance must contain reference to *no other individual whatever*. Otherwise, that other individual would have to exist in order to give the original substance part of its complete notion. The description of an interaction however, must refer to other individuals, and so there can be no interaction between substances.

Cause and effect, which involve interactions, are appearances which arise from the preestablished harmony among things. What is actually happening is that independent substances are generating changes within themselves. These changes run parallel to one another in such a way that one thing seems to have an effect on another.

By way of the doctrine of the complete notion, substances can be logically independent—each could be the only individual—only if they are also causally independent of one another. You will, I am sure, note that the doctrine of the complete notion rules out the distinction between identifying and nonidentifying properties. In Leibniz's system, all the properties of a genuine substance are identifying properties.[29]

The unreality of causal interaction provides further reason for denying that matter can be substantial. For bodies act on one another from without. Worse, they do not change *except* under the influence of external forces. Matter is passive, stodgy, inert, and 'brute'. Mind, on the other hand, has the power of spontaneously initiating changes. It is *active*. In that facet of the mind we know as the will, we have an image of the true source of change: inner, self-moving alteration.

Basic particulars are simple and independent and active. So they must be mental in nature, primitive simple minds or, in a word, monads. Classical atomism has made quite the wrong choice of basic particulars. Furthermore, atomism admits the void, which Leibniz repudiated, for in his view a void involves a gap in space. Hence, the system of atoms can be no more than a scientific theory useful in giving an account of how the spatial world of appearance behaves. It cannot be a true cosmology.

To answer the question raised by Spinoza's system—Why is there more than one monad?—Leibniz appeals to the creative generosity of God. God creates as much as possible; infinitely many isolated individuals are possible together, and so this is what we have. Against Spinoza's monism we set Leibniz's form of pluralism: there is only one *kind* of substance, active mentality, but there are infinitely many *instances* of it, the monads, which build into forms which underlie the variety of the experienced world.

---

29. We could ask in passing how 'created by God' would belong to the complete notion of a substance, and how the creative interaction of God with monads is possible. For all His centrality in Leibniz's thought, God sits very uneasily (and in my opinion inconsistently) in the system.

THE LESSONS OF LEIBNIZ'S COSMOLOGY

Leibniz's metaphysical system is clearly at odds with atomism at many points. These differences are instructive; we can see more clearly from them what the philosophical commitments of a cosmology like atomism really are. We have already found that atomism requires interaction among substances, and this in turn requires the distinction between identifying and nonidentifying properties. In both Spinoza and Leibniz the impossibility of interaction is proved on the basis that all properties are identifying ones.

Now further, Leibniz teaches us something about the parts of simple substances. One ground of his objection to material atoms is that, being extended, they must have parts and so cannot be simple. Let us examine this more closely. Is it true that anything extended must be complex? There is indeed one sense of 'parts' in which any extended thing must have parts. It must have a left and a right side, for example. But there are two situations to consider. The left side might itself be a substance or it might not. That is, the left side might be itself capable of independent existence, or it might exist only as one side of something greater.

To mark this distinction, let us call parts which are themselves substances *real parts*. Anything which has real parts is not simple but complex. Nothing with real parts can be a basic particular, for any such thing depends on the existence of the real parts.

Now it does not follow that just because a thing is extended it must have real parts. Indeed a classical atom is supposed to be, precisely, an extended thing with no real parts. For there is no way of dividing such an atom, according to the theory. So there are no circumstances in which the left side of an atom could exist except as one side of something greater. So an atom does not depend on the existence of its left side, but vice versa.

In cosmology, what matters for simplicity and independence is not having no parts of any kind, but having no real parts. And a thing can be extended, yet have no real parts. So a thing can be extended and yet be a basic particular, and Leibniz's objection fails.

To put this another way, if a thing is divisible in reality, it has real parts and cannot be simple. But if it is only divisible in thought, it has parts which are merely ideal, and these do not count. That we can think of the various parts of a structure on their own does not show that these parts can exist on their own. Hence basic particulars can be complex in idea without thereby ceasing to be simple in the sense required. Atoms can be basic particulars after all.

The distinction between identifying and nonidentifying properties seems to apply to basic particulars as much as to any other kind. The distinction between real and merely ideal parts seems a legitimate one. These two distinctions enable us to resist the powerful arguments of Spinoza and Leibniz. We are not forced to accept their conclusions. Provided the distinctions are sound, neither Spinoza nor Leibniz furnishes reasons against atomism sufficiently strong to demolish it.

But we are not yet out of trouble. There is a further difficulty in any system which has extended substances. Any cosmology resting on basic particulars of finite size, such as atomism, faces an embarrassing problem: what holds the parts of an atom together? What super-strong force binds an atom's ideal parts to one another so tightly that no natural process can overcome it? Why does this force only operate *within* an atom? Why is it so powerful? In cosmology we are seeking an account of the world which leaves the fewest unanswered questions. While we would look to scientific theory for hypotheses about cohesion, it seems that here we would have to pass beyond the limits of atomism as classically understood. Reflection on scientific theory, reflection seeking to settle the extent of a theory's explanatory power, reflection of a philosophical kind, is an essential aspect of cosmology. Such reflection works here to point up a weakness in any atomism as the last word. The problem of what binds together any particle of finite volume leads us naturally on to a review of Boscovich's cosmology.

BOSCOVICH

Roger Boscovich, in addition to being a philosopher, was a scientist and engineer, mathematician and poet, priest and diplomat. Celebrated in his own time, his thought subsequently fell into an undeserved obscurity from which it has recently emerged. The greatest of his many works is the *Theoria Philosophiae Naturalis*, a translation of which is now readily available.[30]

Boscovich's theory bases itself on *material points* with no volume, no shape, no parts, and no mass, which act on one another at a distance in accordance with a single law of repulsion and attraction. We could describe his points either as atoms reduced to the vanishing point or as monads located in ordinary physical space, which interact and conform to mechanical laws rather than changing from within on account of the mindlike *appetition* or will of Leibniz's system. And indeed Boscovich draws attention to just those aspects of his doctrine; the marginal commentaries on two early paragraphs of the *Theory of Natural Philosophy* are the superbly self-confident "How [the theory] differs from, and surpasses, the theory of Leibniz" and "How it differs from, and surpasses, the theory of Newton."

In Boscovich's philosophy of matter there is a void in which float material points. There are indefinitely many of these, but all familiar bodies contain only a finite number of them. These points are all alike, and all affect the velocities of all others in a single standard fashion which depends only on the distance between them. The effects produced are accelerations. They are either attractive or repulsive depending on the distance separating the points, and they occur

---

30. R.J. Boscovich, *A Theory of Natural Philosophy*. The theory is set out in part 1 of this work.

along the line joining them. These accelerations are most conveniently set forth in this graph:[31]

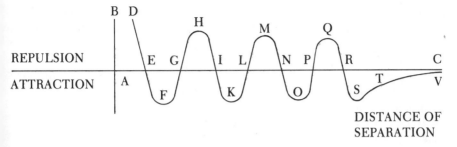

We suppose one point to be at the origin A. As the distance between any two points becomes smaller and smaller, then the repulsion between them becomes indefinitely large—the curve is asymptotic to the ordinate AB. At somewhat greater, though still very small distances, the effect produced is either an attraction or a repulsion of finite magnitude. The details of this part of the curve are as yet unknown; it is in this region that we will find, we hope, explanations for the cohesion of bodies, for viscosity, for strength of materials, for the peculiarities of chemical combination, for magnetic phenomena, and so forth. The distance AS is approximately the radius which a Newtonian atom would have if there were any such things. Beyond this distance, points attract pretty much in accord with Newton's gravitational law; the attraction declines continuously with the increasing distance without ever becoming zero—the curve is asymptotic to the abscissa AC in this direction.[32]

At distances AE, AG, AL, and so on, where the curve crosses the abscissa, the mutual acceleration of two points is zero. But external influences will rapidly disturb these equilibrium states.

No points can ever come into contact. No matter how fast two points approach, an indefinitely strong mutual repulsion builds up between them and their approach is halted at some finite separation. This is just as well, since points with no volume cannot touch without being at exactly the same place at the same time—which would seem to make them one point, not two.

The points have no surface and no solidity; there is no region about any point into which another point, approaching with sufficient velocity, cannot reach. This is an aspect of Boscovich's theory which should make it congenial in the context of nuclear physics and experimentation with particle accelerators, where this seems indeed to be the situation.

---

31. This graph is a version of that appearing in *Theoria Philosophiae Naturalis* by Roger Joseph Boscovich. Reprinted by permission of The Open Court Publishing Company, La Salle, Illinois, © 1922.

32. Ibid. In part 3. § 399 the author suggests that gravity extends only to the farther reaches of the solar system.

The graph is a graph of accelerations rather than forces. We read in the subtitle that Boscovich offers a *Theory of Natural Philosophy Reduced to a Single Law of Forces*, but *force*, in Newtonian physics, is proportional to mass. The points have no mass, and so even a finite force exerted on one point by another would produce an infinite acceleration. We could say, if we like, that Boscovich's material points have "virtual mass"; they exert finite forces on one another which produce finite accelerations. But it is more economical to do without force and mass and to assert as a fundamental truth that the accelerations produced in one point by another are finite and as represented in the graph.

So for Boscovich the fundamental primary qualities are few indeed: just position, mobility, countability, and the power to produce accelerations. Size, shape, solidity, mass are all features of complexes which must be reduced, as consequential primaries, to these features of the basic particulars.

THE MERITS OF THE THEORY: (i) ELEGANCE

Cohesion. Boscovich's cosmology is splendid in its elegance and economy. By giving his basic particulars no volume, he completely avoids the nagging problem about the cohesion of any ordinary, extended particles. Even if we do succeed in 'splitting the atom' as Rutherford did, and so open the way to an investigation of the binding forces in an atom, we do not escape the problem. For if the particles into which the atom is split have any size whatever, the cohesion problem at once arises all over again, this time for the particles. What keeps *their* parts together? But a Boscovich point has no parts at all, and so this question does not arise.

Collision. Boscovich can deal with a problem in classical atomism which concerns elastic collision. Consider the collision of two complex objects, like billiard balls. One approaches, then makes contact with the other, and both move off at altered velocities. But the impact and change of velocity do not occur instantaneously. They take a short time. During this period the first ball is rapidly slowed down; its trailing surface catches up with the leading surface a little; the surface of the second ball into which it is colliding "gives" a little, absorbing the shock; and then the second ball, as it springs back to its normal shape, is rapidly accelerated to its new velocity. This is all possible because billiard balls can be slightly compressed and deformed.

Now consider two *atoms* colliding. Atoms are of infinite hardness; they can not be compressed at all (there is no room inside them to permit compression). Nor can they be deformed (they have no real parts which can change position relative to one another). So in the collision of two atoms, the first must be slowed down, and the second speeded up, *instantaneously*. If the impact occurs at time t, a graph of the velocity of the second atom would look like this:

ALTERNATIVE PARTICULARIST SYSTEMS

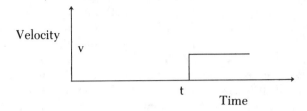

But this means that at time t the atom is *both* at rest and in motion simultaneously. Moreover, at t the atom has simultaneously all the infinitely many different velocities between zero and v. Boscovich thought this was absurd, and I don't blame him. He held that it violated a cardinal law of nature, the principle of continuity ("Nothing happens by jumps") according to which all transitions in location, direction, or speed occur smoothly, passing in succession through the intermediate values between initial and final states.[33]

Now on the theory of material points, there is no difficulty. Suppose point A is approaching point B. The nearer A gets, *without touching*, the more strongly it accelerates B away from itself along the line of approach. And equally, the closer A gets, the more strongly B slows A down by accelerating A backwards along the same line of approach. The net result, velocity sharing, conforms with the laws of elastic collision.[34]

Solidity. In Boscovich's system there are no real surfaces, that is, no planes (or three-dimensional curves) with matter on one side of them and void on the other. But of course familiar perceptible objects have surfaces, that is, limits beyond which other objects cannot penetrate, where, unless something breaks, approaching objects either stop or bounce or start to move that with which they come in contact. That is an aspect of the appearances from which we begin. It is something any philosophy of matter must account for. Atomism can account for it. According to that theory, a 'solid' such as a table is not filled through and through with matter. Nevertheless its surface is a place at which, suddenly, many table atoms begin to be encountered. And these table atoms have real, entire, strictly impenetrable surfaces. So do the atoms which compose a book, say, which approaches the table. The book presents an array of these minisurfaces at its 'surface', they contact the minisurfaces of the atoms of the table's 'surface', and so we get the familiar macroscopic phenomena of solidity. In short, in the atomic theory tables seem to have surfaces because the basic particulars composing them have real surfaces.

---

33. Modern physical theory, with its doctrine of the 'quantum of action', seems to have abandoned the principle of continuity. In which case we should be given an answer to objections of the kind Boscovich makes.

34. Joseph Priestley, in *Disquisitions Relating to Matter and Spirit*, sections 1 and 2, also argues against the possibility of genuine contact and in favor of repulsive forces at small distances. In support, he cites experiments in electrical conductivity and the contraction of mechanically incompressible bodies on cooling.

This way of dealing with the problem is not open to Boscovich. A material point has no surface anywhere, either where it strictly *is* or in any surrounding local region. There is no part of nature which excludes other objects by itself filling the space it occupies. Material points, unlike atoms, do not fill any space and do not absolutely exclude other particulars from any region around them, no matter how small. It just gets harder and harder, but never impossible, to approach a place taken by a material point. The mutual exclusion displayed by solids cannot be explained by appeal to real surfaces.

The points at or near the 'surface' of a table are so arranged that together they present something of a united front. This is a thin horizontal slice of space in which the joint repulsive effect of the many points which make up the table rapidly increases. The points in books, lamps, or heads present similar united fronts in their turn. So books, lamps, and heads cannot pass easily into and through tables. They stop, break, or bounce off.

The 'top surface' of the table is not an absolutely inviolable plane. It is a thin horizontal layer, and falling objects enter more or less deeply into it, depending on their momentum. The idea that the surface of a table is an absolutely definite limit is an illusion springing from the crudity of our everyday investigations of such matters.

Complex objects can therefore have virtual surfaces and exhibit exclusion behavior even though their constituent parts have no distinct surface of any kind. Solidity, like perceptible size and variation of shape, emerges in Boscovich's theory as a feature peculiar to macroobjects and not present in basic particulars.

The idea of material points leaves many people uneasy. They think, reasonably enough, that matter takes up space, one way or another, and if these points are really material, they should take up some space too. Descartes[35] made it a leading principle of his philosophy that whatever is material is extended (and vice versa), and Locke held, as we have seen, that volume and solidity belong to the essence of matter. We can construct arguments from imaginary cases to support this point of view. But these arguments fail, and their failure is instructive.

MECHANICAL MARTIANS AND GHOSTS

One fine day a spaceship lands and out steps its commander. He has an approximately human form, with head, trunk, and limbs, but composed of plastic, steel, and glass. By good fortune he speaks English, and we eagerly question him about, among other matters, his own nature. He tells us that he has an immaterial mind located inside a box in his chest. We skeptical materialists are invited to confirm this for ourselves. As his body is mechanical, we give him no inconvenience if we dismantle him. We find a plastic box in his chest into which myriad strings run. These strings, pulled from inside the box, give his mind control of his body. An X-ray of the box shows the thickness of its walls. Otherwise it

---

35. R. Descartes, *Principles of Philosophy.*

seems to be empty. We check the weight of box plus mind. It exactly equals the weight that the box alone should have. So his mind is weightless, but perhaps it is made of some strange, weightless matter. We cut the box open. Within, there is nothing to be seen or detected by instruments. So his mind is invisible, but perhaps it is material nevertheless. Finally we fill the box with water. It receives the exact quantity which would fill the box if empty. Since he continues to function as well as ever, his mind was not some gas we have expelled. His mind takes up no space at all, neither excluding nor being excluded by the water. This is the deciding factor. We conclude that he does indeed have an immaterial mind. So, it seems, matter must be extended.

One fine night we meet a strange person. He is wearing a green cloak, makes a noise as of rattling chains, and emits the odor of sanctity. All that is acceptable enough. It is the way he passes from room to room without using the doors that we find unnerving. Objects which can pass through walls without damage to either themselves or the wall are not solid. They have no surface, virtual or otherwise. That is enough for us. We conclude that our stranger is a ghost, an immaterial object.

Both cases seem to support the idea that solidity and exclusion are essential to material things. Solidity requires a surface, and surfaces require size and shape. Boscovich's material points, so called, have no size, no shape, and no solidity. So they cannot be material things, and his whole project is a disaster.

This conclusion is premature. For suppose that the world of matter *were* as Boscovich describes it. Then our encounters with the mechanical man and the ghost would have the same outcome. A material mind composed of points which repel at close range would act on the similar points composing the water in such a way that either not as many water points could get into the box, or the mind points would be pushed out. If neither happens, there are no matter points other than water ones in the box. And if the mind is still there, that mind is immaterial.

Likewise anything made up of matter points would have a destructive effect on a wall made up of such points, or would come to rest "against" (that is, very close to) those wall points, or would itself break up. Our ghost did none of these things. So it is not composed of material points—that is, it is not material.

Our cases, therefore, do not refute Boscovich. That minds and strangers like these are not material is a consequence of his theory, not an embarrassment for it. What has gone wrong? The cases show that, to qualify as material, complex *macro*objects must have at least virtual surfaces and hence size and shape. They must exhibit exclusion behavior, which our Martian mind and our ghost failed to do. But fundamental microparticulars such as points do not need in turn to have size, shape, and surface. They only require some features by virtue of which, alone or collectively, they can monopolize regions of space. And Boscovich's points, with their indefinitely increasing mutual repulsion, can do just that. He has shown how complex bodies can be extended, even though their basic constituents are not. For complex bodies have an extent fixed and limited by their virtual surfaces. But these virtual surfaces are the product of the joint action of many points, no one of which has either extent or surface.

This illustrates again the complexity of primary quality predication.[36] Boscovich is offering an alternative account of the nature N in which macroobjects have shape, size, and solidity. Neither the Martian and ghostly cases considered here, nor any others so far as I can tell, show that this alternative is illegitimate.

THE MERITS OF THE THEORY: (ii) FLEXIBILITY

Boscovich's theory is outstandingly flexible. The acceleration curve specifying the effect of one point on another has an intermediate zone of alternative attraction and repulsion, between the indefinitely increasing repulsion at close range and the indefinitely decreasing attraction over large distances. This intermediate zone on the curve can be modified in many ways to meet experimental results. The alternations can be more violent, or more numerous, or more uneven. The curve can be adjusted to account for many different types of molecular clusters of points, each type with its own coherence and distinctive effect on its environment.

By modifying our picture of the intermediate zone we can incorporate new developments in physics and chemistry which on the atomic theory require the postulation of new basic forces. There is room for maneuver on the aggrangement of the points or the details of their effect on one another; we can hold that where previously we had thought there was but one point we now believe there to be several, relating to one another and to the environment according to a rather different pattern of attractions and repulsions. This is a change of detail; it involves no new fundamental properties or forces.

In the case of light, for example, we see how strong the Boscovichian position is. If light is particulate in nature, as Newton believed, the likelihood is that light particles would be altogether smaller and less massive than ordinary material atoms. Indeed, in contemporary theory of light, its particles, the photons, are distinct from all other types. Atomic theory needs to be complicated with a new kind of particle to deal with light. But this is not a problem for material points. Material points are quite small enough to be constituents of light as well as matter. To give a beam of light its distinctive properties, we would need only to postulate a distinctive density of points in it, traveling in distinctive groups, and this could very likely be done by suitable adjustment to the distances and intensities of attraction and repulsion in the intermediate zone of the acceleration curve.

There is of course no absolute guarantee of success here. It may prove impossible to find a single curve which will cover all phenomena. The requirements in one field, of chemistry say, may be in irreconcilable conflict with the requirements of, say, optics. That would show that there are at least two different sorts of material points and would require a departure in substance, not merely in detail, from the initial theory. Boscovich's system, like every serious claim concerning the world's constitution, runs a real risk of refutation. For it belongs

---

36. See above, chapter 5.

to the scientific tradition in which a cosmology undertakes to explain why the world behaves in one way and not some other. What it claims, it claims to be true as a matter of fact, but not of necessity.

A DIFFICULTY IN BOSCOVICH'S THEORY

In atomism, the question What are material things made of? has a clear answer: atoms. The question What are atoms made of? has a less comprehensive but still acceptable answer: matter, that is, a massy, space-filling stuff. Just how or why matter fills space is left unexplained. But perhaps we should not complain of that, for explanations must stop somewhere, and it is acceptable to let them rest on matter just being what it is.[37]

When we turn to Boscovich's theory, what do we find? To the question What are material things made of? we again get a clear answer: material points. But what are material points made of? They are not *made of* anything. They do not have any intrinsic features, like mass, or hardness, or solidity, or shape, or size in virtue of which we could give them a nature. Their only feature, other than location, is that they accelerate other points.

Then what is at a material point? What distinguishes a location in space where there is a point from one where there is no such thing? All we can say is: At a material point there is something which accelerates other somethings which in turn accelerate somethings (including the first) which in turn . . . . But what an odd object this is; its *only* feature is to have an effect on things which have an effect on things which have an effect on things which . . . . We seem to be caught in a regress or circle, forever unable to say just what these things *are* which have an effect on each other.

We meet here a notorious conundrum in metaphysics. Is it possible for anything to be constituted by nothing but causal powers? Whatever the answer to *that* question, I doubt very much whether it is possible for *everything* to be constituted by nothing but causal powers. But that seems to be the situation in Boscovich's system. When one point moves another, all that has been shifted is a power to shift powers to shift. . . . But powers to shift *what?* To be coherent, I consider that Boscovich's points must be *somethings* which have the power to shift one another. They must have some intrinsic features which make them things in their own right, and they must in addition have the power to shift one another. Then, and only then, will there be something to move about. There must be some answer to the question What is at a point? independent of accelerative capacity.

---

37. That matter fills space tends to become one of its explicative, almost defining, characteristics (see chapter 3 above). And there is no accounting for explicative features without descending to a lower, more basic theory. So in an *atomic* theory of matter, the materiality of the atoms will not be explained. But this is acceptable because we are describing atoms in terms of features familiar to us from our experience of human-scale bodies.

Put it this way: we do not understand Boscovich's theory until we know just how a universe with exactly one material point in it would differ from a universe containing none at all. For one material point cannot accelerate anything.

One way out of the dilemma is to invent a new property expressly to meet the case. This could me *materiality* considered as a primitive and fundamental quality, and things with this feature accelerate one another through space. But here materiality has been cut off from the familiar meaning it gets through experience. It is a new primitive, and calling it by the familiar title 'materiality' is just a public relations exercise to calm our suspicions. It deserves equally to be called *punctitude*, which is somewhat less convincing. For an air of profundity, an invented word would serve well—*acceleroretardacity* perhaps.

We might suggest *energy* and hold that this is an intrinsic quality, concentrated and focused into points, which results in mutual accelerations. But here again we have severed connections with the notion of energy as a relational rather than intrinsic capacity for doing work, which is its original meaning.

A theological variant of this ad hoc procedure is to accord to the points a feature given them in their creation. We could try *being* or *created concrete particularity*.

All these labels pick out just *that intrinsic quality, whatever it is, which material points have and other points lack*.

None of this is very satisfactory. Indeed, I consider that the best way of approaching the problem of what is at a material point is not to solve but to circumvent it. To explain this, we need to look at recent developments in physics.

7 *Atomism and Modern Physics*

From the point of view of atomist cosmology, there have been three phases in the evolution of physics since the beginning of the nineteenth century. There were the developments in chemistry and particle physics which imposed successive complications and successive changes in which items were held to be genuinely atomic. There were the discoveries of creation and annihilation of particles as matter and energy transform into one another. And there was the development, in general relativity, of a different cosmological scheme altogether. So we can see atomism as entering a period of difficulty through which its basic structure nevertheless does survive, then encountering evidence which makes any recognizable atomism untenable, and finally being superseded by a holistic cosmic outlook which is very reminiscent of Spinoza's view.

DALTON'S ATOMIC CHEMISTRY

In the early years of the nineteenth century, Dalton tackled the problem of explaining the law of constant proportions, which specifies that in any chemical compound, the proportions of its constituents are always exactly the same.[1] His proposal, so familiar to us now, was that each *elementary* chemical substance exists in a minimum quantity, an atom, and that each chemical compound is made up of molecules containing a fixed number of atoms of its elementary constituents. On this theory the law of constant proportions is a straightforward consequence. And furthermore, all the untold thousands of different chemical substances are identified as different combinations of a strictly limited number of basic or elementary kinds of stuff (we now recognize a hundred odd elements).

---

1. We owe this law more to Lavoisier than any other single person. Lavoisier was a French aristocrat executed during the French Revolution.

This immensely successful and fruitful theory has been the cornerstone of chemistry ever since. It provides a matchless key by which to probe the structure and nature of the immense variety of material which we find in the world about us. But on this theory, the atoms of each element are all exactly like one another, and all unlike the atoms of each other element. They have different masses, different patterns of combination with other elements (different valences), different degrees of vigor and tenacity in combining with other atoms; indeed, they differ in almost every way. It is these differences which make them atoms of one particular element rather than another.

So if these minimum units of chemical reaction are truly atoms, truly corpuscles or minimum bodies of matter, then we must recognize about one hundred irreducibly distinct varieties of matter. These varieties of corpuscles would each have *some* value of the Newtonian primaries—shape, size, mass, mobility, and so on. But they need not all have the same size, shape, or mass. And further, they would need (in all probability) further distinguishing features which determine their combining powers.

This position, that chemical atoms are true indivisible, unstructured atoms of matter, which exists in a hundred distinct varieties, is a considerable complication of the ideal of classical atomism. But it is still clearly a variant of an atomism of concrete particulars.

On the other hand, we could suppose the "atoms" of chemistry are themselves complex structures, composed in one hundred various ways, of the true atoms of physics. This path, which you recognize as the one which speculation did in fact follow, leaves open the possibility that there is at bottom only one kind of matter. It leaves it open in theory, that the true atoms which make up chemical "atoms" are all exactly alike. And these true atoms could all have Newtonian primary qualities. But they would need to have new basic powers, operating at very short range, to explain why none of the mechanical or chemical processes which can dissolve or break up larger objects can sunder the atoms which combine together to form the "atoms" of a chemical element.

The unitary nature of fundamental matter could be preserved in this way. But only at the price of a departure from pure classical atomism. Such a departure is not fatal, for the theory would still be, plainly, an atomism. Yet even this price was insufficient to save the unity of fundamental matter.

ELECTRICITY AND MAGNETISM

Something had been known of magnetism—the lodestone and the compass needle—for centuries. Something had been known of static electricity also. Boscovich, for example, discusses these forces in the eighteenth century as well-established aspects of matter. In a strict classical atomism, these would be merely complex manifestations of the better understood mechanical relationships between matter.

During the nineteenth century, thanks largely to the work of Ampère, Ohm, and Faraday, current electricity was brought under experimental control. The relationship among magnetism, electricity, and motion familiar in the dynamo and electric motor was established. And electric theory developed the notion of *charge*. Charge was a new primitive primary quality. It attached to the basic units (atoms?) taking part in electric processes—in batteries, for example. And charge comes in two species, positive and negative. So once more the underlying unity of matter is threatened. An atomism with all basic particulars alike is as far off as ever.

And another development occurred, pregnant with significance for atomistic ways of thought. This was the introduction of the idea of an electromagnetic field. It is not easy to say what a field is.

To illustrate, think of a magnet; in the space around a magnet odd things happen—compass needles turn then steady, currents flow in moving loops of wire, iron objects are attracted, and so on. We can say either that the magnet has *in* itself powers to act on suitable objects at a distance from it (as Boscovich claimed for his points), or we can say that the magnet sets up in the space *about* itself something (a magnetic field) which acts on suitable objects because they are in that field.

Just what a field is remains elusive; it is a *something* described in terms of its powers to affect the course of events. It is a something which pervades space, which contains stresses or tensions of some kind within it, and which can transmit energy. It is a medium by which electric or magnetic objects can have an effect over distance.

Perhaps it is a very thin soup, a subtle unorthodox fluid, an ether or imponderable (massless) matter. Whatever it is, we can take fields seriously. That is, we can think of fields as real things, not just as convenient ideas for describing the pattern of effects which some objects can produce on others at a distance. And in that case, it is a physical something very different in constitution from a complex of ordinary material atoms.

James Clerk Maxwell found the equations governing the propagation of waves of radiation in the electromagnetic field (light and radiant heat, for example) and was able to show that they could not be reduced to any combination of mechanical forces (compressions, tensions, or twists).

So here again was something that was not going to fit into the classical picture of the material world. The picture was going to need complicating. Further, and even more importantly, here is the beginning of the breakdown of the old dichotomy of atoms and void. Between, among, and perhaps even through the atoms there is not nothing. There is something with unfamiliar physical characteristics. The vacuum, where there is no ordinary matter, is not a void, but a region with features over and above geometric position and volume. The end of the absolute distinction between matter and void leads ultimately to the end of any satisfactory atomism. But this process involves several further changes in basic physics.

ATOMIC PHYSICS

The development and mastery of electrical equipment set the stage for investigation into those fragments of chemical "atoms" which might prove the ultimate constituents of matter. J.J. Thompson and Ernest Rutherford, using electronic tubes, detected the protons and electrons of modern theory. With more powerful and more sophisticated equipment, other particles were discovered—the neutron, the positron, then a bewildering variety of particles, with different charge or 'spin' or 'strangeness' or other mystifying fundamental characteristics. There are now several dozen of these distinct particles, found or made in ever more powerful probings of the nucleus of the chemical atom. Investigations of radioactivity added their measure of complexity to the picture.

In the ever renewed search for simplicity of theory, history is repeating itself. The "atoms" of Dalton's theory were too various to be satisfactory. The diversity of chemical elements inspired a search for an underlying complexity in their structure. It was proposed to account for the many different "atoms" in terms of various combinations of some very few basic types of subatomic particle. And in precisely similar spirit, it is now proposed to account for the many different subatomic particles in terms of various combinations of just three types of sub-subatomic particle, or *quark* as they have been called.

This proposal is perfectly in the spirit of atomism. It seeks, in discrete, distinct, real parts of things the basis of their constitution. It seeks to exhibit the larger as deriving from the smallest units which will be fundamental. For all that has so far been said, the theory of quarks could be the culmination of atomistic cosmology.

The hunting of the quark has now fairly begun, and some even claim success in the search. But however that may be, I do not think that even quarks, if there are any such things, should be regarded as basic concrete particulars in the traditional sense. For there are other developments to consider.

QUANTUM PHYSICS: ATOMS DISSOLVED

In the early years of this century physics faced several perplexing questions: Why do electrons leave metals under the incidence of light, with a fixed maximum velocity?[2] Why doesn't an atom collapse under electrical attraction? Why does emission of radiation occur at some definite intensities and not others? Why do different elements emit radiation at distinct wavelengths?

These phenomena were accounted for in the theory that energy of all types occurs in quanta, or minimal packets. That was a surprise, involving revision of earlier views, but not in itself a discovery with great cosmological implications. However, the theory involved, in its elaboration, a quite new view of the character of atomic particles. The theory incorporated Heisenberg's celebrated uncertainty principle, according to which a particle does not have, simultaneous-

---

2. A. Einstein, *Annalen der Physik*.

ly, definite position and definite momentum.[3] Particles no longer have the definite size, shape, or position classical speculation had given them. They get "smudged."[4] And they acquire "wave" characteristics, having a maximum presence in one ill-defined locality but some diminishing presence roundabout. The boundary between matter and void is further dissolved. Do not think of a single, definite, located item affecting other such items. Think of an approximately located "wavepacket" or stable effect of the interactions of waves in fields which bear and transmit the forces of nature.

BOSCOVICH TURNED INSIDE OUT

In Boscovich's system, point objects with an absolutely definite position affect each other, according to the graph of accelerations, *across* space. They act on each other at a distance. The precise manner of their action is expressed in the details of the acceleration graph. We can modify this system by saying each point particle acts on a field which fills the space about it, and by acting on the field, acts indirectly through the field, rather than directly at a distance, on other point particles. Perhaps we would need more than one field associated with a given point, if it turns out that all the effects of points on one another cannot be reduced to a single acceleration curve, the same for all particles. Modern physics deals with gravitational, electromagnetic, weak and strong nuclear forces and so with four possible fields about each point. But whether one or more, we can give fields a place in Boscovich's theory.

Suppose we gave them first place. Suppose, that is, that instead of thinking of the points as real, and any talk of fields just a convenient way of describing the effect a point would have on another point if another point happened to be at this place or that in the surrounding space (as Boscovich would have done), or of thinking of both point and field as real, we thought of the field as a real physical entity, with stresses and powers distributed through space, and the point as a mere mathematical abstraction. Then the point is a center of symmetry of the field. The values of the field build up symmetrically towards this center.

The field associated with one 'point' has an effect on the field associated with each other point, to alter their centers of symmetry in regular ways. This is what we used to describe as the acceleration of one point particle by another. The interplay of these fields, which interpenetrate one another, gives rise to the observable phenomena of nature.

This field interpretation of Boscovich has its attractions. It completely eliminates the stubborn residual problem with which Boscovich's own system leaves us: what is at a point? What distinguishes a place with a material point

---

3. This puts the matter in realistic terms. In some interpretations the uncertainty is in our knowledge, not in the things themselves. I accept the realistic view, but this is not the place to argue the question. Cf. J.J.C. Smart, *Between Science and Philosophy*.
4. W. Heisenberg, *Quantenmechanik*.

from a place without one? For by turning Boscovich inside out we no longer have any point object. The point is only a center for a field, which is a spread out physical existent.

And if we now introduce some indefiniteness into the fields, holding that their features cannot be specified to closer than a certain range of precision, then their centers of symmetry become blurred, their regions of maximum value become indistinctly bounded, and we thereby give a description which fits the uncertainty principle of quantum physics.[5] We can go on to specify which particular values the quantities of the fields can take, and we describe the processes of nature as proceeding by the "quantum of action," the minimum transitions of quantum theory.

Every atomic cosmology presents the world as composed, in the last resort, of discrete particles like grains of sand. Quantum physics requires at least that the boundaries between particle and surrounding space be made indistinct, after the fashion of crunchy peanut butter. And when we cannot fix the location of a particle within its enclosing field, it seems more economical to strive for a unitary view in which the "particle" appears as just a special region of a much more extensive field. The field is taken to be the fundamental reality.

All that remains of atomism in this way of looking at things is pluralism, the thesis that the fundamental items are many in number, logically independent, each capable of existing on its own, none composed of anything more basic. Yet this way of looking at things, this transformation of particles into unusual regions of an indefinitely extensive, unfamiliar physical somewhat, is not sufficiently motivated by indistinctness of the boundary between the inside and the outside of a particle. The boundaries of a flame are indistinct, but it does not follow just from that that the flame is merely a center in an unbounded fiery extent. To move definitively away from the concept of a particle as a basic particular, we need to suppose that what lies on either side of this indistinct boundary shares a common nature.

And this further step has indeed occurred. Moreover, it has occurred in such a way that even the pluralism, the last vestige of atomism, should also be abandoned.

MASS-ENERGY TRANSFORMATIONS: THE FINAL END OF ATOMISM

In nuclear reactions, particles are transformed. Some decay into others, of less mass, with the emission of large quantities of energy. In other processes, pairs of particles (for example the electron and its positively charged counterpart, the positron) collide and annihilate one another. In yet other processes, a suitable arrangement of radiation can result in the creation of electron/positron pairs. It is thought that every kind of material particle has its antimatter counterpart with

---

5. Cf. De Broglie, *Nature*, p. 441. In the new wave theory of matter, "the material point is conceived as a singularity in a wave."

ATOMISM AND MODERN PHYSICS

which it would be well advised not to collide. The transformations of energy into matter and back are governed by Einstein's famous formula:

$$E = mc^2$$

An atomic bomb is a device which exploits the possibility of converting mass into energy.

There are, in short, circumstances in which particles do not perdure. They fail to retain their identity through all the changes into which they enter. So they cannot be basic particulars, the substances of concrete particularism. They are one possible manifestation of some yet more fundamental bedrock of the world, which takes on now one form, now another.

And in the mass-energy transformations we are speaking of, if massy particles disappear, what appears in their place is radiation, wavelike propagation of energy across fields. The massy stuff "inside" a particle transforms into the wavy stuff "outside." And vice versa, massy particles are created at the expense of energy in fields "about" the particles. This is what lends attraction to the idea of turning Boscovich inside out.

But that idea will not do. For in these nuclear reactions we are considering, the entire particle together with its surrounding field disappears in favor of alterations in *other* energy values, of gamma rays, for example. So even if we did turn Boscovich inside out and thought of something spread-out in place of a localized particle, what we would arrive at would be something which itself disappears in a nuclear reaction. The spread-out counterpart of a particle perdures no more than a particle does. So even these spread-out counterparts must give way to something yet more fundamental, which does perdure and of which the particulate character of mass/energy is a manifestation. That something is space itself.

RUSSELL'S COSMOLOGY

In *The Analysis of Matter* Bertrand Russell tackled this issue head on.[6] He resolves the physical world into particulars, after the manner of concrete particularism. His particulars are simple, unstructured, and exhaustive. They are the ultimate elements of which all else consists.

But they are not concrete particulars, for they have no perduration whatever. They are not things. They do not survive beyond the first change which occurs to them. They are *events*, the occurrence, in a small region of space, during a short period of time (that is, over a small space-time interval), of a physical magnitude.[7] What the primitive physical magnitudes actually are is left to physics to determine. Regular clusters and chains of these events make up the world of

---

6. B. Russell, *The Analysis of Matter*, part 3, esp. chapters 27–29.
7. Cf. chapter 3 above, under "The Cosmology of Events."

spatiotemporal nature. No thing is basic, for every thing is a complex structure of events. And as we have just seen, every one of these complex structures is liable to have a life shorter than the whole cosmos's, for there is some process in which any one of these can be created or annihilated.

This system gets right away from the perplexing problems of dealing with 'things' which lack clearly defined boundaries, with 'things' which transform into energy which is not thinglike, with changes which occur indeterministically as quantal events are said to do. Clusters and chains of events allow of much more flexibility and variety of structure than genuine things, which hold properties together in comparatively rigid ways. They can start and stop, jump, transform in character, even perhaps double back on themselves; they can crisscross and interpenetrate, divide and recombine, without metaphysical embarrassment. But things, especially basic things, require a stable perduring character.

Yet these advantages do not seem to me to be sufficient. We have already recorded reservations about whether it would be possible to maintain a system of events of finite extension, which did not resolve in turn down to instantaneous events, and pointed out that such a system has no resources for explaining how or why the transformation of one event into another occurs (the problem of change).[8] Still more serious, in my opinion, is that events as Russell conceives them cannot be properly independent. In the first place, the *location* of an event is an identifying feature of it, for just that distinguishes it from the occurrence of an equal degree of the same physical magnitude somewhere else in space-time. But if, as seems probable, there is no absolute frame of coordinates for space and time, the location of an event can only be specified by reference to other events. More than that, it does not have a place except in relation to other events, so far in such direction in space-time from such and such other events. So an event is the event it is only through relation to other events. And so the space-time frame of the world is not fundamentally built out of previously specified events, as Russell proposes in chapter 29 of *The Analysis of Matter*. On the contrary, the whole space-time world is the basic reality, and particular events are logically secondary existents which are constructed by limitations on the whole.

In the second place—and the argument here follows the same path—perhaps the particular value of every physical magnitude at every place in space-time depends upon the values of that magnitude at all other places. This is a generalization of Mach's principle, which proposed that the inertial mass of a body depended on the quantity of matter in the universe.[9] If this is so, then as before, the events will depend for their character on the nature of all other events in space-time. So they will not be properly independent. The only properly independent reality will be the entire space-time frame.

---

8. Chapter 3 above.

9. For a discussion of this see Misner, Thorne, and Wheeler, *Gravitation*, sections 21–22.

GENERAL RELATIVITY: THE RETURN OF SPINOZA

The line of thought leading to the view that only the whole cosmos can be a satisfactory basic reality in the philosophy of matter finds its triumphant vindication in the theory of general relativity, or geometrodynamics.[10] In this theory, space-time is no longer viewed as a static, neutral, bland background against which the forces of nature play out their drama. It is itself a participant, having more qualities than traditionally recognized, differing in these qualities from place to place and transforming from one condition to another over time. These qualities, and in particular *curvature* (the quantity determining the character of straight lines, the behavior of parallel lines, the relation of length to area, and in general, the geometry of the space), are specified in a mathematical structure known as a *tensor*, G. And this tensor determines the density of mass/energy T at a place (the modern equivalent of "quantity of matter") according to Einstein's breathtakingly simple equation:

$$G = 8\pi T$$

The quantity of matter and the curvature of space-time mutually determine one another. What more natural than to hold that here are but two different ways of speaking of the same phenomenon? Matter and curvature of the cosmos are one and the same.[11] Perhaps the tensor G determines total quantity of mass/energy, but not its particular form. Then we can suppose some other, more traditionally physical magnitude to be a character of space which does determine this.[12] In that event, too, particular things are not separate, discrete existences, but local peculiarities of the single overarching totality. Spatial regions are clearly not independent existences of the type envisaged by concrete particularism. Only the whole world satisfies that requirement. And even it can satisfy that requirement and incorporate the findings of quantum theory only by supposing fluctuations in the geometry which destroy its deterministic character at tiny distances.[13]

But that does not affect the basic cosmological claim that the whole cosmos is the only viable basic concrete particular in the philosophy of matter—though now perhaps our theme deserves the new title of philosophy of space, of which matter is one aspect. The atomistic distinction between matter and void is quite superseded. Each is a variety of a space much more substantial than a pure

---

10. A wealth of material on this difficult topic is to be found in ibid.

11. Misner, Thorne, and Wheeler say that space is the key element in general relativity, while space-time is the particular hero of special relativity only. That issue does not affect the point being made here.

12. Wheeler, however, speaks of Einstein's vision of a purely geometric basis for physics as at a higher state of development than ever before. (J.A. Wheeler, *Geometrodynamics*.)

13. Misner, Thorne and Wheeler, *Gravitation*, section 43.4. There are unsolved problems in this area.

"Newtonian" expanse. In Wheeler's words ". . . elementary particles do not form a really basic starting point for the description of nature. Instead, they represent a first-order correction to vacuum physics."[14]

You will readily appreciate how this holistic, monistic, totalistic view echoes the conclusions of Spinoza. There is but one substance, and it embraces all reality; familiar bodies are but finite modes of extension. It does not, of course, recapitulate Spinoza's determinism or his pantheism, and to this point has nothing to say about the integration of mind in the whole scheme. Nevertheless, the resemblance of the natural cosmology of general relativity with Spinoza's world is striking enough.

SUMMARY AND UNFINISHED BUSINESS

Concrete particularism is a natural program in the philosophy of matter, and we have followed its vicissitudes from the foundations of atomism through ever more unfamiliar cosmologies to a culmination in the Spinozism of contemporary theory. In following atomism's fortunes, we have found it necessary to distinguish primary from secondary qualities and have seen how atomism can survive criticism on that basis. We have looked at alternative systems, of Spinoza and Leibniz, whose foundations we criticized. We have looked at more closely allied intellectual constructions, of Boscovich and Russell, but found reason not to prefer them. We have ended in a position closer to Spinoza than to the atomism from which we set out, for reasons which derive from the course of scientific advance and the cosmological conclusions which that advance invites.

Now although the discussion of secondary qualities was carried out with reference to atomism, the same problems arise in connection with a cosmos seen in the light of general relativity. If there is no reduction for color in atomism, there is no reduction in unified curved space either, and human experience gets the same kind of subjective, mental interpretation.

This leads to our unfinished business. What place in the scheme of things should we assign to the knowing mind which apprehends the world of space, time, and matter and constructs theories of them? What should we make of life and mind?

Over the last century or so, the whole climate of opinion in the biological sciences has altered. Whereas the earlier orthodoxy was that matter in living things followed distinctive patterns irreducible to ordinary material behavior, the contemporary assumption is quite the reverse. Scientists in these fields now work on the hypothesis that vital functions are biochemically determined, and biochemistry is taken to be just the (normal) chemistry of abnormally complex molecular structures. In the language of the nineteenth century, mechanism has triumphed over vitalism—for the moment, at least.

This being the case, the existence of *living creatures* does not, at the moment,

---

14. Wheeler, *Geometrodynamics*. See also Einstein, *The Evolution of Physics*.

require any addition to the cosmological theses which the study of inanimate nature sustains. Here is an astonishing reduction indeed. At first sight, no distinction could be more striking, more likely to indicate a fundamental duality in our world, than the contrast between the living and the nonliving. To the common sense and common ignorance of mankind, the idea of a special indwelling, propelling, and controlling force setting the living apart from the rest and accounting for its extaordinary behavior is an extremely natural one. We still record that notion in our vocabulary of the *animate*, or soul endowed, and the inanimate.

Yet our current theory of these matters holds the distinction to be one of complexity only. And as such it supports no new ontology, no new range of beings, as did the theory of animation.

The course of the biological sciences has thus taken a turn which is *negative* in the philosophy of nature: contrary to reasonable initial expectation, the living division of nature requires, qua living, no distinctive ontology. No vegetable or animal souls need figure among our basic concrete particulars.

In the case of mind the situation is more controversial. The program of contemporary materialism is to demonstrate that the situation of mind is the same as that of life; that is, the mental reduces to the physical. Materialism has gained a certain amount of plausibility in this century by the so far uniformly successful attempts to relate mental processes to brain functions. But whether nervous tissue, considered as living biochemical substance, exhausts the nature of the mind is an enormous topic, perhaps the most interesting question in the philosophy of mind.[15]

Not the least of our difficulties concern the status of the secondary qualities themselves. But suppose we do take materialism as giving an adequate account of human nature. Then we are the same as our bodies. And they emerge, on the new Spinozistic view, not as distinct and independent things but as temporally and spatially restricted fragments of the whole.

How can such a fragment develop and represent within itself a theory encompassing the whole of which it is a part? What ground have we for any presumptuous confidence that a mere fragment is capable of comprehending and attaining any real understanding of the whole? There is nothing like science to both inspire and chasten the metaphysical ambition of mankind.

---

15. For an account of these problems, see K. Campbell, *Body and Mind*, and the references therein.

III
A FIRST SURVEY
OF ONTOLOGY

8 The Tasks of Ontology

CATEGORIES

D.C. Williams divides the field of metaphysics into two broad subdivisions, *speculative cosmology* and *analytic ontology*.[1] Speculative cosmology has been our theme in part II; it is concerned with developing the best general description of ourselves and our world that we can devise. Cosmology deals with questions of what manner of world this is. In particularist systems it answers these questions in terms of what kinds of thing we must recognize and how these relate to each other.

But there is another kind of question, even more abstract and general, to which cosmology leads us. We find ourselves asking just what is a *thing* anyway? Are there any entities other than things? If so, what are they? Granted that there are, for example, causal connections in our world, just what is involved in a *causal* relationship? These general, structural problems belong to analytic ontology.

The problems of analytic ontology can be pursued in large measure independently of cosmology—indeed for most of this century they have almost monopolized metaphysics. But philosophy is a seamless garment, and problems of one kind lead to problems of the other. In part II, in discussing cosmological issues, we had to touch on ontological questions. Just what is a concrete particular? What is a reduction? Is a thing anything more than a collection of qualities? Can anything have only relational powers and no intrinsic qualities? And here in part III, we will find that although ontology is our theme, cosmological issues will crop up. So the division of metaphysics into two departments is a convenience for study, rather than an absolute distinction.

---

1. D.C. Williams, *Principles of Empirical Realism*, p. 74.

Let us begin with the question, Are there any entities which are not things, or are concrete particulars the only item on a complete schedule of distinct *categories of being?* What about events, spaces, periods of time, properties, numbers, relations, or tendencies—do these all reduce, somehow, to things? If so, how? In asking about categories, we are asking about the basic varieties of existence. That is why this study goes by the name of ontology, or the science of being.[2]

METHOD IN ONTOLOGY: THE CONNECTION WITH LOGIC

It is not at all obvious where to begin in ontology. How do we find out whether there are such entities as concrete or abstract particulars, events or universals? In this study we will use what is to my mind the most promising method, the *method of logical analysis*. That is, first we find out which types of statement-making sentence we require to express our knowledge. Then we analyze specimens of such sentences to reveal their structure. We lay bare the various logical elements of which the sentence is composed, the elements which in combination enable the sentence to make a claim about the world. The guiding idea of the method of logical analysis is that the various ontological elements, the categories which we seek, correspond to the various logical elements in our sentences.

Thus if sentences of some indispensible type can be true only if there are concrete particulars, periods of time, and events, then we must recognize concrete particulars, times, and events among the categories of being.

We approach the ontological problem by attempting to settle the logical questions of which sentence types are indispensable, what is their correct analysis, and which categories this analysis involves. The route to ontology is through logic.[3]

Perhaps an example can make all this plainer.

SUBJECT-PREDICATE SENTENCES

Our task is to determine which sentence forms are indispensable and which categories such sentences involve. An inviting point of departure is the *subject-*

---

2. To establish a reasoned inventory of the categories would be achievement enough. Indeed, I do not think that any more is possible in ontology. But you should be aware that in both the Thomist and the existentialist traditions something further is attempted: the task of finding some structure or nature common to everything that exists, no matter what its category, in virtue of which it enjoys being.

3. This is a standard approach in contemporary analytical philosophy. Not everyone accepts it. The only way to test the method is to discover what it can do. The whole of this part of the book is an illustration of the method.

THE TASKS OF ONTOLOGY 109

predicate form. This is a very simple and very familiar type of sentence. It is used by everyone who speaks English or any remotely similar natural language. It seems to occur, inevitably, in the thought, speech, and research report of every investigator, no matter what his theme. We are quite convinced that myriads of subject-predicate sentences are true.

Take an example:

Julius Caesar was bald.

We can parse this as in school grammar: this sentence has a *subject*, 'Julius Caesar', and a *predicate*, 'was bald'. The subject picks out an item (an object) about which we are going to make some claim. The predicate, on the other hand, does not pick out an object in this way, but makes a claim concerning the item which the subject picks out. In our example, the object picked out is a celebrated Roman military man, and the claim made about him is that he was lacking in hair on the head.

There is an alternative way of analyzing our sentence. We can hold that the predicate is not 'was bald' in its entirety, but just 'bald'. On this account, 'was' is a mere logical link, a *copula* or joiner, necessary to bind the two terms into a statement-making sentence. This alternative has some advantages—for example, it enables us to isolate *tense* for separate treatment more readily. It also has some drawbacks—it makes it harder to grasp the claim-making role of the predicate, and there are difficulties about how to treat sentences with intransitive verbs as predicates, such as

Julius Caesar sleeps.

The differences between these two analyses do not matter at this stage.

We will proceed with the original two-part analysis. The subject, 'Julius Caesar' is a *singular term*. More precisely, it is a *definite singular term*. That is to say, it is used in this sentence to name, pick out, or refer to exactly one concrete particular object. The sentence is a failure if there is no object to which 'Julius Caesar' refers, or if there is more than one. (It doesn't matter that the object isn't here *now*. When we say there *is* an object for this singular term to refer to, we use 'is' *tenselessly;* it doesn't mean 'is now' but rather 'is to be found among those things which at some time exist'.)

The predicate, 'was bald', on the other hand, is a *general term*.[4] General terms are not restricted in application to exactly one object. Indeed many objects, although not all, are bald. General terms can apply in many instances, as with 'bald', or, as it happens, in just one instance ('president of the United States between 1970 and 1972') or to none at all ('dies in his 257th year'). General terms do not name or refer to particular objects, as singular terms do.

---

4. Sometimes we call 'bald' alone the general term. In the two-part analysis of subject-predicate sentences, this is just a convenient abbreviation. It is strictly correct, of course, in the three-part analysis.

There are two different accounts given of how general terms work. In the first, they refer to a special *abstract object*, such as the *property of being bald*, or *baldness*, which in some way belongs to Julius Caesar. In the second, general terms are linked in a direct but nonunique way to ordinary objects like Caesar. The general term 'bald' applies to Caesar and also, as it happens, many other things as well. We say 'bald' is *true of* every one of a certain collection of men.

Which of these accounts is correct is a most controversial question, and we will postpone it. Let us follow Quine in the meantime and take the second account.[5] Then the sentence

Julius Caesar is bald

claims that 'bald' is true of, or applies to, Julius Caesar.

Now we can state, quite generally, the *truth conditions* for any subject-predicate sentence:

A subject-predicate sentence is true if and only if the general term is true of the object to which the singular term refers.[6]

Thus the logical analysis of subject-predicate sentences distinguishes two distinct elements, singular terms and general terms. And these elements are mentioned when we state the truth conditions for sentences of that type. No logical analysis is satisfactory unless it enables us to state truth conditions. Further, this analysis, together with the account given of singular and general terms, provides guidance in matters of ontology. For what categories of being must there be to ensure the truth of a subject-predicate sentence? On the Quinean account, only concrete particulars. There must be concrete particulars for singular terms to refer to. Equally, there must be concrete particulars for the general terms to be true of. These are the only kind of entity required.[7]

Other accounts of the role of general terms would give other ontological results. Suppose we held, for example, that general terms refer to properties. Then the truth condition for subject-predicate sentences would run:

A subject-predicate sentence is true if and only if the object referred to by the singular term has the property referred to by the general term.

This account involves commitment to two categories: concrete particulars, like Julius Caesar, and *abstract objects*, such as baldness.

---

5. W.V. Quine, *Word and Object*, pp. 239f.
6. Ibid., p. 96.
7. We neglect, for the time being, the fact that there must be *words* and *sentences* in order for sentences to be true. These are sometimes treated as *sets* of concrete particulars (blobs of ink, sounds) of which more later.

THE TASKS OF ONTOLOGY

To say what an abstract object is, is no easy task. The secret seems to lie in absence of definite spatiotemporal location. Baldness is not *itself* at any place, not even at every place filled by a bald man. It cannot be shifted about and probably cannot be destroyed, even by the invention and use of hair restorer. The distinguishing mark of abstract objects, or at any rate of properties, is that they can be simultaneously completely present in many locations.

In any event, baldness is a different kettle of fish from any, and even every, bald man. So a *property* account of general terms involves at least a two-category ontology. Quine's analysis of subject-predicate sentences, which links general terms directly to concrete particulars through the relation *true of*, yields a single-category ontology, and so unless there are compelling reasons against it, it is to be preferred on grounds of economy.[8]

The analysis of subject-predicate sentences can be readily generalized to cover *relational* sentences—those with a transitive verb, which school grammar held to contain a subject, a predicate, and a third linguistic item, unfortunately called an 'object'.

> Wellington defeated Napoleon.

This sentence has two definite singular terms and a general term which applies to objects not singly but in pairs. Such sentences are true if and only if the general term is true of the objects referred to by the singular terms taken in order, in this case, in the order in which their names occur in the sentence. We need this proviso about order, since of course Napoleon did *not* defeat Wellington.

This treatment can be extended:

> Wellington defeated Napoleon at Waterloo.

> Wellington defeated Napoleon at Waterloo with the help of Blucher.

In all cases of this type the true-of account confines ontic commitment to a single category.[9]

ONTOLOGICAL PRINCIPLES OF THE SUBJECT-PREDICATE FORM

Our investigation so far suggests these two principles:

---

8. This is an application of Occam's razor: Entities are not to be multiplied beyond necessity. If properties are not necessary, they are superfluous.

9. I use 'ontological' as the adjective 'pertaining to (the science or study of) ontology', and 'ontic' as 'pertaining to being or existence'.

1. The use of the subject-predicate form requires at least the category of concrete particulars.

2. Within the category of concrete particulars, there are (exist) objects corresponding to the subject(s) of every true subject-predicate sentence.

We have already treated the reasons for the first principle. The second rests simply on the idea that sauce for the goose is sauce for the gander. We offer a single account of the truth conditions of all subject-predicate sentences. It applies to all alike, and it requires, for the truth of all such sentences, objects for the singular term to refer to.

There is no getting away from it; every true subject-predicate sentence, in any plausible interpretation, carries an ontic commitment in the referring function of its singular terms. Yet in this very fact lie the seeds of disaster for any responsible cosmology.

PROBLEMS WITH THE SUBJECT-PREDICATE FORM

This heading is a bit misleading, since this section deals rather with problems arising if the subject-predicate form is taken as a guide in ontic matters. For the second principle introduced above rapidly fills our world with most bizarre and unwelcome denizens.

(i) **Fiction and Myth.** Here is a subject-predicate sentence:

Medusa had snakes for hair.

Does this involve the existence of Medusa? If the sentence is true, yes it does. But perhaps we can wriggle out: The sentence is false, since there never were any Gorgons, and false subject-predicate sentences carry no ontic commitment.

Very well, here is another sentence:

Medusa was a mythical woman with snakes for hair.

This sentence is *true* and in subject-predicate form. So by the second principle, it commits us to Medusa. There is only one way out here: to insist that despite superficial appearances this sentence is not *really* in subject-predicate form at all. Thus we could argue that 'mythical' is a very nonstandard sort of adjective. It does not apply to objects in the direct way that, for example, 'feminine' does. A better treatment of our sentence would be:

In myth, Medusa had snakes for hair.

This in turn is expanded as

THE TASKS OF ONTOLOGY

> There is a story (told by the ancients, which we do not believe) in which a snake-haired woman called 'Medusa' figures.

And the falsehood

> Medusa was a mythical winged horse

is counted as false not because there were no Gorgons but because there is no Greek story featuring a winged horse called Medusa.[10]

Much the same device can be used in fictional cases. There is a sense in which

> Mr. Pickwick spent Christmas at Dingley Dell

is true, while

> Mr. Pickwick married Mrs. Bardell

is false. But strictly, the truth of the former entails the existence of Mr. Pickwick and of Dingley Dell. We think of it as true because we are confusing it with

> Dickens wrote a story containing sentences from which 'Mr. Pickwick spent Christmas at Dingley Dell' can be inferred.

We can shorten this to

> In Dicken's novel, Mr. Pickwick spent Christmas at Dingley Dell.

(ii) **Negations.** Our problems are by no means over. If

> Vulcan is nearest the sun

is false, then we would expect

> Vulcan is not nearest the sun

to be true. But it isn't. Neither of these sentences is true, for 'nearest the sun' is *not* true of the object referred to by 'Vulcan' and nor is 'not nearest the sun'. Here we have a case of two sentences, one the negation of the other, which are both false. So they must be contraries rather than contradictories.

---

10. This is a sample of the strategy of claiming that in logic, things are not as they seem. Here the claim is that not all apparently subject-predicate sentences really are such, or really have their apparent subjects as referring terms. This general strategy is crucially important to ontology. Wittgenstein said that ordinary language is perfectly in order as it is. Do not believe him.

The usual way to treat this is to distinguish two varieties of negation, 'internal' and 'external'. In the internal negation of a sentence the predicate is negated and applied to the original subject. The result is a sentence contrary to the original. In external negation the whole sentence, not just the predicate, is negated, and the result is the contradictory, which must be true if the original sentence is false.

In our case, then, since

> Vulcan is nearest the sun

is false, its external negation

> It is not the case that Vulcan is nearest the sun

must be true. Now when we state the truth conditions of this last sentence we must just say that they are the reverse of those for

> Vulcan is nearest the sun.

We cannot state the truth conditions directly. Otherwise, we will find ourselves claiming that

> It is not the case that Vulcan is nearest the sun

is true if and only if 'nearest the sun' does not apply to the object referred to by 'Vulcan'. These are the truth conditions for the internal negation. And they get us back to a commitment to the existence of a nonexistent planet.

There is nothing in itself intolerable about stating the truth conditions for external negation indirectly. But a consequence of this is that the external negations of subject-predicate sentences are not themselves of subject-predicate form. We have already noticed that in fiction and myth, sentences which seem to be subject-predicate sentences must actually have a different form. Now we find that some negative subject-predicate sentences are misleading as to form too. The subject-predicate form is proving to be an unreliable instrument for investigations in ontology.

(iii) **Passive Constructions.** Historians assure us that

> The Scandinavians worshiped Thor.

This is a two-place, relational, subject-predicate sentence (to outward appearance, at least), and its truth commits us to the existence of Scandinavians and of Thor. An unfortunate result. To avoid it, we could treat the so-called intensional verbs, involving beliefs and attitudes which may be wildly astray, as not properly relational. Then our original sentence would be considered a misleading way of saying

The Scandinavians were Thor worshipers,

which commits us only to Scandinavians, telling us something about their religion.

But this strategy, which makes our original sentence true, strikes trouble with the passive form.

Thor was worshiped by the Scandinavians.

Either Thor is real, or this sentence is false. If we take the second alternative, as everyone does nowadays, then the purely grammatical conversion from active to passive voice can convert a truth into a falsehood.

This is most unsatisfactory, and definite singular terms are at the root of the trouble. For they enter our language *whether or not they refer*. This is the basic reason why it is not a good idea to take subject-predicate sentences as a starting point in ontological investigations.[11] For of course it is only if they *do* refer that they can carry any ontic weight.

Some rigorous philosophers have proposed that definite singular terms should be admitted to our language only after it has been established that they refer.[12] There are two objections to this procedure. In the first place, it prevents anyone from denying the existence of anything. We cannot correct our friend's error by saying "Pegasus does not exist," since this denial must itself use the forbidden term 'Pegasus'. In the second place, it prevents us from discussing possibilities, from entertaining hypotheses, from saying, for example, "I wonder whether Ulysses was a real person?" For we could not even form the question until reference is established for the definite singular term, that is, until we knew that Ulysses was real.

(iv) **Abstract Subjects.** English, and languages like it, are very hospitable in their permissible sentence constructions. In particular, they allow subject-predicate sentences to be formed whose subject(s) are not terms referring to concrete particulars. It may be true, as Pope claims, that

Hope springs eternal in the human breast.

And if so, then our account of the truth conditions of subject-predicate sentences requires that there be an object to which the singular term 'hope' can refer. In discussing general terms above, we tried to avoid commitment to such intangible, elusive, unlocated objects; we made general terms true of the ordinary objects referred to by singular terms. But here no escape route is open. For the *singular* term 'hope' must refer in true subject-predicate sentences of which it is

---

11. This insight lies behind Russell's celebrated theory of definite descriptions, which systematically treats subject-predicate sentences as really having a quite different form. See below, chapter 10.

12. D. Hilbert and P. Bernays, in *Grundlagen der Mathematik*, place such a requirement on a formal language.

the subject; and it seems most probable that the object 'hope' refers to is the universal connected with the general terms 'hopes', 'is hopeful', and 'is hoping'.

Sentences with abstract subjects are by no means rare in English. The psalmist is confident that goodness and mercy shall follow him all the days of his life, while Shakespeare draws our attention not just to mercy, but to its quality. We refer constantly to freedom, justice, order, and power. We catalogue virtues and vices, whose names are abstract singular terms.

Yet there is an air of artificiality, of pedantry even, in the suggestion that this convenient way of expressing ourselves involves admitting the existence of squadrons of mysterious entities, existing somehow beyond space and time and so immune from direct experimental investigation.[13] The use of abstract singular terms, we feel, is only a stylistic matter. When Pope spoke of hope springing, he was not really referring to hope. He was making a claim about *men*, a claim concerning their tendencies to be hopeful. There are men, and they are irrepressibly hopeful, but there is no such thing as hope. This line of thought requires for its vindication a proof that whatever can be truly said using the term 'hope' can be equally well or better expressed without using it. This in turn requires a method for finding substitutes for sentences with an abstract subject, which do the same work (or at least all the legitimate work of the abstract sentences), yet contain no abstract singular terms. That task is harder than it might at first glance appear; some aspects of it are taken up below.[14]

The existence of abstract subjects apparently begs a most important question in ontology: Is there a category of abstract entities? We find here yet again that not English or any other natural language, as it stands, but only a purified and ordered language, can serve as the proper basis for investigation in ontology.

(v) **Generalizations and Existence Sentences.** Not all sentences are in subject-predicate form, whatever their superficial grammar may suggest. Generalizations are an important class here. Treating generalizations as subject-predicate sentences yields jokes reminiscent of *Alice in Wonderland* or *The Goon Show*:

> I passed nobody on the way. That's odd, for nobody walks faster than you do.
>
> Somebody must finish last in every race. Then he's a fool to go on competing.
>
> Since 1957, the average plumber has been getting slightly younger every year. Lucky chap.
>
> Cats have three tails, for every cat has one more tail than no cat, and no cat has two tails.

---

13. Plato is the greatest philosopher to take the opposite view. In his ontology, abstract entities such as hope are taken utterly seriously. The world of forms, which contains only such things, is the highest of realities.

14. Chapter 14.

'A', 'an', 'some', 'no', 'all', 'every', 'any' are called *indefinite singular terms,* and sentences containing them are not subject-predicate sentences of any ordinary kind. Some attempts have been made to treat them as compounds of subject-predicate sentences;[15] thus

>Every man is mortal

would be analyzed as

>Socrates is mortal and Plato is mortal and Aristotle is mortal and Descartes is mortal and . . . ,

while

>Some man is mortal

emerges as

>Socrates is mortal or Plato is mortal or Aristotle is mortal or Descartes is mortal or . . .

and

>Everybody loves somebody

would be a complex combination of conjunction with disjunction. But this will not do. The conjunction is sure to have the same truth value as the 'every' sentence only if, after listing every individual man and saying he is mortal, we add ". . . and that is all the men." But this last component is not a subject-predicate sentence. The same point applies to the 'some' sentence.

We must find a place for *generalizations,* as sentences with indefinite singular terms are called, in our ontological investigations.

>Some things are quasars

is as ontic a sentence as one could hope to find. And if

>Some things have no name at all

is true, any attempt to get by in ontology with the subject-predicate form alone is bound to be inadequate.

Existence sentences are peculiarly relevant here. They are apparently of subject-predicate form:

---

15. Cf L.Wittgenstein, *Tractatus Logico-Philosophicus.*

Julius Caesar exists.

Medusa does not exist.

But treating them in the subject-predicate way is a shortcut to disaster. If it is a subject-predicate sentence, then

Julius Caesar exists

is true provided 'exists' applies to the object referred to by 'Julius Caesar'. But if there *is* an object referred to, then 'exists' applies automatically. It is a "predicate" which adds nothing.
And on the other hand,

Medusa does not exist,

taken as an internal negation, is true provided 'does not exist' is true of the object referred to by 'Medusa'. If there is any such object, 'does not exist' does *not* apply to it. So

Medusa does not exist

would not be true. If there is no such object, then again

Medusa does not exist,

having a subject term which lacks reference, would not be true. All genuine subject-predicate sentences have an internal negation, so if existence sentences are of subject predicate form they have one, for which we could use the general expression.

X has nonexistence.

As we have seen from the case of Medusa, *every* such sentence must be false. But this is madness. We all know, to put it paradoxically, that there are lots of things that don't exist. So existence sentences are not subject-predicate sentences. They are better understood as generalizations:

Something is Julius Caesar.

Something is Medusa.

These behave better. The first is true and makes no pretense of describing Julius Caeser by means of a predicate. The second is false; nothing is Medusa. The importance of generalizations for ontology could not be more plain that it is here; existence sentences themselves, which we should expect to be crucial to questions of existence, prove on analysis to be generalizations in disguise.

THE TASKS OF ONTOLOGY

THE OVERPOPULATED WORLD

A philosopher once said that even if there *were* more things in heaven and earth than were dreamt of in his philosophy, he preferred it that way to the other way around. And with natural languages such as English, even if we confine ourselves to the clear central cases among subject-predicate sentences, we rapidly find ourselves with an embarras de richesses from the ontic point of view. Here are just half a dozen sentences, every one of which should give a philosopher some uneasiness:

> The center of the orbit lies within the sun.
>
> The trends in population growth show no repetitive pattern.
>
> The plot of *Tom Jones* is complicated.
>
> The national purpose will be subverted by this measure.
>
> The reason for saying this lies in the probability of the plan's discouraging the cooperative movement.
>
> The ideal would be, of course, no infant mortality whatever.

Now if these sentences, or myriads like them, are true, and if they are subject-predicate sentences, then it seems we are landed with a world of centers, trends, plots, ideals, and Lord knows what else. We feel, rightly in my opinion, that somehow a mere turn of phrase is committing us to all manner of entities. But if we stick with the standard subject-predicate analysis we cannot avoid the commitment. It is mere frivolity to claim to eat one's cake and have it too. It will not do to say

> Of course there are no such things as trends, but the trend of population is giving me deep concern.

In these troublesome cases, the subject position is filled by a 'the' construction, or *definite description*. But this is not the source of the problem about trends or ideals. For nothing is simpler than to introduce a proper name which has the same reference as any given definite description.

Our centers, trends, and plots can be called Adam, Cain, and Abel, and we are back where we started, with an overpopulated universe.

Nor is it satisfactory to attempt to use only *logically proper names*. A logically proper name is one with two peculiarities: it is introduced in such a way as to be guaranteed a reference (unlike 'Julius Caesar'), and it has a purely referential function, with no descriptive content whatever (unlike 'John Jones, Jr.').

When Russell was developing ideas about logically proper names as the philosophy of *logical atomism,* he reached the conclusion that only *demonstratives,* such as 'this' and 'that', applied to minimal elements in perception, were genuine proper names. The fatal defect of such a result, from the point of view of ontology, is that it carries the consequence that only what is perceptible is real. That *might* be true, but it is illegitimate to adopt a method of analysis which guarantees it. The proposal to use only sentences with logically proper names begs the question against the reality of anything not given to human sense. There are no more centers, trends, or plots to clutter up the world, which is all very well. But there are no protons, electrons, or cosmic rays either, which should make us suspicious. How could mere logic show such things to be impossible?

OTHER PROBLEMS IN NATURAL LANGUAGE

To sum up our progress so far, a natural language is in a state of logical and ontic chaos. It contains many sorts of construction, and many sorts of term, which subvert attempts to use the traditional subject-predicate analysis as the foundation for a rational ontology.

There are other defects in natural language, too, which also call for changes towards an artificial philosophical language.

Ambiguity. Natural languages contain ambiguities. Some of these depend solely on ambiguous *terms*, words of identical form with the same kind of function but different meanings as in

> I went to the bank and drew my balance,

which can involve painting by the riverside or a financial transaction with a teller. In other cases, ambiguity turns on alternative interpretations of a sentence's structure, as in

> The robber dropped four feet from his perch on the roof.

Similarly,

> There is a time before any other time

can mean either that there is or that there isn't a first moment of time, depending on how much 'any' is stressed.

Until ambiguities are resolved, there is doubt about the truth value of sentences and further doubt about what they imply, both of which affect metaphysics.

Truth-Value Gaps. Some grammatical English sentences do not satisfactorily fit into our classifications either as true or as false. Perhaps sentences with nonreferring singular terms are of this kind. We held that if every member of a cricket team is bareheaded, then

> The team member in the top hat is keeping wickets

is false. Some writers, of whom P.F. Strawson is the most eminent, argue that such sentences are neither true nor false. In such cases, where the singular term does not refer, the question of truth or falsity just does not arise.[16]

Another candiate for truth-value gap is the conditional whose antecedent is unfulfilled and unconnected to the consequent, such as

> If the moon is made of green cheese, then it is cold on Pluto.

Yet other candidates are sentences which combine terms so foreign to each other that some kind of nonsense is produced (sentences committing what Gilbert Ryle calls 'category mistakes'):

> Saturday is in bed.
>
> Serendipity drinks procrastination.[17]

Like ambiguity, truth-value gaps frustrate attempts to get a clear view of the ontic implications of what we believe.

Fluctuation of Truth-Value. Many sentences in English are inconstant in truth value; that is, they are true when used on some occasions and false on others. The most familiar of these are sentences containing terms which change their reference depending on who uses them and when, such as 'I' and 'you', 'here' and 'now', 'yesterday' and 'tomorrow'.

> I was with you here yesterday

can be either true or false depending on who says it, when he says it, to whom it is addressed, and where it is spoken.

The tense element in verbs has the same character; given that at some time or other you become my acquaintance,

> I have already met you

may be either true or false.

We also use sentences in which a term's reference depends on what has been said in earlier sentences. Thus the sentence

> The man involved was a great general

says something true about the Duke of Marlborough if it follows the sentence

---

16. P.F. Strawson, *Introduction to Logical Theory*, pp. 175ff. W.V. Quine, in *Word and Object*, suggests that this is a normal way of treating such sentences in ordinary English.

17. G. Ryle, *The Concept of Mind*, pp. 16ff.

122 A FIRST SURVEY OF ONTOLOGY

Sarah married a Churchill.

But it says something false about Sir Winston if it follows the sentence

Clementine married a Churchill.

This sort of situation is not at all unusual.

Fluctuation in truth value is one more nuisance in logic and ontology. If we cannot clarify which sentences we hold true and what they involve, we will never get a clear picture of our ontic commitments. So philosophers have set about devising an improved language, or *canonical notation*. The idea here is that careful restrictions on the kinds of sentence which can be formed, and on the vocabulary which can be used, will enable us to avoid the problems of the subject-predicate form in English and the other nuisances and shortcomings of natural language which we have discussed in this chapter.

CANONICAL NOTATIONS

The program of developing a canonical notation is a modest modern version of earlier programs to devise a *perfect language*. A canonical notation is perhaps not a perfect language, but it is at least an improvement on the natural languages of ordinary life and of the sciences. We have already found ample scope for improvement in natural languages, for taking the form of natural sentences at face value results in ontic chaos.

In a canonical notation the form of every sentence must be made perfectly clear. Then an account of these forms must be given which will make plain just what they imply. In ontology we are chiefly interested in what must exist in order for them to be true, especially in what categories they involve. The best canonical notation will have the minimum of such implications.

In all of this, intellectual hygiene is the motive. We need to know where we stand. And the principle of economy, requiring that commitments be kept to a minimum, guards against introducing into our thought and belief elements which are gratuitous and for which, therefore, there is no sufficient basis.

Although the term *canonical notation* is a new one,[18] the attempt to devise such notations has always been on the philosohers' agenda. In the *Aristotelian* canonical notation, the standard form for any sentence involves two general terms which are joined to make a sentence by a *copula* expressing quality (affirmative or negative) and quantity (some or all).

The basic Aristotelian forms are thus four different generalizations, the affirmative and negative universal, such as

---

18. Quine gave it currency.

THE TASKS OF ONTOLOGY

All penguins are swimmers

and

No cats play guitars

and the affirmative and negative particular, of which examples are

Some tigers are fierce

and

Some bridges are not timber.

Sentences of these types came to be known as *a*, *e*, *i*, and *o* propositions; in each type the two general terms are related to each other in a distinctive way. These relations can be expressed using a letter for the copula between the general terms, so that in place of these four examples we would write

Penguins *a* swimmers.

Cats *e* guitar players.

Tigers *i* fierce.

Bridges *o* timber.

The notation based on these four forms enjoyed a very long period of supremacy and is still worth investigating. But we will not be pursuing it, for a notation which springs out of modern logic is, in my opinion, better able to deal with problems about definite singular terms, about complicated relations, and about numbers.

There is an *idealist* canonical notation, at least in embryo, in Bradley's dictum that the Absolute is the true subject of all affirmations. This would be quite different in its approach from the Aristotelian system. On the idealist view all sentences should take the form

Reality is such that. . . .

And in place of

All penguins are swimmers,

we would perhaps write

Reality is such that it contains only the swimming variety of penguinhood.

What categories this involves us in is not very clear, but it certainly seems to move away from the familiar ground of concrete particulars.

As yet a third alternative to be found in philosophical tradition, there is a *logical atomist* canonical notation. This relies solely on subject-predicate sentences in which a definite singular term is joined to a general term. And the sentences must be of the special kind which use only logically proper names as subjects. It is extremely difficult to produce any actual sentences of this notation which would replace an ordinary claim like

All penguins swim.

Besides, we have already seen that this notation has trouble dealing with generalizations of any type. And we have seen what difficulties we encounter in ontology if we take any version of the subject-predicate form as our standard guide.

So the notation which we will study is *Quine's*. It is based on bound variables and general terms. Because it contains no proper names and has a standard method for dealing with definite descriptions, it is the most promising point of departure for an inquiry into categories.

9 Quine's Canonical Notation

A canonical notation is a language, clearer and simpler than a natural language, but a language nevertheless.[1] And to give an exact account of it, we specify a *vocabulary*, setting out what kinds of symbols belong to the language; a *syntax*, laying down which combinations of symbols are well formed (i.e., grammatical) sentences; and a *semantics*, setting forth the interpretation of the grammatical sentences.

VOCABULARY

Logical particles. The standard Russellian notation is used, and so we have

∼	negation
·	conjunction
∨	disjunction
⊃	material implication
≡	material equivalence
(,)	parentheses

---

[1] What matters in a canonical notation is what elements there are and how they fit together. It does not, of course, matter at all how these elements are *written*. The use of unfamiliar symbols is for convenience and accuracy, and what they look like is a trivial matter. Insofar as it suggests otherwise, the phrase 'canonical notation' is unfortunate.

A FIRST SURVEY OF ONTOLOGY

Individual Variables. Individual variables are lower-case letters, x, y, z, w, with prime marks added, x', x'', ..., if need be, to ensure that we never run out of distinct individual variables.

Quantifiers. Quantifiers are technical versions of the *indefinite* singular terms 'something,' 'everything', 'nothing', 'most'. Quine's notation uses just two kinds of quantifier, the *universal* (written by enclosing an individual variable in parentheses) and the *existential* (written using an inverted capital E and individual variable within parentheses). These quantifiers are read as "for all ..." and "for some ..." respectively.

Predicates. Predicates form the remaining element in the vocabulary of the notation. They supply all the specific content which gives one sentence a different subject matter from others. Whether our talk is of dogs or gods depends on the predicates our sentences contain, and whether we say of them that they are great or small again turns on which predicates are present.

The traditional school grammar idea that a subject term introduces a topic upon which the predicate makes a comment, disappears in Quine's canonical notation. Predicates do all the work of both introducing topics and commenting on them, as we shall see.

In discussing the notation itself, it is generally irrelevant whether sheep or goats or anything else is the subject matter of the sentence. And we prevent this irrelevant question from cluttering our minds by using *dummy predicate letters*, capitals F, G, H ..., in place of real predicates. And again we use superscripted prime marks (F', G'', ...) if need be, to assure us of an inexhaustible supply of different symbols.

Dummy predicate letters are not variables. F, G, H, and so on are definite fixed predicates, like 'frog', 'grog', and 'hog', but we just do not care which. We are interested, when considering the notation itself, in how a predicate behaves just because it is a predicate. To avoid being distracted from this, we write not 'fat', 'frosty', or 'fortyish', but just F.

Most of the predicates we naturally think of are one-place predicates; they apply to individuals considered singly, such as 'red', 'round', or 'rusty'. But there can, of course, be two-, three-, or more-placed predicates asserting relations between objects, like 'redder than', 'rustier than', 'between ——— and ———', 'bought from ——— with ——— borrowed from ———'. All such multiplaced predicates also appear as dummy letters. By convention, they are placed in front of the variables with which they are associated. So we write Fx, Gxy, $Hxyz$, and so on.

FORMATION RULES

In the canonical notation, then, we have logical particles, individual variables, quantifiers, and predicates. Sentences are built up from these vocabulary elements according to some definite, simple rules. There are two basic types of sentences, open and closed; each type can be simple or compound.

Open sentences. Simple open sentences are formed by *concatenating* (writing together in order) an *n*-place predicate followed by *n* individual variables, for example

$$Fx$$

$$Gxy$$

Because variables are involved, these sentences do not say of any definite object that it is F, or of any two definite objects that they are related G-wise. So although they are called sentences, they are neither true nor false, for they make no definite statement.[2]

Open sentences can be more complicated in various ways. Simple open sentences can be joined by logical connectives, giving, for example

$$Fx \ . \ Gxy$$

or

$$Fx \supset Gxy$$

or

$$(Fx \ . \ Gxy) \supset Hz.$$

There is no upper limit to this process of combination.

In English, predicates can themselves be combined by 'truth-functional' connectives. We can regard the predicate 'woman', for example, as just a shorthand way of writing 'human . female . adult'. So we might expect our canonical language to include open sentences such as

$$(F \ . \ G) \, x$$

and

$$(G \supset H) \, y.$$

But all such constructions can be "dissolved away," in Quine's expression, leaving us with simple predicates only, as in the open sentences

---

2. Calling such formulas 'sentences' is somewhat at odds with the traditional notion of a sentence as a minimum combination of symbols expressing a complete thought. But they are essential combinations of symbols in the building of complete sentences, and 'open sentences' is the name they have been given.

$Fx \cdot Gx$

and

$Gy \supset Hy.$[3]

Closed Sentences. Closed sentences are complete sentences, and they do have a truth value.[4] They are formed by *closing* an open sentence with the right number of the right quantifiers, either existential or universal, or by combining already closed sentences using truth functions.

Simple open sentences are closed when they are preceded by one quantifier for each distinct individual variable in the sentence.

For example, from

Fx

we can get

$(x)Fx$ (Everything is F)

or

$(\exists x)(Fx)$ (Something is F).

From

Gxy

come

$(x)(y)(Gxy),$
$(\exists x)(\exists y)(Gxy),$

and others with a mixture of existential and universal quantifiers.

Even in thise simple cases, if we have both existential and universal quantifiers to deal with, the order in which they occur makes a difference.

Everybody loves somebody

becomes

---

3. Quine, *Word and Object*, p. 175

4. That is, they are either true or false. Some logicians have allowed complete sentences to take other values, perhaps intermediate between truth and falsity. But Quine's system is two-valued.

QUINE'S CANONICAL NOTATION 129

$(x)(\exists y)(\text{Loves } xy),$[5]

while

There is somebody everyone loves

which means something quite different, we express by

$(\exists y)(x)(\text{Loves } x\, y).$

Somebody loves everyone

is different again. It appears in the canonical notation as

$(\exists x)(y)(\text{Loves } x\, y).$

And we can say that

Everyone has someone who loves them

using

$(y)\,(\exists x)\,(\text{Loves } x\, y).$

In more complicated cases, even the order of two quantifiers of the same type can make a difference.

Closed sentences can be more complex in various ways; separate closed sentences can be combined by truth functions:

$(\exists x)\, Fx\,.\,(y)Hy$

$(x)\, Fx \supset (\exists y)Hy$

and so on.[6]

Compound open sentences can be closed:

$(x)\,(\exists y)(Fx \supset Gy).$

An open sentence with a closed component can be closed:

---

5. In these examples, we are using the quantifiers to mean 'for every *person*,' 'for some *person*' rather than the unrestricted *thing*. This is just a convenience. We could state explicitly that the things involved were persons if we wanted to.

6. Brackets around *simple* open sentences can be omitted.

$(\exists y)(Fy \cdot (x)(Gx))$.

Sentences of any of these kinds can be in turn combined using truth functions. It is possible to have too many quantifiers or to have the wrong ones. Thus we might get

$(z)(\exists x)Fx$.

This is a closed sentence with a superfluous, idle quantifier (z) which does no work. This sentence is equivalent to

$(\exists x) Fx$.

Or suppose we had

$(\exists y)(z) Fxy$.

Here we have the right number of quantifiers, but the wrong ones. It is equivalent to the *open* (i.e., not completely closed) sentence

$(\exists y) Fxy$.

We can, by building up more and more complex sentences in all the ways described above, form infinitely many well-formed sentences in the canonical notation. This is just as it should be. For there are indefinitely many different English sentences, and if there were a finite limit to the number of canonical sentences, we would know at once that the canonical notation is inadequate as a satisfactory, and ontologically superior, alternative to English. As it is, we know that there is no *numerical* barrier to the acceptability of the canonical notation. The crucial question will be: Are there any *kinds* of English sentence, which we cannot do without, for which there are no satisfactory analogs in the canonical language?

THE SEMANTICS OF THE CANONICAL NOTATION

We have so far specified in the vocabulary what kinds of words are to be found in the canonical language, and the formation rules lay down what combinations of these words count as sentences. What we must now do is set forth precisely the circumstances under which those sentences are true. We do this by explaining in a *metalanguage* how various components of the canonical language are connected with the world which the language describes, and how these connections determine the truth of canonical sentences.[7] To do this is to provide a semantics for the language.

Domain or Universe of Discourse. Our basic conception for

---

7. A metalanguage is a higher-level language used to talk about a given language—in this case, our metalanguage is English.

this purpose is that of a large and somewhat unspecified field of objects, called a *domain* or *universe of discourse*. It can, in theory, contain anything we fancy—numbers, angels, saints, chessmen, characters of fiction. . . . But our purpose is the sober one of truly describing the actual world. We do not know, certainly not at this stage, exactly what the actual world contains.

So we proceed cautiously, saying only that there is a universe of individual objects, the precise nature of which remains to be spelled out, which will form the field of the assertions which we make in the canonical language.

Predicates. Predicates are the only nonlogical constants in Quine's notation. Let us deal with them first. Every one-place predicate has assigned to it a subclass of items from the domain. The members of this subclass are exactly those objects of which the predicate is true. This subclass, which contains just the objects to which the predicate applies, is often dubbed the term's *extension*.

In theory, any predicate can be made to apply to any collection of objects. This is suggested by using the term 'assign'. But where a predicate is taken over from English, we take over with it the extension which has already been more or less precisely determined for it. Unless we want to spread wanton confusion, we assign to the predicate 'horse' the class containing all and only horses.

When we are introducing a new technical term, then we can be as highhanded as Humpty Dumpty was with Alice. We can make a new term mean exactly what we choose it to mean, no more and no less. That is, we can assign to it as its extension whatever subclass of the domain best suits our purposes. In so doing, we specify just which objects it is true of; we fix its application by fiat.

Both the null class and the universe class of the domain count as subclasses here. The extension of 'Chinese Pope' is null; that predicate is true of nothing—nothing is both Chinese and Pope, at least so far. And if, suppose, nothing lasts forever, then 'transitory' is true of everything; its extension is the same class as the entire domain.[8] The extensions of two-place and three-place predicates are classes of ordered pairs and triples from the domain. And so on for predicates of any number of places.

Even at this first stage in setting up a semantics, we seem to be already involved with the ontic category of individual objects. We do not have any definite singular terms in subject position, but in giving predicates an extension containing individual objects, we seem to be committed to some form of concrete particularism. It is important to realize that this commitment to concrete individual objects, horses or penguins for example, is so far only provisional. The whole matter depends on which predicates we ultimately include in our system. So long as 'horse' and 'penguin' remain, individual objects for them to be true of will be required. But perhaps these predicates belong only to the world's manifest image. Perhaps when the world is described correctly, these predicates give place to other, more fundamental predicates which are true of some

---

8. Some philosophers working in the Aristotelian tradition deny the legitimacy of empty and universal terms. I regard this as exposing a defect in their tradition rather than casting doubt on the propriety of such terms.

category of entity other than the concrete particular. A term like 'sulphur', for example, seems to require the category of *kind of stuff* rather than concrete particular.

To avoid begging questions in ontology, we must avoid *assuming* that any one variety of predicate is essential. For which predicates prove ultimately to be essential determines the ontological questions.

Individual Variables and Quantifiers. The individual variables of the canonical notation ($x, y, z, \ldots$) are attached to a predicate to form an open sentence. They therefore fill the same sort of place in open sentences as definite singular terms in subject position fill in subject-predicate sentences. So variables are some kind of singular term. Not definite singular terms, of course; there is no unique object picked out or referred to by them on every occasion of their use. So we must give an alternative account of how these terms relate to the objects in the domain.

We start from the notion of an *assignment* of objects to variables. Take the variable x, for example. It can be in turn assigned to each of the items in the domain. The celebrated Roman military man is assigned to 'Julius Caesar' on a permanent basis; but variables are linked to particular objects only under some assignment. *Under the assignment*, a variable acts like a proper name for the object assigned to it. In this it is like a singular term. But of course under any other assignment it would act as a proper name for some different object. That is the way in which variables are variable. Objects assigned to variables are called the *values* of the variable.

To attain a *complete* assignment, we proceed to link object with variable until every variable is linked to some object in the domain. No variable is to have more than one value, but the same object can be the value of different variables.

Now variables are closely linked with quantifiers. It is by the use of a quantifier containing the correct variable letter that *free* variables (those in simple open sentences or the open parts of mixed ones) become *bound* (that is, tied to a quantifier in the formation of a closed, complete sentence). Once the idea of assignment of values to variables has been introduced, we can describe the role of quantifiers with precision.

Consider all the possible different complete assignments. Then for simple existentially closed sentences, such as

$$(\exists x)\, Fx,$$

we can state general truth conditions thus: Such a sentence is true if and only if there is at least one assignment in which the value of x is an object of which F is true.

Analogously, for

$$(x)\, Fx$$

the truth conditions stipulate that in *every* assignment the object linked to x have F true of it.

Since everything in the domain is linked to x in at least one assignment, these truth conditions require, as we should expect, that $(x)\, Fx$ is true if and only if everything is F.[9]

The more complex cases work out as we would expect;

$$(x)\,(Fx \supset Gx),$$

for example, is true provided that in every assignment, the value assigned to x is either not F or both F and G.

$$(x)\,(y)\,(\text{Loves } x\, y)$$

requires that under every assignemnt the value assigned to x loves the value assigned to y.

Assignments, Binding, and Scope. A quantifier can be called 'x-binding' (or 'y-binding' or whatever) according to which variable letter it contains. And binding is a constraint on the freedom with which assignments can be made. Within a canonical sentence we use and reuse the same variable letter to indicate just where the same assignment must be made or some different one is permitted.

Thus

$$Fx\, .\, Gx$$

is an open sentence with two positions for free variables, which happen to contain the same variable letter. If we now close this sentence, obtaining for example

$$(\exists x)\,(Fx\, .\, Gx),$$

then the fact that x occurs after both F and G requires that the same assignment be made in each place. This sentence is true only if there is some *one* thing (or group of things) which is both F and G. It would not do to have some thing F and some *other* thing G. That situation is covered by the sentence

$$(\exists x)\,(\exists y)\,(Fx\, .\, Gy).$$

We say that a quantifier binds all the variables of its type (indicated by the variable letter it contains) which fall within its *scope*.

---

9. Note that in the metalanguage, we operate freely here with the ideas of 'something', 'at least one', 'everything', 'all', and so on. The quantitative ideas can be defined in terms of one another to a certain extent, but they cannot be eliminated. In our metalanguage they appear undefined, and are used here in our semantical explanation of the quantitative elements of the canonical language.

'Binding' and 'scope' are correlative terms. On the one hand, a quantifier binds all and only the appropriate free variables falling within its scope. The scope of a quantifier, conversely, is that fragment of what follows within which the quantifier controls permissible variation in assignments. In the canonical notation we use brackets to indicate scope.

We saw that in

$$(\exists x)(Fx \cdot Gx)$$

the assignments must be the same for each occurrence of the variable x. But in

$$(\exists x)(Fx \cdot (\exists x) Gx)$$

the first quantifier does not control assignment beyond the conjunction sign '.'. The value of the x associated with G can be quite different from that of the x associated with F. The whole sentence is equivalent to

$$(\exists x)(\exists y)(Fx \cdot Gy),$$

where the thing which is G may or may not be the same as the thing which is F.

On the same principle,

$$(x)(Fx \supset (\exists y)Gy) \quad \text{(If anything is } F\text{, then something is } G\text{)}$$

is equivalent to

$$(x)(Fx \supset (\exists x)Gx).$$

Here, although the x associated with G does fall within the scope of (x), it is not a free occurrence, for it is bound by $(\exists x)$. So it is not bound by (x). We are at liberty to give the x with G a different value from the x with F. It is merely to avoid confusion that the use of y is to be preferred here.

We can describe this whole situation succinctly by saying that under an assignment, variables *refer* to values in the universe of discourse *beyond* the sentence, and, independently of any particular assignment, the same variables *cross-refer, within* the sentence, to one another and to the key letter in the quantifier, if the same quantifier binds them both. Only by saying all this can we reach the position of being able to specify truth conditions for all varieties of canonical sentence.[10]

---

10. This account of variables and quantifiers goes by the name of 'objectual quantification'. Either this account, or some other which relates quantified sentences to a domain, is best adapted for consideration of ontological questions. But there is an alternative treatment of variables, known as 'substitutional quantification', which relates variables not to objects but to proper names which might go in the variable's place in a sentence. For substitutional quantification, see Quine, *Ontological Relativity*.

Whenever a semantics gives an account of predicates in terms of an extension in a domain, and an account of variables in terms of values, it falls naturally into speaking of individuals in the domain. And everybody's first thought, when thinking what individuals might be, is of concrete particulars.

So there is at least a suspicion that this canonical notation, with its semantics given in this way, assumes the existence of concrete particulars. To avoid this, we need to be alert to the possibility of there being more kinds of individuals than concrete particulars. In chapter 14 below we explore one such alternative.

Quine himself would not be embarrassed if his canonical notation assumes the existence of concrete particulars. For this is one of the two categories he recognizes. In specifying his own ontology, he comes out in favor of fundamental particles and collections of them, that is, in favor of concrete particulars. Sets are the other category in Quine's ontology.[11]

THE REASONS FOR CHOOSING THIS CANONICAL NOTATION

Quine has two fundamental reasons for adopting this particular language as canonical. First, this language is a concrete version of a *first-order predicate logic with identity*. Logical systems of this kind have been thoroughly investigated. A great deal is known about them, and it is all to their credit. They are consistent; that is, using their inference rules will never lead us into contradiction. They have a clear and adequate semantics, the elements of which we have just been discussing. Their formal structure can be completely axiomatized, so that the extent of legitimate deductive inference in them, though infinite, can be stated in a finite way. And they are extensional—that is, if two expressions have the same semantics, one can be substituted for the other in any sentence at all without changing the truth value of that sentence.[12]

The canonical language, then, is a comparatively simple and manageable language whose logic is clearly understood and clearly in a satisfactory condition.

Quine's second reason is simply that this canonical notation is all we need; we can make any claim worth making about the world in this language if in any.[13] Any further elaboration of this canonical language would be superfluous, and with languages, as with ontologies, economy is a rule of reason; it is folly to do with more what can equally be done with less. Quine holds that the canonical language is the minimum sufficient for giving expression to scientific and all other knowledge. No simpler language is adequate, but provided a properly rich

---

11. Quine, *The Ways of Paradox*, chapters 19, 20.
12. English, by contrast, is not extensional. Suppose Jack the Ripper is the milkman. Then 'Jack the Ripper' and 'the milkman' have the same semantics. But we cannot substitute one for the other in 'Sherlock Holmes knows that Jack the Ripper is a murderer'. For this may well be true and yet 'Holmes knows that the milkman is a murderer' be false. Constructions with 'know', 'believe', 'hope for', and others are not extensional but *intensional*. See below, chapter 11.
13. Quine, *Word and Object*, p. 228.

stock of predicates is available, the sentence forms of the canonical language do suffice for this task.

No one disputes that if the canonical notation *is* adequate then it is acceptable. The contentious question is whether it is genuinely adequate. That is the topic to which we now turn.

10 *Regimentation or Paraphrase*

If we are to use Quine's canonical notation as a basis for investigation in ontology, we must first be assured that it is an adequate notation. It must be possible to say whatever can be said in English as well or better in the canonical language. Otherwise, any review of the ontic implications of the canonical language may well be ignoring crucial elements from that part of English with which the canonical language cannot deal.

The demonstration that the canonical language is adequate proceeds in two stages. First, all legitimate varieties of English construction are distinguished and set out. Then second, a canonical alternative is proposed for each distinct variety of English sentence. The process goes by the name of *regimentation*, which suggests that English is going to be *put in order*. This is a somewhat misleading suggestion, for what is happening is rather that alongside the natural language is arranged an orderly *alternative*, namely the well-disciplined ranks of sentences in canonical form. As he himself often expresses the matter, what Quine is offering is a set of *paraphrases* of English sentences. We do not go to work on English in an attempt to transform it, but to set up a parallel system of expressions which is claimed to be superior.[1]

This program is open, in principle, to two lines of criticism: that the account of English is defective, and that the paraphrases proposed, or any canonical alternatives, are unable to capture the full legitimate content of the sentences which they paraphrase.

It is the second line of criticism that has attracted the most attention and will occupy us.

---

1. W.V. Quine, *Word and Object*, pp. 159ff.

THE LANGUAGE TO BE PARAPHRASED

The object of study, the candidate for paraphrase, is the statement-making fragment of English, unadorned. It is the plain, literal, prosaic, spare system of sentences in which we make straightforward claims as to how the world is. We exclude from consideration all ornament, all figures of speech, all irony, all exaggeration, all poetic license. This in itself is a source of problems. It is a serious question whether we can actually get along without metaphor in science, for example, where we grapple with the problem of describing the new and exotic sides of nature. What does the use of metaphor involve? Is there a way of saying in literal terms whatever can be said by way of metaphor? Is metaphor merely a superfluous grace, or is it actually essential to a decently flexible language?

Again, there is an important tradition in philosophical theology according to which no literally applicable descriptions of God are available to mankind. On this view, all talk of God is essentially and unalterably analogical but is nevertheless significant and informative. Perhaps plain, literal English is insufficient for the expression of belief. We must just note that there are important issues here, and pass on.

We will also ignore the qualifications, linking expressions, and signposts in expository prose. "It seems likely that . . .", "As is shown above . . .", "Finally . . .", "We are now in a position to state our central thesis, namely . . .", and many similar turns of phrase are invaluable aids to the setting forth of a reasonable system of belief. But they do not themselves make any contribution to the actual content of a belief structure. They are not elements in the statement-making function itself. No attempt is made to provide direct canonical equivalents for them.

Our target language is thus a simplified version of English. It is a version of *English* for no profound metaphysical reasons, but simply because that is Quine's and our native tongue. The same program of canonical paraphrases could be adopted for any natural language and would be equally interesting for any language adequate, as English is, to serve the world of learning. Whether German, Russian, or Japanese would prove resistant to paraphrase where English is not, is a fascinating question which once more we cannot broach here.

PARAPHRASES:

Generalizations. Sentences with 'some', 'every', and 'none' are the most directly paraphrased:

Some penguins dance

becomes

$(\exists x)$ (penguin x . dances x).

The statement

> Every author is vain

is, in canonical language, a conditional rather than a conjunction (everything is such that if it is an author then it is vain) :

> (x) (author $x \supset$ vain x).

The statement

> No snakes have legs

can be dealt with at two levels. At the first, it is paraphrased as

> $\sim (\exists x)$ (snake x . has legs x)

or, equivalently,

> (x) (snake $x \supset \sim$ has legs x).

Then we can go on to analyze 'has legs' (or 'legged') in terms of legs, to get simpler predicates:

> (x) (snake $x \supset \sim (\exists y)$ (y is a leg . x has y)).

Particular negative claims, such as

> Not all timber floats

get the treatment we would expect:

> $(\exists x)$ (timber x . $\sim$ floats x).

But most paraphrasing is not so direct.

Feature-Placing Sentences. When someone is panning shingle and cries "Gold!" or takes a sip and says "Chateau Lafite 1957!", he is using a very simple sentence form in which he identifies a particular segment of his environment, made clear by the context, as being of a certain character.[2] Such sentences have no direct paraphrases, for "F" and "G" are not well-formed sentences.

---

2. Mass terms such as 'gold' or 'water', which do not pick out countable individuals, are common in feature-placing sentences. But other terms can also be used, as in 'Fred's Volkswagen!' or 'The French!'.

So what we have to do is first find alternative English sentences which make equivalent claims and paraphrase them. In this case the best course is to replace "Gold!" by

Here is some gold,[3]

which in turn becomes

There is something here which is golden

(that is, composed of gold, not merely of the same color as gold). This sentence can be paraphrased as

($\exists\, x$) (x is here . x is golden).

We leave that as it stands in the meantime, but eventually the indicator 'here' will have to go. For it is a source of truth-value fluctuation and so must disappear in a fully canonical notation, which contains only truth-value constant or eternal sentences.

Paraphrase in two or more stages is by no means uncommon. We find the same situation arising with

Chateau Lafite 1957!

which we first transform into

Here is some wine made at Chateau Lafite in 1957,

then into

($\exists\, x$) (x is here . x is wine . x is made at Chateau Lafite in 1957).

This is still not properly canonical. The proper name 'Chateau Lafite' should strictly disappear from the predicate. And 'in 1957', which makes the present predicate complex, must be given a separate place of its own. For the treatment of demonstratives, proper names, and times, see below.

Indefinite Singular Terms and Pronouns. Indefinite singular terms, such as 'some cow', 'no fish', 'any man' occur in generalizations and can be paraphrased using quantifiers.

Any man can swim

is treated as a universal conditional

---

3. Neglecting the 'now' which is strictly required as well.

Everything is such that if it is a man then it can swim,

which becomes

(x) (man $x \supset$ can swim x).

The English version has two occurrences of the pronoun 'it' which refer back to 'everything'. In the canonical language version, their place is taken by variables bound by the same universal quantifier. This use of pronouns, referring back to an indefinite singular term such as 'everything', is the use most directly reproduced in the paraphrases.

It is sometimes said that pronouns merely stand in place of their antecedent noun to prevent tedious repetition. This is sometimes the case, where the antecedent is a definite singular term, as in

I saw the Statue of Liberty and you saw it too,

where 'it' can be replaced by 'the Statue of Liberty' at the cost of elegance.

But with indefinite singular antecedent, pronouns are not just devices for avoiding repetition; the reference of a pronoun is fixed by the preceding part of the sentence in more complex ways.

I met a gangster and you met him too

is not equivalent to

I met a gangster and you met a gangster too.

But the first is equivalent to

I met a gangster and you met that gangster too.

In the canonical language we distinguish these by our choice of variables, as

$(\exists x)(\exists y)(\exists z)$ (x is me . y is you. z is a gangster . met $x\ z$. met $y\ z$),

and

$(\exists x)(\exists y)(\exists z)(\exists w)$ (x is me. y is you. z is a gangster. w is a gangster. met $x\ z$. met $y\ w$).

If we want to say explicitly that we met different gangsters, we have to add

$z \neq w$

Similarly,

> Every snake is male or it is female

does not mean the same as

> Every snake is male or every snake is female.

In this case we distinguish the two sentences by the scope of the quantifiers. The first, the truth, is paraphrased as

$$(x)\,(x \text{ is a snake} \supset (x \text{ is male} \vee x \text{ is female})),$$

while the second, the falsehood, takes the form

$$(x)\,(x \text{ is a snake} \supset x \text{ is male}) \vee (x)\,(x \text{ is a snake} \supset x \text{ is female}).$$

Pronouns cross-referring beyond their own sentence can be troublesome. The two sentences

> The lunar environment is hostile.
>
> It is full of meteorites,

can either be treated together by joining them with 'and', or the 'it' in the second sentence can be replaced with 'the lunar environment'.

Where we have this kind of cross-reference with *indefinite* singular antecedents, as in

> A man came into the room. He was burly and tough,

if we just repeat 'a man' in the second sentence, we lose the implication that the same man both came into the room and was burly and tough. One way to preserve that implication is to join the sentences with 'and' before proceeding to paraphrase.

Definite Singular Terms: Russell's Theory of Definite Descriptions. With definite singular terms we come to that aspect of English which originally inspired the program of canonical paraphrase which Quine has pursued. For it was Bertrand Russell's treatment of definite descriptions which began it all.

Russell was dissatisfied with straightforward subject-predicate analyses of sentences whose subjects were definite descriptions, because definite descriptions ('the' constructions) can fail to refer and yet be perfectly meaningful.[4] An example is

---

4. B. Russell, "On Denoting."

The present king of France is bald.

The account of this which he rejected held that 'the present king of France' is the subject of the sentence, the role of a subject term is to refer, and such a term means what it refers to. If that were correct, since the term 'the present king of France' lacks a reference, it must lack a meaning, and so the whole sentence must be nonsense.

As the sentence is obviously *not* nonsense, Russell concluded that it is not really a subject-predicate sentence.[5] Instead, Russell held that definite descriptions are *incomplete symbols* to be given *contextual definition*. This means that in logical analysis, they are not to be treated in isolation as complete units, but rather the whole sentences in which they occur are to be replaced by other whole sentences which do the same statement-making work but do not contain definite descriptions.

In Russell's account,

The present king of France is bald

amounts to three distinct but connected assertions:

(1) There is a present king of France,

(2) There is only one present king of France,

(3) He is bald.

Russell viewed these three sentences as revealing what the original sentence really means all along, but keeps hidden. Quine takes over the threefold account but treats it as furnishing a paraphrase, a superior alternative, to the original. The sentences of the threefold account contain no definite descriptions. And they can be expressed in the canonical notation without difficulty.

We need the *predicate* 'being a present king of France'. Let us abbreviate that to *PKF*. Sentence (1) appears as an existentially quantified closed sentence:

(1') $(\exists x)(PKF\ x)$.

Sentence (2) is the uniqueness clause; the use of 'the' implies that there is only one thing which the description fits. We see this when we notice that the phrase 'the Member of Parliament', for example, gives trouble not because nothing is an M.P. but because more than one thing is. So any account of definite descriptions requires a uniqueness clause. What we need to say is that anything whatever which is *PKF* is the very thing which we said was *PKF* in (1'). That will ensure that there is only one of them. We express this using a universal quantifier and the identity predicate '=' (is the same thing as):

---

5. He might have concluded instead that the meaning of a singular term must be something different from its reference —which is the line Strawson takes—but he did not. See P.F. Strawson, "On Referring."

$(2')$ $(y)(PKF\ y \supset (y = x))$

and this must be placed within the scope of the existential quantifier binding x in $(1')$.

Sentence (3) says this thing is bald, reproducing the predicate of the original sentence

The present king of France is bald.

So Sentence (3) appears as just

$(3')$ Bald x,

and again this must be placed within the scope of the original existential quantifier so that we claim that the very thing which is PKF is also bald.

So our complete sentence reads:

(4) $(\exists x)(PKF\ x.\ (y)(PKF\ y \supset (y = x)).\ \text{Bald}\ x)$.

It turns out that this can be simplified to

$(\exists x)(y)\ (PKFy \equiv (x = y).\ \text{Bald}\ x)$,

and that is the form in which you will sometimes find it written.

Both these sentences are canonical. In both, all the material content is in predicative position. Subject positions are filled by variables. The original problem of the reference of the expression

The present king of France

disappears, because that expression disappears. And our complete sentence (4) is perfectly meaningful but false. It is false because $(\exists x)(PKF\ x)$ is false (there is no present king of France). All most satisfactory.

We give the same treatment to all sentences with definite descriptions in subject position. A true specimen, such as

The earth is an oblate spheroid

is replaced by

$(\exists x)$ (earth x. (y) (earth $y \supset (y = x)$. oblate spheroid x),

which is true. We can, that is, assign values to variables in such a way that x's value is an oblately spheroidal earth, and whatever y's value, if that thing is an earth, it is also the value of x. Again, all most satisfactory.

REGIMENTATION OR PARAPHRASE 145

There has been a good deal of discussion of Russell's account of definite descriptions. Some of this revolves about how precisely the threefold analysis captures the use of 'the' constructions in English. It has been pointed out that we use sentences like

> The table is in the corner,

knowing full well that there is more than one table and more than one corner.[6] We rely on the context in which we speak to fix which table and which corner we are referring to. But Russell's theory makes

> The table is in the corner

false, since in his theory this sentence entails that there is but one table and but one corner.

The reply to this criticism is that the canonical language admits only sentences which are independent of context. So we must first supply supplementary descriptions of the table and the corner which single them out from all others and then paraphrase this expanded sentence, which might begin

> The circular cedar pedestal table finished by Snug the Joiner on October 4, 1837 . . .

This program of expanding the description until it becomes an *identifying description*, that is, a description fitting just one thing and no other, clearly depends on there *being*, at least in principle, a distinct and unique description for each different thing. This in turn requires that every thing differs from every other thing in a way which can be expressed using just predicates and not, for example, gestures which depend on context for their force.

This principle, that every different thing does have a unique identifying description, is the principle of the *identity of indiscernibles*. Here it is expressed the other way about as the *discernibility of diverses:* if two items are distinct, they can be discerned, that is, distinguished from one another by distinguishing descriptions. This is a controversial principle, which is discussed below.[7] Quine is clearly and explicitly committed to it, and here, in the use of Russell's theory of descriptions, we see one reason for this.[8]

Donellan points out that there are two distinguishable uses of definite descriptions in English.[9] On one of these, when I say, for example,

> The murderer wears size ten boots,

---

6. Cf. P.F. Strawson, *Introduction to Logical Theory*, p. 186.
7. Chapter 14.
8. Quine, *Word and Object*, p. 230.
9. K. Donellan, "Proper Names and Identity Descriptions."

I may be a detective investigating the case, searching for clues, but quite unaware of who, precisely, the murderer is. Otherwise, of course, I could proceed directly to the arrest. In this case I do not speak of any *particular* person in that, because I do not know who the murderer is, I cannot myself deliberately refer to him as the murderer. My sentence means:

> Some one person committed the murder, and *whoever* it is, that person wears size ten boots.

And *this* is what the Russell theory makes our original sentence containing a definite description say.

But there is also a use of definite descriptions as much more like names. In this second use, the definite description serves to pick out some particular object. It is used among people who know exactly which object is referred to, and so can even misdescribe that object without thereby involving some *other* object which, as it happens, is truly described. Thus, to use Donellan's example, if I say in the courtroom at the trial of Jones for the murder,

> The murderer is insane,

then I mean Jones, the man in the dock, is insane. I can make this even clearer by jerking my thumb in his direction. And I mean that Jones is insane even if he is innocent and no murderer at all. I do not mean that someone else, Brown, who is the actual murderer, is insane.

Likewise, when at a party convention the nominator gives the delegates "the next president of the United States," he gives them their candidate, not any rival, even though a rival may in fact be the next president.

This kind of use of definite descriptions to make a particular reference cannot be reproduced within Russell's account of the matter. In Russell's account,

> The F is G

becomes

$$(\exists\, x)\, (Fx.\, (y)\, (Fy \supset (x = y)))\, .\, Gx$$

which is interpreted as

> Somewhere among the things in the universe is one which alone is F, and that thing, whatever it may be, is also G.

There is no particular reference here. This sentence does nothing to answer the question, But which thing *is* it that is uniquely F? We may or may not be able to find the F. The sentence itself carries no promise on that score.

When the definite description is used to make a particular reference, however, we *can* say, nontrivially, which thing is indicated. In the murderer example, it is the man over there, or the prisoner at the bar.

Let us admit that not all ways of using definite descriptions are reproduced in the Russellian paraphrases. Does this discredit Quine's canonical notation? *Not for purposes of ontology.* For there is no question of the 'missing' use somehow involving new and different objects.

For so far as ontic implications are concerned,

> Somewhere there is a unique F which is G

is absolutely on a par with

> This thing here is the only F, and it is G.

Provided the individual variables of the canonical language range over items which include the thing referred to by the definite description, sentences involving definite descriptions can be replaced by the threefold canonical sentences of Russell's theory with no loss of ontic implication.

Proper Names. There are various ways of tackling proper names. Russell favored the idea that no one could use a name unless he knew a set of descriptions which together identified the object named. So that, for example, unless I know that he was the pupil of Plato and the teacher of Alexander, (or some description which equally well singles him out,) I cannot use the name 'Aristotle' to mean the Greek philosopher.

So Russell dispensed with proper names in two stages: first he replaced them by compound definite descriptions, and then these descriptions were subjected to the threefold analysis already discussed.

There are several objections to this line of approach, which equates proper names with compound definite descriptions. Consider mistakes about people, dogs, mountains, planets, or whatever we give proper names to. Suppose that I think, wrongly, that Aristotle was married to Xantippe. Then according to Russell's doctrine, when I say

> Aristotle wrote the *Posterior Analytics*

(which is true), I am really saying

> Someone was pupil of Plato, husband of Xantippe, . . . and wrote the *Posterior Analytics*

(which is false).

There is a further difficulty urged by some, that we can successfully use a proper name, for example 'Moses', even though we know *no* definite descriptions concerning this person—if, for example, I come into a room and hear you discussing Moses, of whom I have never heard until this moment, and say, truthfully and correctly,

I have never heard of Moses until this moment.

But it seems this can be answered by pointing out that I must know at least that Moses is

The person or thing called 'Moses'.

So we will not press this point. The previous objection that false belief about any one feature of the named object makes all statements about that object false, is itself sufficiently serious.

Quine takes a different tack.[10] He is just as determined as Russell, if not more, to banish singular terms from his canonical language, and proper names are singular terms par excellence.

First, we notice that we can manipulate English into a stilted semi-English in which every proper name occurs immediately after the identity sign. For this we use the 'such that' locution.[11] Wherever a proper name occurs in a sentence, it can be picked out by the 'such that' device and set down after the identity sign, as the following examples show.

Jack built a house

can be expressed as

Someone is such that he = Jack and he built a house.

A rat lived with Jack

becomes

Someone is such that he = Jack and a rat lived with him.

A rat ate malt in Jack's house

becomes

Someone is such that he = Jack and he had a house and a rat ate malt in it.

---

10. Quine, *Word and Object*, p. 178.
11. Quine himself gets all proper names into a position after '=' not through the 'such that' construction but by appeal to a logical theorem applied to canonical sentences.

Once this conversion into semi-English has been completed, the sentence admits of direct paraphrase in canonical form. The last sentence emerges, for example, as

($\exists\ x$)($\exists\ y$)($\exists\ z$)($\exists\ w$)(x = Jack. y is a house. x owned y. z is a rat. w is a malt. w is in y. z ate w).[12]

The useful but self-denying phrase 'such that' disappears entirely.

Now we are left with proper names in just one sort of context—after the identity sign. Let us symbolize any proper name by a. Then the piece of text with which we must deal is '$=a$', where what comes before the '=' is always a variable.

Quine's procedure is short and decisive: treat '$=a$' as a *simple*, unstructured *predicate* attaching to the variable which immediately precedes it. Think of '=Jack', for instance, as rather like

is called 'Jack',

except that quotation is not a canonical device. To avoid any suspicion of covertly importing quotation marks, think of '= Jack' as 'Jackizes'.

We get a new predicate for every proper name. Some of the more celebrated are Pegasizing, Socratizing, and Nelsonizing. We treat an earlier example now as

Someone who Aristotleizes wrote something which *Posterior Analyticizes*.

This at once breaks right through the difficulties in Russell's position which arise from different, or faulty, or highly attenuated conceptions of Aristotle. And it works beautifully for dealing with those problems of nonreferring proper names (which parallel the problems of nonreferring definite descriptions like 'the present king of France') and which so bedevil any approach to ontology based on singular terms.

Hercules was bald

becomes simply

($\exists\ x$) (x Herculizes. x was bald).

Or, if we wish to make explicit the idea implicit in the use of proper names, that just one object is involved, then we add a uniqueness clause:

($\exists\ x$) (y) (x Herculizes. y Herculizes $\supset$ (y = x). x was bald).

---

12. To be quite accurate, we should state that Jack had just one house, and insert a uniqueness clause in the paraphrase.

In both cases, the canonical sentence is false, and it involves no reference to Hercules, which is as it should be.

Hercules does not exist

becomes merely

$\sim (\exists x)(x \text{ Herculizes})$,

which is true and does not tie us up in the knot of trying to attribute nonexistence, somehow, to something that doesn't exist.

Despite these plain merits, however, Quine's proposal tends to encounter resistance from those who are hearing of it for the first time. They feel that some fraud, some sleight of hand, is involved. Singular terms are transformed into general terms before their very eyes. There must be a trick. What lies behind this feeling?

The artificial predicates, 'Herculizes', 'Socratizes', and so on, must be taught and learned in exactly the way singular terms are. The term is introduced, by way of acquaintance with or description of the one object which it describes (or names). It is not understood unless the learner realizes that it applies to that one object and no other. If how a term is introduced settled its logical status, it would indeed be a fraud to try to convert a singular term into a general term without altering its manner of introduction. But as Quine points out, a term's logical status depends not on its mode of introduction but on its relation to other terms in its context. And we can change from 'Nelson', which occupies the position a variable can occupy, to 'Nelsonizes', which does *not* occupy a position open to variables but a position of predication with a variable. This change is a change from a singular term to a general one. For 'Nelsonizes' fits into sentences in the same way as 'sails', 'loves', or 'commands the flagship'.

Again, it is sometimes objected that these artificial predicates made up from names apply to one thing only, while general terms apply to many things. But on the contrary, general terms can be true of none, or one, or several things. 'Is a Chinese Pope', 'is captain of a trans-Atlantic expedition in 1492', 'is a water molecule' are cases in point.

Again, it is objected that these predicates deriving from names have their uniqueness of application built into their meaning, whereas it is a matter not of meaning but of fact that some general terms apply to exactly one item. To this it can be replied that 'Pegasizes' *doesn't* apply to exactly one object, whatever is supposed to be built into its meaning. This does not satisfy the objector. His idea is that proper names are special in that they have *at most* one bearer, as a matter of meaning. But this is not a special distinguishing mark of proper names: the general terms 'is a mountain taller than any other', or 'is a city at exactly 40°N,0°E', have as much purport of uniqueness as any proper name.

In any event, says Quine, if you insist that every general term have multiple application, cut Socrates up into thin slices, Socrates-during-an-hour-of-his-life.

There are as many of these as hours Socrates was alive. Let 'Socratizes' truly describe each one, and there is your multiple application.

So the reasons advanced for not accepting Quine's method of eliminating proper names are not conclusive—or even convincing. Underlying them all is the sense that a genuine predicate must represent, or correspond to, some real quality of the thing described. It should tell what that thing is *like*, give us information as to its nature, and the artificial predicates formed from proper names do not do this. Just as anything can be given any name, so any predicate like 'Nelsonizes' gives us no clue to the characteristics of the object it appears to describe. 'Nelsonizes' *does* differ from 'is a sea captain' in this respect: whether or not one thing is a sea captain depends on how much, and in what way, it resembles other things that have been given that description, whereas 'Nelsonizes' is subject to no such constraint. But this makes a difference to how much we can learn from the application of a general term. It does not make a difference to whether or not a general term has been applied.

The crux is that proper names are used, typically, to make particularizing reference to specific items. And we have seen that the canonical language is ill-fitted to make particularizing reference, since its variables range over all items and its existentially quantified sentences consequently speak only of some item(s) from among the heap. But as was urged there, this is no criticism of the canonical language's adequacy for ontology.

Exactly one Nelsonizer had one arm

leaves out of account nothing included by

Nelson had one arm.

And we are in a position to establish the truth of the first if we know when 'Nelsonizer' applies, that is, in exactly those cases where we understand the particularizing reference of 'Nelson'.

In summary, Quine's artificial measures with proper names succeed in banishing them from canonical discourse without loss for ontological purposes.

Indicators. The remaining singular terms of English belong to the class of *indicator* words. Indicators get their name from their use to indicate things by reference to the speaker's situation. Examples are 'I', 'you', 'here', 'there', 'now', 'then', 'today', 'tomorrow', 'next week'. Russell called them *egocentric particulars*, because what they refer to when I use them depends on my situation with respect to place, time, and audience. Reichenbach's name was *token-reflexive* terms, for their reference is dependent on the place, time, and circumstances in which the particular specimens (tokens) of the words are uttered and is determined by *reflecting back* on these circumstances of utterance.

When you say 'today', the stretch of time you are speaking of varies with when you say it—a familiar fact exploited by Lewis Carroll in the joke about jam yesterday and jam tomorrow, but never jam today.

There are several varieties of indicators, most of them singular terms. The singular terms must be eliminated by paraphrase in any case, but all indicator words must go, in constructing a canonical language, because they are a source of truth-value fluctuation.

>I am going to the dentist today

is, we are pleased to agree, not always true, although it sometimes is. The same can be said of most sentences involving indicators, with the teasing exceptions beloved of Descartes:

>I think,
>
>I exist,

and some others:

>I am not dead
>
>I am right here now (the logician's preservative against ever getting lost).

Indicators are a source of truth-value fluctuation, and truth-value fluctuation sabotages the effort to develop a single and generally applicable system of logical inference. So it is important to determine whether we can get along, for theoretical purposes, without them. But most indicators do not involve any question of a distinct category of being, and we can therefore be summary in our mention of their paraphrases.

Demonstratives 'This' and 'that' are demonstrative pronouns. They occur in demonstrative descriptions, such as 'this apple' and 'that apple'. These are changed to 'the apple here' and 'the apple there', which contain other indicators which will be treated in their turn.

Plain 'this' and 'that' go over into 'the thing here' and 'the thing there', with 'thing' operating as a dummy noun which disappears into a variable.

>This is a Ferrari

becomes

>$(\exists x)(x$ is here. x is a Ferrari$)$.

Adverbs of Place 'Here' and 'there' are indicators. Quine holds that they are, or can be treated as, general terms in their own right. Not *canonical* general terms, of course, because they introduce truth-value fluctuation. They have no general paraphrase, but are replaced, on each particular occasion, by some nonindicator description which picks out the same place as that particular use of 'here' or 'there'.

Pronouns   Pronouns, particularly the personal variety, often function as indicator words. 'I' and 'you' standardly serve as subject terms in their own right. So do 'he', 'she', and 'it' when not serving a cross-referential function. They are singular terms, and their reference fluctuates with the occasion of their use. They thus generate truth-value fluctuation of the sentences in which they occur.

They are paraphrased away, as we would expect, in a way quite comparable to the way taken with 'here' and 'there'. In each particular case, a name or definite description must be found which has, always, the reference which the pronoun has on this occasion.

The name or definite description which replaces the pronoun is then treated according to Russell's theory of descriptions or Quine's short way with names.

'Now' and 'Then'   Quine holds that 'now' and 'then', unlike 'here' and 'there', are singular terms. The basis for this distinction is obscure to me, for the temporal terms seem to work largely parallel with the locational ones. It is true we don't say things like "The apple is now," while "The apple is here" is quite acceptable. But "The train is here now" is perfectly good English, apparently according 'here' and 'now' the same status. And "The place is here; the time is now" also suggests 'here' and 'now' are on the same footing. And to correspond with

> Now is the winter of our discontent made glorious summer by this sun of York

or

> Now is the time for all good men to come to the aid of the party,

we find

> There's rosemary; that's for remembrance

or

> Here comes the bride.

But whether 'now' and 'then' are singular or general terms in English is not a matter of great consequence. The question is whether their functions can be discharged by other means in a language without indicators.

Take 'now' and 'then' to be singular terms naming *epochs*. Epochs are periods of time. Epochs seem to form a new category, distinct from concrete particulars, sets, or whatever else we finally recognize. For time is not a thing, or at least not a thing in the same way that a shoe, ship, or lump of sealing wax is. And a slice of time, an epoch, would seem to share time's character. But in Quine's philosophy the difference between epochs and more familiar objects is not so sharp.

Consider the four-dimensional 'block' world of Minkowski's interpretation of Einstein's special theory of relativity. This has three spatial and one temporal dimension. In this two-dimensional representation of a three-dimensional representation of this world it appears as a picture of a cuboid box, with the temporal dimension the longer one:

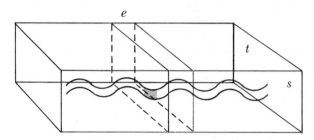

Object s and epoch e have a common part (shaded).

A familiar material object, such as a ship, appears on this scheme as an elongated 'space-time worm'. The bends and curves of the worm correspond to the ship's journeys from one place to another. A stationary object appears as a long, straight 'worm', like a piece of wire, for it is at the same place at many different times. Changes in shape and size appear as differences in the cross-section of the 'worm' at different points along its extent in the temporal dimension. Changes in color or constitution emerge as a 'zebra-striped' effect, as if the worm were wearing a hooped football jersey.

A familiar material object is, in this model, a small portion of the whole space-time world taken more or less parallel to the time axis.

An epoch, on the other hand, is a slice of the block world which cuts *across* the time axis. It is the whole world during some limited period. Just which parts of the whole world belong to the same period depends on the reference frame, according to relativity theory. But any slice is always a legitimate object, though perhaps not an object containing simultaneous events. A slice which does contain simultaneous events, in a given frame, is an epoch, for that frame.

Epochs are artificial objects. They can be of various thicknesses according to our purposes, just as areas can be of various extents. The fifteenth century, the ides of March, 44 B.C., and this minute are all epochs.

'Now' names an epoch: one of the indefinitely many epochs which contain its own event of being uttered. It will be the second in which it is uttered in the case of

The race is starting now,

and, depending on political stability, the day, month, or year in which it is uttered in the case of

The center-left coalition is now in office.

To paraphrase sentences containing 'now', we can use the *at-locution*. There can be two objects which overlap. That is, they can have a part in common. Part of the Pacific Ocean, for example, is the water in Sydney Harbor. And that same water is part of Sydney Harbor—the remainder being the surrounding land. To refer to this water, we speak of the Pacific Ocean *at* Sydney Harbor. This is not the *only* use of 'at', which sometimes relates things to places, but it is one legitimate use. The gold at Bendigo is that (scattered) object which is both part of Bendigo and part of all the world's gold. Likewise the leaves at the top of the tree. In all these cases, the objects which overlap or intersect are 'spatial' in character. But an epoch also intersects, has a common part with, every space-time worm which extends through it. And we can use the at-locution to speak of this common part.

When we are paraphrasing

Nelson is now commanding attack,

we first rewrite this as

Nelson at now commands attack.

In this sentence, 'Nelson at now' is a complex singular term which refers to the intersection of the space-time worm Nelson and the epoch now. It is this common part of Nelson and an epoch, this rather short fraction of Nelson's life, which is doing the commanding.

To eliminate the complex singular term 'Nelson at now' we proceed as follows:

Nelson at now commands attack,

gives way to

$(\exists x)(\exists y)(\exists z)$ (x Nelsonizes. y is now. z is the common part of x and y. z commands attack).

This is canonical in form, but it contains the indicator predicate 'is now', which is true of epochs. As with 'here', 'now' must be replaced by a description true of that epoch wherein it is uttered.

This can be done in a standard way by setting up a dating system. To do this, we select one specific temporal origin point, zero hour, and describe y as 'an epoch t hours later than 0' (or t hours earlier as the case may be). A dating system can be set up independent of indicator terms if the origin, the zero hour, can be singled out by a description which itself contains no indicator terms.

The usual manner of attempting this is to pick on a notable and unrepeated event, such as the founding of our city, the birth of our redeemer, or the establishment of our republic, and date everything from some conveniently short epoch containing that event. Apart from such public and spectacular events, most of us can identify many epochs by something unusual which happened to us, for example: "You remember 1957—that was the year you got married/ joined the army/broke the bank at Monte Carlo/stood for Parliament/bought a fur coat/. . . ." If any of these descriptions is indeed true of just one event, it can serve to establish the origin for a dating system.

The problem in this mode of procedure is that it does assume that at least one event is never repeated. We are dealing here with a special case of the identity of indiscernibles—the identity of indiscernible epochs. For a dating system is *ambiguous*, and therefore useless, unless the specification of the origin is unique. And an origin can be uniquely specified by a description containing no indicator words, if but only if there are not two different epochs which both fit that description.

For any two epochs to be discernible, it is necessary and sufficient that there be at least one happening, no matter how simple or complex, which is not matched by an exactly similar happening at some other time. Call such an event U. Then any two epochs, even if they match exactly with respect to their internal constitution, will differ in bearing different relations of earlier or later to U.

So if just one event U has no exact match at any other time, every diverse epoch will be discernible. To put that the other way about, the identity of indiscernibles will hold for epochs. The rub is, however, that there is no guarantee that any U exists. The 'concertina' worlds discussed below (chapter 14) provide a counterinstance, and we may live in a concertina world.

Without a U, the origin of a dating system can be fixed unambiguously *only with the help of indicator words*. 'Now' or 'the epoch of this utterance' or 'The epoch of this (demonstratively indicated) event', or some expression depending equally on indicators, will be required.

Once an origin is successfully pinpointed, indicator words are not needed to specify epochs. If we cannot rely on the identity of indiscernibles for epochs, however, indicators are needed to pinpoint the origin. The problem for space of setting up systems of spatial coordinates is closely parallel.

If this is our situation, then indicators play a vital role, not *in* the canonical language, but in establishing its capacity to describe reality. Perhaps all information can be set down using just the canonical indicator-free expressions. But perhaps the canonical expresssions can achieve this because noncanonical indicator terms exist outside the canonical circle. If so, the canonical language will depend on noncanonical elements, which will therefore be dispensable only in the narrower sense that we do not need to use them in canonical sentences themselves. They are not dispensable in the sense that we could do without them altogether. For without them, in noncanonical expressions, the canonical language would have no origin-related descriptions of places or times, and so it would be defective.

But however that may be, it seems that we will need to take account of epochs in our ontology of categories.

      Tense. English, along with many natural languages, is partial towards time. Indications of temporal relationship are incorporated into the main verbs of sentences, in the shape of tense. But spatial relationships must be separately and explicitly specified by additional predicative material ('in front of', 'behind', 'to the left of', and so on).

This is objectionable on two counts: it suggests that there is some crucial distinction in nature between spatial and temporal dimensions, which runs counter to the spirit of relativity theory, and it requires the introduction of quite new principles in logic. For the logic of the canonical language, the first-order predicate calculus with identity, states rules governing the derivation of expressions from one another in terms of the predicates they contain. Now different consequences flow from

          Our admiral was victorious

and

          Our admiral will be victorious,

and so the predicates 'was victorious' and 'will be victorious' must be different predicates. Yet it would be a mistake to think of these two predicates as no more closely related than 'spider' and 'cider'. So we should try to separate the temporal element, and the peculiarities of consequence which each tense involves, from the victorious element. The temporal element must be given separate expression in a predicate of its own instead of being buried in other verbs.

      The first step is to remove temporal implication from the verb. This is done by using the so-called *timeless present*, the tense of mathematics. When we say two plus two *are* four, or triangles *have* three sides, we do not mean that it is something special to the present. It has nothing to do with one time rather than another. It has present *tense* without any connection with the present *time*. Hence its name, the timeless present.

      The second step is to indicate time. We do this using 'at', relating objects to epochs as in 'at t', 'at now', 'at then', and using the before-and-after locutions, 'before t', 'before now', 'after 1976', which relate epochs to epochs.

      Thus for

          I am walking

we write

          I at now walk,

with the 'walk' understood timelessly.

For the other indicative tenses we use 'before' or 'after' as well as 'at'.

I was walking, I have been walking: ($\exists\, t$) (t is before now. I at t walk)

I will be walking: ($\exists\, t$) (now is before t. I at t walk)

I had been walking when the inspector arrived: ($\exists\, t$) ($\exists\, u$) (t is before u. u is before now. I at t walk. the inspector at u arrives)

I will have been walking when the inspector arrives. ($\exists\, t$) ($\exists\, u$) (now is before t. t is before u. I at t walk. the inspector at u arrives).

The problems of tense in inferences can be resolved in these ways, although the matter is more complicated than Quine suggests.[13]

In all these paraphrases, we have been seeking ways to express canonically what is expressed in English using constructions which are not available in the canonical language. The purpose of seeking paraphrases is to test whether the canonical language is satisfactory for expressing our beliefs. And the purpose of establishing that the canonical language is satisfactory is so that we can use this simplified and clear language in giving an answer to the question, Which categories of being are we required to acknowledge as essential, in the sense that they must be real if our statements are to be true?

Before we continue in assessing the adequacy of the canonical notation, we must take stock, asking what exactly the relation is between English sentences and canonical paraphrase.

THE PARAPHRASE RELATION

Take a straightforward example of a paraphrase; for the statement

Some dogs are fierce,

we write

($\exists\, x$) (dog x . fierce x).

What logical relation holds between a sentence and its paraphrase? The straightforward examples encourage us to believe that the two are not merely equivalent (true or false together), but, more closely, amount to the same thing, mean the same, are synonyms. And this in turn has led to the idea that the

---

13. Quine, *Word and Object*, pp. 170–171. H. Lacey, "Quine on the Logic and Ontology of Time."

canonical sentence gives the *analysis*, that is, makes manifest the true but hidden content of the English sentence.[14]

Quine has special difficulty in accepting any such view, since he regards the concepts of synonymy and translation between languages as inherently illegitimate.[15] But leaving that difficulty aside, there are still plenty of good reasons for holding that a paraphrase is, in general, not an analysis or clear version of the original sentence but a superior *alternative* to it.

In the first place, the canonical language uses descriptions where natural language uses demonstratives. If we have to paraphrase

>That chap over there is an admiral,

we have to provide a specification of 'over there' using general terms. What we choose depends on the circumstances in which the sentence is spoken. Suppose in this case the admiral is standing on the quarterdeck of the flagship. Then we would offer as a paraphrase of the original sentence:

>($\exists$ x) (x is a chap. x is on the quarterdeck of the flagship. x is an admiral).

This is also of course our paraphrase of

>There is an admiral on the quarterdeck of the flagship.

So we have the same paraphrase for two different, nonsynonymous English sentences. In at least one case, therefore, the paraphrase cannot be synonymous with its original.

Again ambiguity, truth-value gaps, and truth-value fluctuation characterize English. But we are trying to get rid of these defects in the canonical language. Synonymous paraphrases, however, would just reproduce the ambiguity, or truth-value gap, or truth-value fluctuation which they were designed to remove.

Thus

>The king commands the bishop to marry all his daughters

is multiply ambiguous and has several different paraphrases, one corresponding to each interpretation and each true under different conditions. These

---

14. This was Bertrand Russell's view of the paraphrases he offered for sentences containing definite descriptions ('the' constructions) in English. See Russell, "On Denoting."

15. Basically, this is because in his opinion the available data —what words are used on what occasions—could never possibly distinguish one of several possible translations as the correct one. See Quine, *Word and Object*, chapter 2.

paraphrases are not synonymous with one another and, not being ambiguous, not synonymous with the original English sentence either.[16]

And if two sentences do not have the same meaning, then one cannot be giving the true, real, hidden meaning of the other. Hence the canonical sentence is not an analysis of the English sentence. So we are confronted with two distinct sentences and must return to our original question, What logical relationship holds between them?

Well, it would seem at first sight that they should at least be *material equivalents*, that is, have the same truth value. Yet even this is too strong. For ambiguous, vague, or truth-value-gap sentences have no one clear truth value to share with their paraphrases. What *is* correct here is that, when an English sentence does have a definite truth value, its paraphrase must have the same value. No paraphrase is acceptable which produces a false analog to a true sentence or vice versa. Call this relationship *quasi-material equivalence*.

But quasi-material equivalence on its own is not a sufficiently intimate connection to provide the whole story. In paraphrasing we aim to provide as much information, and the same information, in a better form. In paraphrasing there must be no sacrifice of subject matter.

But quasi-material equivalence cannot guarantee the provision of as much and the same information. All sorts of dodges in paraphrasing can preserve quasi-material equivalence when preservation of subject matter is lost.

For example, to produce the paraphrase of natural sentence S, first determine S's truth value. When S is true, let its paraphrase be

$(\exists x)(x = x)$ (Something is identical with itself).

When S is false, let its paraphrase be

$(\exists x)(x \neq x)$ (Something is not identical with itself).

This preserves quasi-material equivalence, and yet the canonical language contains the solitary predicate '$=$', which is scarcely sufficient for giving expression to all traits of reality.

So quasi-material equivalence between natural sentence and canonical paraphrase is not enough. The two must be *reality equivalents* also. That is, the very claim about the world legitimately encapsulated in the natural sentence must be reproduced in the canonical one.

The notion of reality equivalence is an intuitive one which resists systematic treatment.[17] Yet so far as I can see, we cannot do without it. And as a result, there

---

16. It might be suggested that the correct paraphrase is the disjunction of alternative interpretations. But I think the English sentence means now one thing, now another, rather than always various alternatives.

17. Furthermore, the claim that two sentences X and Y are reality equivalents seems to be an intensional, not an extensional, claim. A cloud of obscurity hangs over intensional claims, which is why Quine insists on an extensional canonical language. It seems to me that we must use an intensional idea to establish which canonical sentences to affirm, even if those sentences themselves are free from intensional elements. I wish it were not so.

is inevitably some element of judgment in questions of the adequacy of paraphrase and so of the adequacy of a proposed canonical notation. This should not distress us too much; it shows only that in ontology, as in cosmology, the dream of a metaphysics free from doubt and uncertainty is just a dream.

11 Constructions Which Have No Paraphrase

Some considerable fragments of English cannot be reproduced at all, in any recognizable form, in the canonical language. So if we restrict ourselves to canonical resources, we will just have to get along without them. And should it turn out that they alone can discharge some essential task, the canonical language will have been shown to be in that respect defective, in which case it will require modification. Adverbs and adverbial phrases are discussed in Chapter 13 below.

OPAQUE CONSTRUCTIONS

In an ordinary and rather simple sentence like

Napoleon was defeated at Waterloo

we can replace the singular term 'Napoleon' by any other singular term which, as it happens, refers to the same being, without altering the truth value of the original sentence. Thus 'the first Bonaparte emperor' refers to the same being as 'Napoleon', and

The first Bonaparte emperor was defeated at Waterloo

has the same truth value, truth, as our original sentence. Within the context '... was defeated at Waterloo', any coreferring terms can be substituted for one another *salva veritate*, that is, without distrubing the truth value of the whole sentence.

Such a context, call it F for short, conforms to this principle of extensionality:

$$(a = b) \supset (Fa \equiv Fb);$$

that is, where 'a' and 'b' are coreferring terms, 'Fa' and 'Fb' have the same truth value.

Again, in many contexts, a predicate can be replaced salva veritate by another with the same *extension* (that is, another which is, as it happens, true of exactly the same objects). Thus, as it happens, all and only full grown giant kangaroos are marsupials more than eight feet tall. And if the sentence

Some giant kangaroos had long hair

is true, then

Some marsupials more than eight feet tall had long hair

is true too. In contexts such as this one, coextensive predicates may be substituted salva veritate. It conforms to this principle of extensionality:

$$(x)(Fx \equiv Gx) \supset ((\exists x)(Fx \cdot Hx) \equiv (\exists x)(Gx \cdot Hx))$$

or, more schematically and generally:

$$(x)(Fx \equiv Gx) \supset (\ldots F \ldots \equiv \ldots G \ldots).$$

A third principle of extensionality applies to equivalent sentences embedded in other sentences (by the use of truth functions, for example):

$$(p \equiv q) \supset (\ldots p \ldots \equiv \ldots q \ldots).$$

Contexts, which we here represent by dots, satisfying these principles of extensionality are known, of course, as *extensional contexts*.

Now every canonical context is extensional. There is just no way of constructing a canonical sentence which does not satisfy these principles. But the same cannot be said for English. Some sentences in English are not extensional. They are intensional or opaque. Two notable families of opaque constructions are *modal* constructions, which speak of necessity or possibility, and psychological expressions of propositional attitude.

MODAL CONSTRUCTIONS

The queen of England must be a woman. The queen of England is England's reigning monarch. But England's reigning monarch doesn't have to be a woman. Here we cannot substitute the coreferring terms 'the queen of England' and 'England's reigning monarch' one for another salva veritate. Likewise, although nine is the number of planets and nine is necessarily greater than seven, the number of planets is not necessarily greater than seven.

Modal constructions are not extensional. They seem to predicate necessary or possible characteristics of objects, and yet they do not permit substitution of coreferring terms salva veritate. So they have no place in the canonical language.

We could give them a place by following the line favored by Frege.[1] This idea is that modal constructions have a special subject matter. On this approach a modal sentence such as

The queen of England must be a woman

is not about the queen herself, despite appearances. It is about the sense of the expression 'The queen of England'. And this is something different from the sense of the expression 'England's reigning monarch', even though the queen is the same *person* as the reigning monarch.[2] So there is no violation of extensionality. In substituting 'England's reigning monarch' for 'the queen of England' in a modal context, we substitute the name of one sense for the name of another. The terms do *not* corefer, so naturally substituting one for the other cannot be expected to preserve truth value.

Such an approach analyzes modal sentences as introducing a new category, either of senses or of properties. Considerations of economy should make us cautious here. But for Quine, the much more serious problem is that no one can state clearly, in extensional language, just exactly when two candidate properties are really the same property, and when they are actually two. We should have bottomless suspicion of any category of beings for which no identity conditions can be satisfactorily stated.

Quine is unenthusiastic, for quite comparable reasons, about the idea that the subject matter of modal statements is *possibilities*, or *possible worlds*, in some or all of which the queen is a woman.[3]

Modal ideas find no expression in the canonical language, and so it cannot tell us of what must be or might be or might have been, of what is inevitable or what is fortuitous. It can tell us only what is or was or will be. Using the timeless present, it can tell us what is. This is an embarrassingly short way of dealing with the whole problem of necessity. By excluding modal ideas, the canonical notation just bypasses the Scholastic tradition in philosophy, which builds its astonishing edifices on the distinction between contingent and necessary being. But the problem of necessity is a large one in its own right, too large to be dealt with in

---

1. See G. Frege, *Philosophical Writings*.
2. We could also try *the property of being queen of England* in place of *the sense of the expression 'The queen of England'*, etc.
3. For further discussion of modality, see G. Hughes and M. Cresswell, *An Introduction to Modal Logic*, and L. Linsky (ed.), *Reference and Modality*.

passing. Let us continue to explore what the canonical language does make possible (!) in ontology, holding the provisional attitude: Provided nothing is lost by treating modality as a characteristic of expressions rather than of realities . . .

PROPOSITIONAL ATTITUDES

Many psychological verbs with a cognitive component also display failure of extensionality. In Russell's example, George IV wondered whether Scott was the author of *Waverley*. Since Scott did write that novel, 'Scott' and 'the author of *Waverley*' are coreferring terms. But substitution of one for the other in our original truth about George IV results in the falsehood that George IV wondered whether Scott was Scott.

In Quine's example, a poorly instructed Tom believes that Cicero denounced Catiline but not that Tully did, even though Cicero and Tully are the one person.

'Wonders whether' and 'believes that' are verbs generating nonextensional contexts. They are known as verbs of propositional attitude, because belief and wonder are often thought of as attitudes taken by people towards propositions. 'Searches for', 'wishes that', 'hopes that', and 'looks forward to' show nonextensionality too, although it is less natural to think of these verbs as involving an attitude to propositions. I may look forward to meeting my first alligator, and my first alligator may be that which instantly destroys me. Yet I may not be looking forward to meeting that which instantly destroys me.

Attempts to find an extensional way of expressing the great deal of psychological knowledge which we at present set down using the attitude verbs are many, ingenious, complex, and by no means clearly successful.[4] The behaviorist psychology, for example, has constant difficulty with the fact that what an organism does depends not on stimulus merely, but on what the stimulus is taken to be, and on the organism's intentions and purposes, all of which involve nonextensional descriptions of the environment and behavior within it.

Quine suggests handling the matter as a relationship between persons and sentences, but this seems strained and unconvincing for beings which have no language and makes

Ernest is hunting lions

an affair between Ernest and a piece of language.

We cannot go into the issue properly here. The most promising line of development, to my way of thinking, would introduce thoughts. The thought of Scott is not the same as the thought of the author of *Waverley*, and if 'wonders whether' is a verb with thoughts as objects, it would not be legitimate to substitute 'Scott' for 'the author of *Waverley*' after 'wonders whether'. 'Wonders whether' would in this account be an extensional verb. But the question is still a

---

4. See, for example, D.C. Dennett, *Content and Consciousness*.

very open one. It is not known whether it is possible to identify thoughts and distinguish them from one another, except using nonextensional expressions.

What we know of one another's beliefs, hopes, fears, questions, and intentions is much too important, and much too solid, to be just abandoned. If this knowledge cannot be given an extensional form, then so much the worse for our austere canonical notation. And we cannot just blithely add nonextensional expressions to our canonical language. For the semantics, and the consequences in ontology, of intensional constructions are not fully understood. We would not know what we had let ourselves in for.

THE STRONG CONDITIONAL

Conditionals, or 'if-then' statements, are of great importance to us in setting out our views of how the world works. In every endeavor we constantly use them:

> If the oxygen supply is cut off, then the patient will die.
>
> If the plunger is pushed home, then the gelignite will explode.
>
> If the capsule is accelerated for another few seconds, then it will escape the earth's gravitational field.

In the canonical language there is only one conditional term, the hook or material conditional, '$\supset$'. The first sentence above is compounded from two component sentences. Its canonical form would link these two sentences with '$\supset$':

> The oxygen supply is cut off $\supset$ the patient will die,

for the material conditional is the only device available for paraphrasing 'if-then'.

Now '$\supset$' is governed by some familiar rules which cause difficulties when paraphrasing is attempted. Any sentence of the form

$$p \supset q$$

is true provided only that its antecedent, p, is false, or its consequent, q, is true.

But the conditionals of ordinary and scientific thought are not like this. If the plunger is *not* pushed home, then

> The plunger is pushed home $\supset$ the gelignite explodes

is true, but so also is

> The plunger is pushed home $\supset$ the gelignite doesn't explode.

And on the other hand, if the gelignite does indeed explode, then

> The plunger is pushed home ⊃ the gelignite explodes

is true, but so also is

> The plunger is not pushed home ⊃ the gelignite explodes.

Now this is not the way we regard 'if-then' statements. We pick and choose among them, accepting some and rejecting others where, on the material conditional interpretation, all are true.

Take those with unfulfilled antecedent, the *counterfactual* conditionals. We do not accept

> If Hitler had invaded England, the moon would have crashed into the Pacific Ocean,

and we do not accept it even when reminded that Hilter did not invade. Some counterfactuals are not acceptable, which indicates that the conditional in use is not the material one, for every '⊃' sentence with a false antecedent is true.

Again, counterfactuals can compete.

> If Caesar had been in command, he would have used Phantom jets

might win our endorsement. But equally,

> If Caesar had been in command, he would have used catapults

can seem reasonable. But if we are dealing with the material conditional, these two together imply:

> If Caesar had been in command, he would have used Phantom jets and catapults,

which no one thinks for a moment. There can be competing counterfactuals, where accepting both leads to impossible consequences if the conditional involved is the material conditional.

The material conditional requires just a connection between the truth values of the component sentences—it excludes the antecedent being true and the consequent false. So, for example,

> Charlie Chaplin was a comedian ⊃ Mae West was the director of *Birth of a Nation*

is false.

But the strong conditional excludes more. For it requires some connection, as yet unspecified, between the content or meaning of the component sentences.

The counterfactual is the combination of a strong conditional with the *denial* of its antecedent.

> If this liquid had been acid (which it wasn't), then it would have turned the litmus paper red (which it didn't).

But we can also affirm a strong conditional while either leaving open the question of whether the antecedent is fulfilled, or asserting that it is. In these cases we get the open conditional,

> If this liquid is acid, then the litmus paper will turn (or did turn) red,

or the factual conditional or *since* statement,

> Since this liquid is acid, the litmus paper turned red,

which is equivalent to

> If this liquid is acid (and it is), then the litmus paper will turn red (and it did).

Open and factual conditionals contain the strong and not just the material conditional. This is shown by the fact that the truth of antecedent and consequent is not sufficient to establish them.

> If there is oil in Alaska, then the platypus has webbed feet

does not commend itself to us; still less does

> Since there is oil in Alaska, the platypus has webbed feet.

But if these sentences contained the material conditional, they would both be true.

The strong conditional is involved in our understanding of three crucial and related kinds of scientific statement: dispositionals, natural laws, and causal statements.

> This glass is brittle,

a dispositional statement, is often analysed as

> If this glass is suitably sharply struck, then it shatters.

This cannot be the material conditional

> This glass is suitably sharply struck ⊃ this shatters,

for on that account every unstruck object is brittle. Thus

> This lump of putty which is never struck is brittle

would amount to

> This unstruck lump of putty is struck ⊃ this shatters,

which is true because its antecedent is false.

Dispositionals involve the strong conditional. The strong conditional cannot be expressed in the canonical language. So, it would seem, dispositions cannot be spoken of in the canonical language. When we consider the vast range of dispositional ideas in use in common life and science, from irascible to inflammable to mothproof to malleable to stable, this appears a grievous restriction.

Again, statements of natural law involve the strong conditional. Natural law statements are universal generalizations and can be distinguished, as *nomological* generalizations, from mere *factual* generalizations, by their supporting counterfactuals. Thus

> All copper conducts electricity

is a law of nature, since it supports

> If this twig had been copper, it would have conducted electricity,

while on the other hand

> All the coins in my pocket are copper

is not a law of nature, but a mere factual generalization, since it does not support

> If this sovereign had been in my pocket, it would have been copper.

Natural laws are distinctive, then, in their connection with counterfactual strong conditionals.

Again, causal statements are distinguished by their relation to strong conditionals. Post hoc ergo propter hoc is a traditionally recognized fallacy resting on the confusion of mere succession with causal sequence. The difference between the causal

> The switch was pressed, starting the fan

and the merely temporal

> The switch was pressed, then the fan started

is that the first, but not the second, supports the factual strong conditional

> Since the switch was pressed, the fan started.

It would seem a crippling restriction on any language that it cannot deal adequately with dispositions, natural laws, and causal statements. Quine tackles the problem by a strategy of progressive transcendence of the strong conditional idioms.[5]

Take a disposition, say brittleness. Brittleness isn't magic; we don't understand brittleness properly unless we realize that there is some subtle structural property of glass—the peculiar forces bonding its molecules, in this case—on which its reaction to smart blows depends. But this inner structural property can be described directly, without any if-thens, as an enduring, standing property of the glass. And although this more profound description may in its turn involve conditional elements (it may appeal to natural laws, for example), the description would in principle finally resolve into one involving basic categorical features and basic regularities expressed using the material conditional.[6]

Dispositional predicates are what we use and get along with in the meantime, while we lack sufficient knowledge of nature to be able to give a direct description. Everything that *is*, is an actuality, not a possibility. We speak in terms of possibilities while we lack anything better. As we extend our knowledge, we dispense with dispositional terms in favor of categorical ones. The canonical language suffices for setting down how, in the final analysis, things actually are.

In much the same way, the sense of necessity attaching to laws of nature or causal statements springs from our conception of underlying structures or regularities. Any process which changed a twig into copper would have to give it a subtle inner structure of an electrically conductive kind. So we affirm the statement

> If this twig had been copper, it would have conducted electricity.

On the other hand, the process of putting a sovereign in my pocket will not turn it into copper. So we deny the statement

> If this sovereign had been in my pocket, it would have been copper.

---

5. W.V. Quine, *The Ways of Paradox*, pp. 51–54.

6. A categorical description is one which claims flatly that such and such *is* so, rather than conditionally, that it is so provided something else.

Laws of nature are generalizations supported by, and explained by appeal to, more basic underlying regularities. At the bottom of this hierarchy of regularities are those fundamental, for the present, in our scientific theory. But what about fundamental regularities? Let us use as an example,

> All electrons have negative charge.

We hold that they support the corresponding counterfactual

> If this had been an electron, it would have had negative charge.

These fundamental counterfactuals cannot rest on any underlying structure, just because we are dealing with fundamentals. But here the fundamental status of the electron (taken for the sake of argument) comes in. Just because electrons have no structure, there is no way of making an electron which is not also a way of making something with negative charge. Our counterfactual is guaranteed by the whole theoretical structure in which the idea of an electron plays its part.

Some things *must* be thus and so only in this sense: that that is a consequence of being *in fact* as they are. There is no sense in which, at the deepest level, the world had to be as it is. This is Quine's position, and it places him squarely in the tradition of Hume. If he is right on this controversial question, then at the basic level of description, categorical predicates and the material conditional will suffice for setting down the traits of reality. The strong conditional will be, in principle, dispensible.[7]

John Mackie offers an account of the strong conditional which complements Quine's doctrine.[8] Never mind whether we can do without strong conditionals; what are they? What would we do without if we did without them? He answers this question by his *suppositional* theory. When we offer or accept a conditional statement, we are not making an assertion that some rather mysterious hypothetical property belongs to the world. We are not claiming the existence of some metaphysical chain of necessity binding items together. We are *supposing* something (the state of affairs described in the antecedent) and, on that supposition, claiming a consequence (the state of affairs described in the consequence).

> If the liquid is acid, then the litmus paper will turn red

is analyzed as:

> Suppose the liquid is acid. Using this as a premise, more or less

---

7. This result fits neatly with the earlier rejection of modal expressions from the canonical language, for the strong conditional invites analysis in terms of what must be and what cannot be, and both modals and strong conditionals are excluded.

8. J. L. Mackie, *Truth, Probability, and Paradox*, Chapters 3 and 4. For other views, see E. Nagel, *The Structure of Science*, and D. Lewis, *Counterfactuals*.

formal reasoning processes lead us to conclude that the litmus paper will turn red.

We are saying:

Let this liquid be acid. On that basis, the litmus paper will turn red.

We can account, in this view of the matter, for the way we deal with strong conditionals. Not all counterfactuals are acceptable. Take the gelignite example. We cannot ordinarily suppose that the plunger is pushed home yet conclude that there is no explosion. And this is the case even if the plunger is not in fact pushed home. So we reject the statement

If the plunger had been pushed home, the gelignite would not have exploded.

Counterfactuals can compete with one another. The reason for this is that the information provided in the antecedent is often not sufficient on its own to fix just one outcome. And by supplying different implicit supplements we arrive at different conclusions. Hence,

If Caesar had been in command (and the battle had taken place in his time and with his technology), he would have used catapults,

is only apparently at odds with

If Caesar had been in command (and the battle had taken place in our time and with our technology), he would have used Phantoms.

Underlying structural regularities support strong conditionals in just this way. We supply the regularity as an implicit premise for the situation in which our supposition works. When we suppose, for example, that a twig is copper, our theory about copper enters as further information, from which its electrical conductivity is a consequence. And we accept that if the twig had been copper, it would have conducted electricity.

A factual conditional,

Since p, q,

is the fruit of a complex thought process. It involves, at one level, the assertion of both p and q, and at another level, not the *assertion* of any conditional component, but the claim that from the supposition that p, together with the general continuing condition of the world, q could be expected to follow. This is what we dimly apprehend when we feel that the strong conditional involves a connection of content between antecedent and consequent. The antecedent, together with whatever else is implicitly supposed about the situation, must furnish a ground for the consequent in just the sense that its description furnishes premises for a more or less conclusive piece of reasoning.

On Mackie's view, then, strong conditionals are not literally true or false, since they are reasonings not made fully explicit, rather than assertions. Apart from a residual problem about strong conditionals acting as components in other conditionals (since these components must admit assertion or denial in factual or counterfactual conditionals), this theory accounts well for the distinctive way conditionals operate in our thought. It makes perfectly plain why the material conditional is so different and why the differences are what they are.

For Quine, the conditionals give way to statements of underlying truth. For Mackie, the underlying truth does not replace the conditional, but stands as the implicit supplementary premise from which the consequent emerges as consequence of the supposition. This is a less draconian program for conditionals, and so it is to be preferred. And since on Mackie's view conditionals are not assertions, they need not (and indeed cannot) figure in a complete schedule of assertions.

Let them be used, by all means, for they have their uses, just because reasoning has its uses. But there is no good purpose served by including these reasonings among the assertions on which reasoning rests. So such conditionals should not figure in the canonical schedule of assertions, which claims to be complete in principle. It is not a defect but a positive merit of the canonical language that, possessing only the material conditional, it lacks the means of expressing the strong conditional.

THE ADEQUACY OF THE CANONICAL LANGUAGE

This completes a review of the principle patterns of paraphrase and the principal English idioms for which no paraphrase is available.

We have seen that a shadow of doubt lies over the canonical notation so far as modality is concerned. If we do need the idea of necessity, and if that involves ontological consequences, then this will require that conclusions reached using the canonical notation be supplemented.

Much the same situation holds in the area of psychological descriptions. But these problems can be deferred. It is of great value to determine the ontological implications of the canonical language, for it is plain that that language will suffice for a great deal of our statement-making needs.

Indeed, if the strategy outlined above for treatment of the strong conditional—and thereby dispositions, causes, and natural laws—is satisfactory, then the canonical language will suffice at least for the whole of the natural sciences. In this connection, the great merit of the canonical language is that in it, ontological consequences are plain and unambiguous, as the next chapter explains.

12 Ontic Commitment and Reduction to a Minimum Domain

ONTIC COMMITMENT

We use *theories*, or interrelated systems of statement-making sentences, in a variety of ways—sometimes to state the plain and literal truth as we see it, and sometimes as poetry or myth or useful model or a convenient way of expressing ourselves without being quite serious. Even within science, it is often unclear just exactly what a theory implies is to be found in reality. A theory of planetary orbits pretty certainly involves a commitment to the reality of planets, but its commitment to orbits is perhaps not so unconditional. And what must the world contain to validate the random walk theory of stock market prices?

The question of the implications for reality of the various theories or quasi-theories we accept, is the problem of the *ontic commitment* of those theories. But there is often prodigality, frivolity, or plain muddle in the ontic commitment of theories cast in natural or scientific language, which is often fashioned with quite other ends in view than advance in ontology. The canonical language, by contrast, is deliberately constructed in such a way that ontic commitments are clear, unambiguous, and unavoidable.

The canonical language faces us, uncompromisingly, with our ontic commitments. It achieves this by a series of simplifying steps: it does without all figures of speech, and it uses only the very simple syntax of bound variables, predicates, and truth functions. In consequence, it has a clearly and completely statable semantics in which we specify the truth conditions of canonical sentences. And a consideration of these truth conditions yields our precise and crystalline rule of ontic commitment.

To remind you: individual variables take as their values under assignments the entities in the universe of discourse (for serious theory, this is just the world). Any item can, under some assignment, be the value of any variable. Predicates have as their extension the class of those items (or pairs of items, etc.) in the universe of discourse of which they are true. Existentially quantified simple sentences are true if under some assignment the variables have as values items from the extensions of the predicates involved; universally quantified simple sentences are true if this is the case under all assignments. More complicated but equally definite truth conditions can be specified for sentences containing truth functions.

Now the ontic commitments of a theory are shown in its *affirmative, existentially quantified sentences*. A theory containing the sentence

There are green frogs, $(\exists x)(Fx.Gx)$

is committed, naturally enough, to the existence of green frogs. For that sentence cannot be true unless there is some value which 'x' can have which is at once in the extension of 'frog' and of 'green'. Any such item is a green frog.

But a theory which contains the negation of this sentence, namely,

There are no green frogs, $\sim(\exists x)(Fx.Gx)$

is not, so far as that sentence goes, committed to anything. That sentence is true in a world without green frogs, no matter what it contains or even if it contains nothing at all.

Universally quantified sentences are standardly taken to have no ontic commitments;

Every frog is green, $(x)(Fx \supset Gx)$

is treated as equivalent to the negative existential sentence

There are no frogs which are not green, $\sim(\exists x)(Fx . \sim Gx)$.[1]

Bearing in mind, then, that it is the affirmative existential sentences which are going to matter, we can state in general form Quine's rule for the ontic commitment of theories expressed in canonical form:

> R: A theory is committed to all and only those objects which must be values of the variables in order for its sentences to be true.[2]

The universe of discourse contains items, and the variables range over these as values. Some of the items are essential in the sense that without them the

---

1. So a theory of planetary orbits is committed to the existence of planets if it is of the form, There are planets which obey these laws. . . . The laws themselves, being universal, carry no commitment.
2. For example, W.V. Quine, *From a Logical Point of View*, chapter 1.

theory's sentences would not be true. These essential items constitute the ontic commitment of the theory.

Before expanding on R, let us notice the slogan form in which it is sometimes expressed:

To be is to be the value of a variable.

Do not be misled by this. R is not a rule specifying what there is, but what a theory *says* there is. The slogan does not mean that if there had been no thought, no language, and so no variables, nothing would have existed. It means that the way to find out what a theory is commited to as existing or real is to find what items are required as values of variables for the theory to be true.

The rule R specifies what a theory says there is. Of course, it cannot itself settle whether or not a theory is true, and so it cannot tell us what actually exists. But R is connected with the question of what actually exists. It specifies what must be in order for a theory to be true, and when a theory *is* true, its commitments will indeed consist in (some of) those things which *do* exist.

Again, when something is a commitment of our best, most indispensable body of theory, then we have the best possible ground for holding that that thing exists. And a rule such as R is necessary for the interpretation of science which uncovers its ontic import.

R is a rule of ontic commitment. It commits us, not to particular things, but to *kinds* of things. For apart from logical machinery, the canonical language contains only predicates. The ontic commitment is made by affirmative existential sentences, such as

There are green frogs,

and for this to be true we don't need Freddy the green frog, provided we have Freda or Ferdinand or Felicity.[3]

To just which kinds of thing a theory is committed thus depends on the theory's *ideology*, as Quine calls the stock of predicates at its disposal. More particularly, the theory is committed to exactly those kinds of things whose predicates appear in its affirmative existential sentences.

There is nothing to quarrel with here. All the elements in canonical sentences work together in settling the commitment; the signal of commitment is the quantified variable, while the concrete character of the commitment depends on the predicates employed. Many of our well-respected theories are in fact general, dealing only in kinds of things. Such theories are equally well satisfied by many different sets of particulars. And if a theory leaves open what particulars there are, this is quite properly left open by the rule specifying the theory's ontic implications.

---

3. Corresponding to proper names, the canonical language is committed to one-member kinds, such as the Nelsonizers and the Statue-of-Libertyizers.

PROBLEMS WITH THE RULE FOR ONTIC COMMITMENT

R is a rule which concerns theories expressed in the canonical language. So R belongs to the metalanguage of the canonical (object) language. It therefore belongs to a different and perhaps richer language than the canonical one. Nevertheless, some of the restrictions Quine insists on for the canonical language must, in consistency, be applied to the metalanguage also. Chief among these is the *extensionality condition*. Quine holds that nonextensional contexts are inherently obscure and ruin clear inference rules. They should, on these grounds, be banned from the metalanguage no less than from the canonical language itself. So R, which sets out ontic commitments, should be expressed extensionally. But it is not extensional in its original form. All Quine's statements of it mention what is *required*, or what *must* be in the domain, or what the variables *need* to range over. None of these expressions is extensional. Yet when attempts are made to put R in extensional form, difficulties arise.

Following Cartwright, let us take the domain D in which a theory T is interpreted (i.e., over which T's variables range and within which T's predicates have extensions).[4] Various subdomains of items from D will, let us suppose, provide materials sufficient for the truth of T. Let these subdomains be the set of U's which satisfy T (i.e., render true the sentences of T). Thus if T is the single sentence

There are green frogs,

then any subdomain containing any one or more items which are both green and frogs is a U satisfying T.

Now the natural way of expressing the rule R is to say that T is committed to items of kind K provided the only subdomains which satisfy T have Ks in them, and a straightforward extensional formulation of this is:

T is committed to Ks $\equiv (U)$ (U satisfies $T \supset U$ contains Ks)

But this is disastrous. For suppose T is in fact false. Then no U whatever satisfies it. But if no U satisfies T, then for every U whatever, 'U satisfies T' is false, and so

U satisfies $T \supset U$ contains Ks,

which is a material conditional, is true. And it is true no matter what Ks are. Consequently, the theory

There are unicorns

---

4. R.L. Cartwright, "Ontology and the Theory of Meaning."

turns out, on this formulation, to involve a commitment to Ks, *no matter what* Ks *are*. This theory is committed to unicorns all right, but also to monkeys, leopards, lizards, electrons, and furthermore to flying horses, gorgons, and even to married bachelors, since (where U does not satisfy T) it does not have to be true that

U contains Ks

for the statement

U satisfies $T \supset U$ contains Ks

to be true and so for T to be committed to Ks.

We might try to mend matters by excluding this trivial way of fulfilling the condition for commitment. To do this, we would naturally insist that some U's do satisfy T, which gives us

T is committed to Ks $\equiv$ ($\exists$ U) (U satisfies T).

(U)(U satisfies $T \supset U$ contains Ks).

Unhappily, this is just as disastrous. For if T is in fact false, no U will satisfy it, and

($\exists$ U) (U satisfies T)

will be false. So the whole right-hand side will be false, no matter what Ks are. Furthermore, no matter what Ks are, the whole left-hand side will be false. In other words, T will be committed to nothing. Our false theory

There are unicorns

will not be committed to monkeys or leopards, which is all very well, but it will not be committed to unicorns either. This is precisely what we do *not* want. The clear sense of R is that this theory requires unicorns as values of its variables if it is to be true, and so it *is* committed to unicorns. Any other result is quite unacceptable.

This problem, that extensional versions of R involve unacceptable commitments in the case of false theories, has never been satisfactorily cleared up.

Another closely connected problem with extensional versions of R concerns discussion of theories that we do not ourselves accept. One point of R is that it can serve as a guide in cases where we are in doubt over whether to adopt T; we need to be able to ask, among other questions, what ontic commitments T will involve us in. Again, R can be used as a weapon in dispute with someone whose theory we reject—we point out that T has certain ontic commitments that ought not to be accepted, and so furnish a reason for rejecting T. In both cases, we need to be able to specify the ontic commitment of T without ourselves thereby becoming involved in those very commitments. But committing ourselves to the commitments of any theory T under discussion is not easy to avoid if R is given extensional form. An ordinary extensional relational sentence involving unicorns, such as

> Peter is attacked by at least one unicorn,

shows some of its ontic implications in the equivalent

> $(\exists\, x)$ (x is a unicorn. Peter is attacked by x).

And if ontic commitment is an extensional relation, then analogously,

> T is committed to at least one unicorn

invites the formulation

> $(\exists\, x)$ (x is a unicorn. T is committed to x).

But for that to be true, x must range over unicorns. Anyone who says it is therefore *himself* committed to unicorns along with anyone who affirms T.

Putting it mildly, it is pretty unsatisfactory to find oneself committed to unicorns in the very act of criticizing T on the ground that it involves commitment to unicorns. Put generally, the problem here is that no extensional relation can hold except between items which exist, whereas commitment is a 'relation' which can hold between a theory and items which, to speak paradoxically, do not exist.

Finally, the nonextensional character of ontic commitment is plain in cases when, as it happens, two predicates have the same extension. Suppose, for example, that all and only bats are flying placentals, but that I think they are not placentals but marsupials. My theory T is

> Bats are flying marsupials,

and I accept as a canonical paraphrase of this

> $(\exists\, x)$ (x is a bat) . (y) (y is a bat $\supset$ (y flies. y is a marsupial)).

T is immediately committed to bats. It is also, through its consequence

> $(\exists\, x)$ (x flies. x is a marsupial),

committed to flying marsupials.

But it seems quite wrong to say that because I am committed to bats I am thereby committed to flying placentals, even though bats *are* flying placentals.

In my theory I may well want to insist that

> Bats are flying marsupials, and there are no flying placentals.

Yet if commitment is extensional, then

> T is committed to bats

and

> Bats are flying placentals

together entail

> T is committed to flying placentals.

Since this result is unacceptable, we again conclude that statements of ontic commitment cannot have an extensional form. And since it is a cardinal doctrine of Quine that whatever can be legitimately said can be said extensionally, he would seem to be hoist on his own petard.

THE RESOLUTION OF THESE DIFFICULTIES

I think that the key to the resolution of this problem lies in one natural way of putting the rule R of ontic commitment:

> T is committed to Ks ≡ if T is true, then there are Ks which the variables of T range over.

The 'if-then' on the right-hand side here is plainly the *strong conditional*. The falsity of T is surely not sufficient to make the right-hand side true in any interesting way.

Following up this clue, we remember Mackie's suppositional account of the strong conditional. In this account, a strong conditional sentence is not a simple statement but a more complex expression of a piece of reasoning from the antecedent taken as basis. The conditional sentence frame

> If p, then q

receives the interpretation

> Suppose p. Under that supposition, q is a (more or less strongly indicated) consequence.[5]

---

5. That is, by more or less rigorous reasoning, we may pass from p as premise to q as conclusion.

This view of strong conditionals has welcome application here with the problem of the rule for ontic commitment. To determine the ontic commitment of theory T we proceed as follows:

> Suppose T to be true. On that supposition, apply to its sentences the semantical rules laid down in the canonical language. These rules can be applied only if D is of a certain kind. D must contain subdomain(s) U which satisfies T. And if every one of the U's satisfying T contains Ks, than T is committed to Ks.

Put more briefly, T is committed to Ks where the supposition that T is true has as consequence that Ks figure among the values of the variables of T's sentences.

This criterion will take a counterfactual form when we discuss theories we reject, the open conditional form when we are wondering about the merits of a theory, and the factual or 'since' form when we are investigating the commitments of theories to which we already adhere.

The commitments of a theory are on this new view unaltered by whether or not we accept the theory and by whether or not the theory is in fact true or false. For what *follows from* a supposition does not depend on whether that supposition is asserted, entertained, or denied, nor on whether it is true or false. And everything which is in fact true about bats, for example, does not follow from the supposition that there are bats. So we can be committed to bats without being committed to flying placentals.

Since Mackie's account of the strong conditional holds that it is not a sort of *statement*, a strong conditional view of the rule for canonical commitment, interpreted in Mackie's way, is compatible with the view that all statements, even in the metalanguage, are extensional.

So much for the criterion for ontic commitment itself; let us now watch it in action.

ONTIC COMMITMENT AND STRAIGHTFORWARD PARAPHRASES

The canonical paraphrases of ordinary and scientific language are quantified predications. And we have now seen that the ontic commitments of a canonical sentence are shown by the quantifications—the sentence makes a commitment to whatever it quantifies over. So sentences in canonical form display their commitments in an open and unavoidable way. Canonical sentences *confront* us with the ontological issue; they show exactly what sorts of things we are perhaps unwittingly committing ourselves to.

Thus many people would cheerfully and heedlessly assent to

> Hermes was a Greek god.

Yet the straightforward paraphrase of this (neglecting the complication of tense),

182 A FIRST SURVEY OF ONTOLOGY

$(\exists x)(x$ Hermesizes. x is Greek. x is a god),

quantifies over (requires for its truth the existence of) Greek gods and so is ontically committed to them. What this paraphrase forcefully brings home to us is our slack way of thinking about these matters. It treats

Hermes was a Greek god

as sharing its form and type of implications with

Demosthenes was a Greek orator,

whose straightforward paraphrase makes plain the acceptable commitment to Greek orators. Precision of thought requires that we find some other way of saying what is correct but misexpressed in

Hermes was a Greek god,

for that sentence is false if there are no Greek gods. The canonical language and the criterion of ontic commitment bring this out.

There are many other types of sentences with often unsuspected ontic implications on a common interpretation.

Jupiter has more satellites than the earth,

for example, relates the numerousness of the class of earth satellites to that of the class of Jupiter satellites. It involves a commitment to classes (or, in an alternative analysis, to numbers), although such things get no explicit mention in the English sentence. Leaving singular terms undisturbed for simplicity's sake, a paraphrase of the sentence makes this perfectly clear:

$(\exists x)(\exists y)(x$ is a class. $(z)(z \epsilon x \equiv z$ is a satellite of Jupiter). y is a class. $(w)(w \epsilon y \equiv w$ is a satellite of the earth). x has more members than $y)$.

Our original sentence,

The earth has more satellites than Jupiter,

is thus seen to obscure rather than reveal its ontic commitments. Much the same is true of

All red things have something in common,

which looks harmless enough, but whose straightforward paraphrase

ONTIC COMMITMENT AND REDUCTION   183

$$(\exists x)(y)(y \text{ is red} \supset y \text{ has } x)$$

reveals a commitment to some as yet unspecified and rather mysterious item (redness?) to be found wherever red things are.

In other cases, ontic implications are not so much hidden as just not attended to. For example, the editorial pontification

> The reason for the Cabinet reshuffle was the performance of some of the ministers

involves a bizarre prodigality of ontic commitment, as this paraphrase, simplified by the omission of uniqueness clauses, shows:

> $(\exists x)(\exists y)(\exists z)$ (x is a Cabinet. y is a reshuffle of x. z is a performance. $(\exists v)(v$ is a minister. v took part in z). $(v)(v$ took part in $z \supset v$ is a minister). z is a reason for y).

The paraphrase of the editorial pontification quantifies over reshuffles, reasons, and performances as well as ministers and Cabinets. Surely we should be uneasy, if not downright incredulous, at the idea that such items are to be found, as values for variables, alongside shoes, ships, and lumps of sealing wax in our domain or universe of discourse.

Here, as earlier with the Greek gods, the paraphrase rules take a sentence at its literal face value and accord it the same structure as the grammatically parallel

> The cousin of the Mafia boss was the owner of some of the speakeasies,

which has parallel but unembarrassing ontic commitments. And not just common life but science as well yields sentences with this structure and this pattern of commitment:

> The value of the coefficient of friction was the solution of some of the equations.

English is a flexible instrument. We can generate referring expressions in it with no difficulty at all to conveniently cover whatever we have in mind. For ontological purposes, it is all too flexible. A short while back I wrote of the paraphrase of the editorial pontification. A paraphrase of the sentence in which *that* expression occurs would quantify over, and so involve a commitment to, paraphrases and pontifications as well as editors.

But our thought is irresponsible if we think or act as though fertility of referring expressions is not matched by fertility in ontic commitment. Unless there is some specified way in which referring expressions are shown to be mere conveniences which we can do without whenever challenged to do so, they have ontic implications. And in using them we should be prepared to shoulder those commitments. The canonical language, with its uncompromising criterion for ontic commitment, requires us to face this issue. It just will not do to say that although of course there weren't *really* any Greek gods, Hermes was one of them—or anything comparable for classes, properties, reasons, reshuffles, pontifications, or values of coefficients.

REDUCTION PROGRAMS

Straightforward paraphrase reveals, in a way that cannot be ignored, the bizarre, overblown, paradoxical, and generally discreditable ontology which users of English heedlessly espouse. So straightforward paraphrase naturally engenders a search for ways of expressing ourselves which avoid the excessive commitments of ordinary English. Such a search takes the form of attempts to replace embarrassing patterns of expression by others which will do as well, yet be innocent of some of the ontic commitments of what they replace. Such a search is a *reduction program* for the category of items which are not favored. All sentences about Greek gods, for example, might give way to sentences quantifying over stories about Greek gods, or thoughts or beliefs about them, or statues of them, or rustling breezes in olive groves. If this can be accomplished, well and good. Greek gods can be reduced and we are not committed to them. On the other hand, if there is even one true sentence quantifying over Greek gods which resists such treatment, then we are committed to their existence and must just face and accept that fact.

In ontology, the problem concerns very general reduction programs; the question is which *categories*—concrete particulars, events, numbers, properties, classes, facts, propositions, and so forth—must be recognized, and which admit of reduction to others. Rival metaphysical systems each specify a basic universe of discourse comprising those categories which are taken to be fundamental. The variables range over items from these categories and these categories alone. So revised ways must be found for stating what is true but not directly expressible in these terms. These revised ways of expressing ordinary truths then operate as reductions or eliminations of nonfundamental categories. That system deserves our allegiance, which furnishes the most convincing reductions to the clearest and most economical base.

QUINE'S MINIMUM DOMAIN

Economy is one great virtue in theories. Although we have no a priori guarantee that nature is parsimonious and always achieves its results in the most direct and efficient manner, there is good reason always to prefer the more economical of two theories, or bodies of theory, which are equally adequate to the facts with which they deal. For consider the alternative. If we take the less economical view, then we affirm the existence of some elements or forces or laws which are not necessary for our explanation. These extra elements, forces, or laws are therefore doing no work in the explanation. They are idle decorations. And being idle, there can be no evidence for them, since the only evidence there can be for the reality of something lies in the phenomena which it alone can explain. The case is simple when one theory consists in just another theory plus needless additions. It is very much more complex where we have two competing theories which do not share any common content. In this more usual case, judgments of relative economy are often difficult to make. One theory has fewer elements but more complicated laws than the other, perhaps, or one theory purchases overall simplicity at the cost of some local elaboration.

These difficulties notwithstanding, economy remains a desideratum in metaphysics no less than in more special scientific theorizing. This is commonly expressed in the slogan known as Occam's razor: Entities are not to be multiplied beyond necessity. In the branch of ontology presently under consideration, this methodological rule requires a search for a *minimum domain* which will embrace both the minimum number of distinct categories of being and, within them, the minimum number of entities of the least possible number of different kinds.

The specification of a minimum domain is at the same time the specification of the minimum stock of predicates. As we have seen, ontic commitment is carried by the predicates which figure in affirmative existentially quantified sentences, and the minimal set of such predicates thus form the most meager resources adequate to set down the traits of reality. The canonical language is that language with the simplest *structure* adequate to our statement-making needs. Its most austere form, which admits the minimal predicate stock, carries an ontic commitment to the minimum domain.

Quine adopts a two-category domain. It contains sets and concrete particulars. Let us put the sets aside for the time being and look further at the concrete particulars.

Quine's position is physicalist. The basic items are fundamental physical particles. We saw in part II that there is room for dispute over whether such particles are the happiest choice as fundamental particulars, but Quine follows the atomistic tradition and declares for particles rather than fields or a physicalized space-time. So among the predicates of the most economical language will be those applying to fundamental particles—spin, charge, mass, and position, for example—qualified as need be by the indeterminacy relations postulated in quantum theory.

Some of those predicates may prove to be dispensable. They are not strictly needed if they can be defined in terms of others, as velocity can be defined using position and time, and acceleration using velocity and time. Where a predicate is definable, its use is a convenience involving no distinct ontological implications. It can be added to the stock of predicates with a light heart, since it involves no increase in the ontic burden we assume. The definition is our guarantee of that, for the definition guarantees that the new predicate can be eliminated whenever we choose.

Ordinary Things

We can readily get in a tangle when we consider ordinary things, which Quine certainly admits to be real, such as cows and horses, chairs and tables, comets and stars. Do the variables range over such things, or not? None of them is a fundamental particle; none shares any specific property with any particle. So if, among concrete particulars, the variables range over particles and particles alone, then in this system there are *no* cows, horses, chairs, tables, comets, or stars.

Take, for example, the statement

There are green frogs.[6]

Its natural paraphrase is

$(\exists x)(\text{frog } x \, . \, \text{green } x)$.

This is true only if the variable x can have as value something which is both a frog and green. But no particle is a frog, and no particle, at any rate in orthodox physics, is green. So if the variable x can take only particles as values, then our sentence is false, and there are no green frogs.

This is an unfortunate result. What we want to say, of course, is that there *are* green frogs, but green frogs are made up of particles and nothing else. There are two ways of dealing with the situation. We can allow that the variables range over not just particles considered singly but over all groups, heaps, and systems of particles as well, in which case we *retain* the predicates 'frog' and 'green' in our vocabulary, and

$(\exists x)(\text{frog } x \, . \, \text{green } x)$

turns out true just in case some system of particles is both a frog and green.

Alternatively, we can hold that 'frog' and 'green' are predicates which can be definitionally eliminated in favor of some fearsomely complex and unknown predicates which apply strictly to individual particles, and apply in precisely those circumstances where, in vulgar and superficial language, a green frog is present. If we take this second course, 'frog' and 'green' disappear from our minimal predicate stock and

$(\exists x)(\text{frog } x \, . \, \text{green } x)$

is not false so much as unstatable in our most austere language.

---

6. Forget that the color terms have a special and puzzling status. We are using 'green' just as an example of a predicate which applies only to *systems* of particles. 'Greasy' or 'gigantic' or 'grotesque' would do as well, but they all have (equally irrelevant) complications of their own.

I recommend the first alternative. It does, in one sense, increase the number of sorts of things over which the variables are held to range, for it includes groups, heaps, and systems of particles in addition to particles simpliciter. But if I say this does *not* represent any increase in the number of *categories* of the ontology, I am sure you will know what I mean and agree. It is hard indeed to say what makes categories distinct, but lumping many items of one category together will not produce a new one. So this first alternative is not an ontologically inflationary move. And it has two advantages which to my mind are decisive.

First, as already indicated in connection with frogs, we just do not know and are never likely to know exactly what internal state of a system of *particles* is necessary and sufficient for green froghood. If we could do it even for the cells of a frog, this would be a fantastic triumph, and yet each cell in turn contains many millions of particles. So we will never be in a position to actually do without predicates like 'frog'.

Second, there are several levels of 'higher' predicates. Terms like 'migration' apply to systems of organisms, which are systems of cells, which are systems of molecules, which are systems of atoms, which are systems of particles. So even if we got over one stage in eliminating higher predicates, the next would be there to confront us. Furthermore, the higher predicates cover *indefinite* arrangements of constituents. There is an indeterminate range of particular motions of birds which constitute a migration, a similar range of particular structures of cells which constitute a bird, and so forth. So any attempt to do without higher predicates would involve either an indefinitely complex disjunction of lower level descriptions or a new set of indefinite range-covering predicates applying at base level. Neither of these developments is more attractive than retaining higher level predicates.

The relationship between higher and lower is even more complex in the case of predicates such as 'clock' or 'lamp' or 'calculator', where we can have objects of indefinitely many materials arranged in indefinitely many different ways all qualifying for the same predicate.

Higher predicates are not, then, in general eliminable. But this does not mean that we here confront new categories. For the failure of elimination stems from the indefinite and variable relationship between systems of items, taken collectively, and their constituents. The failure does not stem from the presence of a new category of item which higher predicates alone can describe.

In retaining higher predicates, we at the same time let the variables range over both basic and derivative particulars. There is prudence in this, for it may well be that particles prove not to be basic; indeed, any class of item can be basic only provisionally. In part II we saw reason to think that particles will not prove to be, forever, the basic particulars recognized in our world view. But if they are ever superseded as basic particulars, they may remain as derivative ones. And a system quantifying over derivative particulars will not need to be completely replaced to accommodate this change. It can be modified by the introduction of new predicates and new relationships among predicates so that particles take on a status comparable to that of frogs; variables range over them as well as over basic particulars, and predicates apply to them as derivative items.

NATURALISM AND 'FACILE MATERIALISM'

A schedule of categories constitutes an ontology. We have seen, for example, that Quine's ontology contains concrete particulars. The frame of a cosmology is given when the basic kinds of concrete particular are specified. In Quine's case, the concrete particulars are particles; there is as much, but no more, than is recognized by physics. Physics is the master system of the natural world; whatever is physical is real, and whatever is real is physical.

This is an uncompromising version of contemporary materialism. The traditional Western world view allowed of the three great grades of being—God, mind, and matter—but of those three only matter remains in Quine's scheme. If there are any gods, angels, souls, spirits, demons, or minds, then they are, I dare say, concrete particulars. But no such items, Quine holds, figure in the minimum domain. The manner of their banishment varies from case to case. The denial of gods, angels, demons, principalities, and powers, the most exotic and spectacular participants in the cosmic drama, is *naturalism*. And here Quine is a purist; no predicates distinctive of supernatural beings are admitted into affirmative existentially quantified sentences, and in consequence there is no call for the variables to range over such beings.

The case is very different when we consider mind, soul, or spirit. For as already mentioned, the psychological predicates are with us; they discharge an essential function, and there is no eliminating them. There are thinking, sensing, feeling, hoping, desiring, and suffering men just as clearly as there are green frogs. But that does not show that there are special concrete particulars, Minds, distinct from bodies. Quine holds that the mental functions are in fact complex bodily functions, but this is a matter of speculative theory rather than demonstration in our present state of knowledge.

We might have expected that, this being the state of the case, the existence of minds would be, correspondingly, a matter of (opposing) speculative theory too. But no. Even without the painstaking detail work of identifying the particular concrete physical truth which exhausts the reality of, say,

Jones has a headache,

we can, and on principles of economy should, hold that 'has a headache' is a predicate true of the whole man Jones, which man is a complex physical object. Even if they cannot be superseded by sophisticated complexes of ordinary physical predicates, the psychological predicates are best interpreted as applying directly and literally to those entirely physical objects, human or other animal bodies.

By taking this tack, we can restrict the basic kinds of concrete particular to particles and systems of particles. Quine has the grace to dub this position a 'facile physicalization' of mental states.[7]

---

7. Quine, *The Ways of Paradox*, p. 230.

ONTIC COMMITMENT AND REDUCTION 189

MEASURES

Even if we confine ourselves to the physical realm, the ontological texture of common, technical, and scientific thought is still richer than Quine's. Measures are a case in point. Are there such things as miles? Yes, of course; there are more than five hundred of them between Sydney and Melbourne alone. We talk of miles and kilograms, degrees of this and that, poundals, ergs, watts and amps, and so forth, whenever our thought gets even mildly technical.

Yet miles, for example, are strange fish indeed. Why can't they be moved about like normal things? Why do they always have to lie end to end? What would happen if I tried to lay a second, parallel set of miles between Sydney and Melbourne? Why wouldn't that double the number of miles between the cities?

Reflections of this kind encourage parsimonious philosophers to attempt to do without miles, or any other measures, as distinct objects. The crucial question is always, Is it possible to avoid quantifying over miles without sacrificing any real knowledge?

There are two characteristic contexts in which length measures occur: when we say of one thing that it is so many miles long, and when we say of two things that they are so many miles apart.

Let us take Quine's example,

$$\text{Manhattan is eleven miles long.}$$

It will not do to say this quantifies only over islands:

$$(\exists\, x)\,(x \text{ is Manhattan. eleven-miles-long } x).$$

For the hyphens in the predicate eleven-miles-long show that it is a simple, unstructured predicate, like the dummy F. And in that case we cannot conclude that

$$\text{Manhattan is more than eight miles long,}$$

for 'more-than-eight-miles-long' would be another, different, unstructured predicate, say G. And F does not imply G. But it is absolutely crucial to any intelligible and useful employment of measures that such entailments be preserved. Hyphenating is no solution to our problem.

We might be tempted next to try

$$\text{Length of Manhattan} = \text{eleven miles,}$$

for this, together with the principle

$$\text{Eleven miles} > \text{eight miles,}$$

will enable us to say

Length of Manhattan >eight miles

and so reach our conclusion

Manhattan is more than eight miles long.

This preserves the entailment, but at the cost of quantifying over miles, as well as lengths, which are just as dubious. For the canonical expression of

Length of Manhattan = eleven miles,

using the concept of combined length, would say there is one thing x which is the length of Manhattan, and another eleven ys which are miles, and x is equal to the combined length of the ys. But quantifying over miles, or lengths for that matter, is precisely what we wished to avoid.

Quine's solution is to introduce an interrelated set of measure relations: *length in miles of, length in kilometers of,* and so on. Our original

Manhattan is eleven miles long

becomes

Manhattan's length in miles is eleven.

And in canonical form, this quantifies over objects (Manhattan) and numbers (eleven):

$(\exists x)(\exists y)$ (x elevenizes. y Manhattanizes. x is length in miles of y).

Manhattan is a heap of particles, so gives us no qualms. Eleven is a number, and Quine believes that numbers exist, for he holds that numbers are a special sort of set, and sets exist.

And since eleven is greater than eight, we *can* conclude that Manhattan's length in miles is greater than eight, and so that Manhattan is more than eight miles long.

The other typical context for miles, that of *distance between*, can be handled analogously. For

Melbourne is five hundred miles from Sydney

we substitute

The distance in miles between Melbourne and Sydney is five hundred, and this in turn gives way to

($\exists\ x$) ($\exists\ y$) ($\exists\ z$) (x Melbournizes. y Sydneyizes. z five hundredizes. z is distance in miles between x and y),

which quantifies over cities and numbers.
 I am sure you will be able to extend this pattern of analysis to all sentences involving measures. In all cases we end up with quantification over the item(s) measured, and numbers.

GEOMETRICAL OBJECTS

Geometrical objects form another class of entities which have no straightforward place in Quine's ontology, for points, lines, surfaces, and solids are not obviously either particles, or heaps of particles, or sets. The nearest we seem to get to them are the vertices, edges, and surfaces of physical objects, especially precision-made ones in steel or plastic. Yet even here there is difficulty, for the triangles, squares, spheres, and so forth of geometry have a perfection, a "geometrical" precision, expressed in the idea that they are of *no* thickness, or *absolutely* smooth and rigid, or *absolutely* symmetrical, which is not matched by any actual material object. Vertices and edges and surfaces of material things are worrying enough in themselves—if they are distinct realities, why are they inseparable from their owners?—and even if we admit them, they seem to fall short of the perfection geometry requires. Yet geometry quantifies over points, lines, planes, figures in planes, and volumes in 3-space, 4-space, and even n-space, with a prodigality that borders on the indecent.
 One way to cope with this is to introduce a dual ontology for space. We have already allowed space to contain particles in multitudes. Alongside, in, and among the particles we can now recognize an infinity of *purely spatial objects*. We will require *points*, dimensionless items, as basic; lines, shapes, planes, and solids can be treated as various infinite collections of points.
 If we take this line and admit purely spatial items as the true subject matter of geometry, the extensions of geometry to 'spaces' with more dimensions than our world enjoys will have to be regarded as suppositional hypotheses without any genuine ontic content. Such geometries, insofar as they quantify over objects of more dimensions than this world allows, would have to be regarded as fascinating and illuminating systems of falsehoods.
 The introduction of points in addition to particles is one possible way of treating geometrical objects. But it is scarcely an economical one. Can we not, an Occamite philosopher will surely ask, somehow dispense with this duplication?
 There is a way—two in fact. Quine proposes to interpret geometrical propositions as claiming various relations among particles: geodesic lines are treated as minimum distances between particles, triangles emerge as more com-

plex relations among the triads of particles that constitute their vertices, and so forth. This program is made more complicated by the possibility that there may be no particle at the place required.

The alternative takes minimum volumes of space as the basic items. These would have tiny, but finite, dimensions. There is no deficiency of them, for collectively they exhaust the entire space. Some minimum volumes are 'empty', and some are 'full'—that is, have the features which previously we described as belonging to a particle at that place. We can replace particles by 'full' volumes. This prevents a duplication of categories of spatial item. And it prepares the way, through the discovery that the distinction between matter and void is not a sharp one, for the closer assimilation of 'full' and 'empty' volumes. An ontology of minimum volumes can be one step on the way to the idea of all spacetime as one single interconnected item. But taking the many minimum volumes as many distinct items and quantifying over them, we can account for geometry as follows.

These volumes, and strings of them, and sheets of them, and volumes of them, form the subject matter of geometry as points, lines, planes with plane figures, and so forth. But they have a finite thickness and so do not have the exact features of geometrical entities. However, we can treat the axioms and theorems of geometry as constituting a *limit myth* about minimum volumes. In a limit myth we claim that certain features literally and categorically belong to a fictitious class of entities. So a limit myth is literally false. This is not mere falsehood, for it gives us a compact and convenient way of claiming that the more and more closely certain real things approach to the fictitious ideal, the more and more nearly they conform to the ideal description. In this case, minimum volumes and collections of them are in issue; the thinner and thinner such volumes become, the more and more exactly they conform to the statements of geometrical theory.

The technique of limit myths is familiar in other branches of science, as Quine points out. When we develop in mechanics our theories of the frictionless surface, or the body acted on by no forces, or the absolutely rigid body, or the dimensionless mass point, we do not really become committed to such things. Or at least we had better not, for our physical theories themselves imply that there are no frictionless surfaces, isolated bodies, undeformable rods, or mass points. The status of these theories of ideal objects is that of limit myths, describing in succinct and comprehensible ways how the behavior of real things approximates more and more to certain (unattained) norms as they approach certain (unattained) extreme conditions.

Understood as a limit myth, geometry has a real subject matter, minimal volumes, concerning which it does not tell the direct and literal truth. And understood in this way, it calls for no additions to an ontology which may serve for physics and so for all of science if Quine's physicalism is correct.

In this chapter we have considered the category of concrete particular. We have seen that, for Quine at least, there is no need to admit any types of concrete particular other than those required for physics. Neither mental nor spiritual par-

ONTIC COMMITMENT AND REDUCTION 193

ticulars need be recognized. Ancillary particulars, measures, and geometric items can be dispensed with as distinct elements of reality.[8] Let us now raise questions about categories other than the concrete particular.

---

8. In chapter 14 below, a treatment of geometric objects is suggested which takes them to be abstract particulars. In this chapter we looked at the problem of geometry from the standpoint of a system which recognizes only concrete particulars and sets.

13 *Events and Sets*

EVENTS

Concrete particulars are *things* of one kind or another. That is, they endure, at least for some time, and they can change in some or all of their characteristics. But there is another sort of entity recognized in everyday thought, that of the *happening*, the event or process. An event is not any thing which changes but rather the changing itself.

We make reference to events when we speak of races, of fires, floods, droughts, and earthquakes, of occultations and transits. Some things bring a blush to the cheek, a tingle to the spine, or a creep to the flesh. By using such terms we are, at least apparently, referring to events. A direct paraphrase would have us quantifying over blushes as well as cheeks, fires as well as forests, and so on. So we seem to be confronted here by a new category. The question is, Is this a genuinely new and distinct category to be added to our schedule?

We often feel that events and processes are dependent items. It sometimes seems that they could not exist unless the concrete particulars that participate in them existed and changed. When these concrete particulars change, an 'event' is born, but referring to an event is no more than an indirect way of speaking about the changing concrete particulars. This feeling will not take us very far in seeking an answer to our question. It assumes that concrete particulars are a basic category, which has been denied, for example by Russell.[1] Anyway, a category

---

1. See above, chapter 7. There is an ambiguity in the term 'event'. Here we are using it in its ordinary sense to signify a change or series of changes (process). Russell uses the same term to signify the occurrence at a place at a time of some state. In *that* terminology, a change is a sequence of differing events, while the case when nothing happens (no event in our sense here) would be described as one event continuing, or one event succeeded by another similar one. Whitehead, in *Process and Reality*, also develops a system in which events take precedence over concrete particulars.

could, in theory, be dependent and yet distinct and not reducible to what it depends on. For example, roses are roses and not reducible to something divine, although they depend on God in the orthodox Christian scheme.

Furthermore, suppose that direct overt reference to events by definite descriptions such as 'the eclipse', 'the progress of the disease' could be dispensed with in favor of descriptions referring only to moving bodies or multiplying bacteria. Even then, we would by no means be free of commitment to events. Here we must consider the arguments of Davidson, which rest not on the use of definite descriptions referring to events, but on our existing vocabulary of adverbs and modifying clauses.[2]

ADVERBIAL EXPRESSIONS

Let us work with an example borrowed from Davidson:

> Jones buttered the toast slowly, deliberately, masterfully, with a knife, in the bathroom, at 2 A.M.

What happens if we try to put this sentence into canonical form? The canonical language admits only direct and simple predication, of verb, noun, or adjective attached to a variable. It has no place for adverbs or adverbial phrases. So finding a canonical form for our example is not a straightforward problem.

We cannot just fuse the adverbial expression with the verb 'buttered' into a hyphenated whole 'buttered-slowly-deliberately-... at 2 A.M.,' (call that B) and claim that the sentence has the form

> B Jones, the toast.

There are two connected reasons why not. First, we lose the entailments of our original sentence. For example, the original sentence entails

> Jones buttered the toast,

which would appear with an *unrelated* simple predicate as

> C Jones, the toast.

Every intermediate sentence between the full original and this shortest derivative, obtained by omitting one or more of the adverbial expressions from the original, also follows from that original sentence. But these intermediate sentences would all appear as unrelated simple claims about Jones and the toast which we could dub D, E, F, and so on. Any paraphrase which fuses the predicate together with hyphens obscures the logical connections between the full original sentence and others which just leave out some of its information.

---

2. See in particular, D. Davidson, "The Logical Form of Action Statements."

We cannot save this situation, that is, we cannot restore the lost entailments, by introducing a set of subsidiary principles such as

$(x)(y)(Bxy \supset Cxy)$.

From our original sentence

B Jones, the toast,

together with this principle as additional premise, we can infer

C Jones, the toast.

And the separate extra principle

$(x)(y)(Bxy \supset Dxy)$

will enable us to infer

D Jones, the toast.

And similarly, extra principles can be introduced for E, F, and so on. But in theory, there is no upper limit to the number of adverbial expressions which a sentence can contain. So we would need to introduce indefinitely many new, independent, subsidiary principles. These principles would be quasi-logical, for it is no mere fact of nature that if Jones buttered the toast slowly then he buttered the toast. Yet because we can only use the simple distinct predicates D, E, F, and so on, these principles would be all equally mysterious, all equally inexplicable, all equally (apparently) arbitrary. They would be recognizable as valid principles only by reference to unreformed English, with its adverbs and modifying expressions. This is not a convincing position.

There is a second, more profound objection. We can keep on increasing the complexity of sentences such as our toast buttering one by adding further adverbial modifications. In principle, this process can continue without limit. Each one of the hyphenated predicates we have been calling B, C, D, E, and so on, is a new primitive of the canonical language. It is syntactically simple and not definable in other terms. Since the addition of adverbial modifiers can, in principle, proceed without limit, there must be indefinitely many of these independent primitives. But as Davidson has elsewhere so forcefully argued, such a language cannot have a recursive specification of the truth conditions of its sentences from a finite base.[3] Such a language cannot be learned, mastered, or understood in its entirety by finite creatures such as ourselves. No language can have indefinitely

---

3. Davidson, "Theories of Meaning and Learnable Languages." A recursive specification is one showing how, from a finite and fully specified base, by a finite number of mechanical steps, every sentence can be formed.

many independent primitives, and a proposal to paraphrase English which gives the canonical language indefinitely many primitives is unacceptable.

We might try to overcome our difficulties by transferring the qualifications from the buttering of the toast to Jones, the butterer. Can the adverbial phrases appear in paraphrases as adjectives? Some of them can.

> Jones buttered the toast in the bathroom at 2 A.M.

can be dealt with using the 'at' device as

> Jones at 2 A.M. is in the bathroom buttering toast,

which would get the canonical expression (allowing, for the present, the complex predicates 'in the bathroom' and 'buttered toast')

> ($\exists\ x$) ($\exists\ y$) ($\exists\ z$) (x is Jones. y is epoch 2 A.M. z is the common part of x and y. z is in the bathroom. z butters toast).

This approach will not work, however, with all the adverbial modifiers. Take 'with a knife', for example. It is not sufficient to say that Jones is in the bathroom, is buttering toast, and has a knife. We have to say that the knife is not hanging by Jones's side or plunged in his back but is used for buttering. So 'with a knife' is not just a qualification of Jones, but a qualification of Jones's buttering.

And we cannot overcome this difficulty by suggesting that 'butters' is not a two-term relation relating, say, Jones and the toast, but a three-term relation relating Jones, the toast, and some instrument. In this suggestion,

> Jones buttered the toast

is a natural but elliptical way of saying

> Jones buttered the toast with something.

It is a pity this suggestion will not work, for if it did it would provide a basis for the entailment from

> Jones buttered the toast with a knife

to

> Jones buttered the toast (with something),

since this inference would be just an existential generalization.

The suggestion will not work, because we cannot set limits to how many other hidden terms there might be (an instrument, a place, time, manner, frequency,

...). And that being so, we could not specify the real form even of familiar English sentences, such as

> Jones buttered the toast.

Besides, whatever may be the case for buttering, this suggestion is clearly incorrect for other verbs. Take dancing, for example, or eating. We dance sometimes with a partner and sometimes without. So

> Jones dances

cannot be, in all cases, a natural contraction of

> Jones dances with someone.

And similarly we eat sometimes with an instrument and sometimes without, which requires that we cannot make covert reference to some instrument every time we say someone is eating.

These difficulties, which defeat the suggestion that action verbs like 'butters' relate several terms, not just the two that meet the eye, go by the technical name of 'variable and indefinite polyadicity'. And that is somthing verbs had best not be afflicted with.

Furthermore, adverbs which apply to the buttering may not apply as adjectives to the butterer. Jones's buttering is slow and masterful, but Jones himself may be more accurately described as quick but self-effacing. What *is* true of Jones is that he is *slow in buttering, masterful in buttering,* and so forth. But we cannot just use these as hyphenated simple predicates applying to Jones. For if we did, we would lose such implications as that anyone being slow in buttering is in fact buttering. We would be back where we started.

QUANTIFICATION OVER EVENTS

All our difficulties melt away if we allow the variables of quantification to range over events. Then, for our example,

> Jones buttered toast slowly, deliberately, masterfully, with a knife, in the bathroom, at 2 A.M.

we can provide the paraphrase

> There is a buttering of toast, by Jones, which is slow, deliberate, masterful, with a knife, in the bathroom, at 2 A.M.

In canonical notation (neglecting the complications of the complex predicate 'in

EVENTS AND SETS

the bathroom', which do not here concern us) this paraphrase would be expressed

> $(\exists\ x)(\exists\ y)(\exists\ z)(x$ is a buttering. x is by Jones. y is toast. x is of y. x is slow. x is deliberate. x is masterful. z is a knife. x is with z. x is in the bathroom. x is at 2 A.M.).

Here every one of the troublesome modifying expressions appears in its own conjunctive clause. Each one is a simple and direct predication, as required. And all our entailments are preserved in the simplest possible manner. The entailment from

> Jones buttered toast slowly, . . .

to

> Jones buttered toast,

appears as a case of the ordinary conjunctive rule that

> $(\exists\ x)(Fx\ .\ Gx\ .\ .\ .\ )$

entails

> $(\exists\ x)(Fx)$.

By quantifying over events we completely avoid the need for introducing any special premises to preserve entailments.

By Quine's rule for ontic commitment, which Davidson cordially accepts, to quantify over events is to admit them into one's ontology. Davidson agrees and holds that the argument does indeed provide reason for thinking that events are a distinct category of entity. What better proof could there be of this than that events are indispensable for a clear canonical description of what happens?

This line of reasoning is strengthened by a consideration of causes.[4] Causal relations are relations, but between what items? The chief candidates are on the one hand sentences (linked by 'because') and on the other hand some entities from the world rather than from language. Davidson argues that the related items cannot be sentences in a language which remains extensional. He concludes that the natural, common sense opinion that *events* enter causal sequences is the correct one, and that

> The short circuit caused the fire

---

4. Davidson, "Causal Relations."

has the form it seems to have, and has as its paraphrase (neglecting uniqueness clauses for the definite descriptions) the formulation

($\exists\ x$) ($\exists\ y$) (x is a short circuit. y is a fire. x caused y).

Such a sentence is true only if x and y range over events. The need to quantify over events to give an account of causal claims markedly reinforces the claim of events to full status as a distinct category.

Quine suggests, when he considers events at all, that they can be identified with the four-dimensional things-or-processes which he admits as concrete particulars.[5] This would rob events of any claim to be a distinct category, but it is open to serious objection. One objection is that there can be more than one event or process at the same place and time, but only one concrete particular. Thus you may be at one and the same time swimming brilliantly, thinking incompetently, and coughing involuntarily. Since 'brilliant', 'incompetent', and 'involuntary' are incompatible adjectives, they cannot all just apply directly to the four-dimensional you.

Another objection we have already met: 'with a knife' must apply to Jones's buttering, and not just to the four-dimensional Jones, to catch the meaning of 'butters with a knife'.

So alongside concrete particulars, events form another category in our ontology.

SETS OR CLASSES

Sets as Mysterious and Paradoxical. Quine's ontology admits two categories: concrete particulars and sets. We have just been examining reasons for including a third candidate, events, whose associations are with concrete particulars. Now let us turn our attention to sets.

The astonishing thing about sets, at first sight, is that no one can say what they are. No one can say it, that is, with any tolerable degree of clarity, in such a way as to be enlightening to anyone who doesn't already know what they are. Sets are objects usually made up from or out of other objects (their members), yet distinct from those other objects and even from all those other objects taken together. We naturally ask how this can be. Here are some of the answers:

> Cantor: By a 'set' we understand any assembly into a whole—of definite and well-distinguished objects—of our perception or thought.[6]
>
> Allen: A set is a collection of well-defined objects thought of as a whole.[7]

---

5. W.V. Quine, *Word and Object*, p. 171.
6. G. Cantor, *Gesammelte Abhandlungen*.
7. R.G.D. Allen, *Basic Mathematics*.

Quine: Sets are classes. . . . We can say that a class is any aggregate, any collection, any combination of objects of any sort; if this helps, well and good. But even this will be less help than hindrance when we keep clearly in mind that the aggregating or collecting or combining here is to connote no actual displacement of the objects.[8]

I cannot but agree with Black that this situation is most unsatisfactory.[9] But worse follows; in developing the theory of sets as the entities indicated in ways such as the above, Russell discovered one of a series of contradictions, his celebrated paradox of the set of all sets not members of themselves, which can be proven both to be and not to be a member of itself.

The response of mathematicians to this discovery was to admit only those sets whose existence could be proved from certain axioms about sets, axioms carefully chosen *not* to yield the existence of Russell's paradoxical class or anything of the same disastrous character. This strategy keeps our doctrine of sets consistent but does not really settle our worry about what sets actually are. It is not sufficient to say that sets are objects which satisfy (have properties in conformity with) the axioms of set theory. Even ignoring the uncomfortable fact that there are several nonequivalent rival axiomatizations of set theory, no set (!) of axioms ever completely specifies its own subject matter. More than one realm of objects may satisfy the axioms, given suitable reinterpretation of the terms occurring in them. Peano's axioms for elementary number theory, for example, are satisfied by the natural numbers and, on reinterpretation, the even numbers and, on reinterpretation, the fence posts of an indefinitely long fence. In technical language, all axiom sets have nonstandard interpretations. So to the question "What are sets?", the answer "Whatever satisfies the set-theoretic axioms" is a good deal less than adequate.

Yet despite this cloud of uncertainty surrounding abstract, eternal, nonspatiotemporal sets, Quine does not dismiss them. He does not treat them as myths, or fictions, or conveniences, or pretences. He posits their existence as fully and equally as he posits the existence of concrete particulars. Why? The short answer is that sets provide a basis for mathematics, and that mathematics is an essential and integral part of the physics through which alone we can attain any tolerable cosmology. Let us lengthen the answer a little.

Sets and Mathematics. If we quantify over sets, and sets of sets, and so on without other restrictions than those imposed by the set-theoretic axioms, we can give a coherent account of all the dazzling variety of numbers with which mathematicians deal. And numbers are virtually all that a mathematician requires.

---

8. Quine, *Set Theory and Its Logic*.
9. M. Black, "The Elusiveness of Sets."

Algebra, analysis, and analytic geometry can all be expressed as concerned with—that is, quantifying over—complex, real, rational, and natural numbers. And once this has been accomplished, sets play an ever increasing role in investigations into the foundations of mathematics.

Complex numbers can be treated as cunningly chosen classes of real numbers, with the arithmetic operations of addition, multiplication, and so on suitably defined. And real numbers, in the same way, can be defined as classes of rational numbers. In turn, the rational numbers are sets of ordered pairs (themselves sets) of natural numbers.[10]

These developments immensely simplify the ontology of mathematics, which is reduced to natural numbers and sets of natural numbers. Mathematical statements are interpreted as quantifying over sets of natural numbers. In classical mathematics we quantify over sets of infinite membership, as in "There is a real number greater than 10," and over infinitely many sets, as in "Every real number between 9 and 10 is greater than any real number between 6 and 7." After all, if we are going to admit sets, we may as well enjoy all their advantages, including infinitude. In for a penny, in for a pound.

Sets in Natural Number Theory. The role of sets in number theory by no means ends with the reduction of some sorts of numbers to others. We are left with natural numbers at this point. But further, sets can be used in investigation of the foundations of natural number theory itself.

To speak of all the numbers together—that is, of 0, and 0's successor, and its successor, and *its* successor, and so on and on—Frege developed the notion of the *ancestral* of the successor of a number, and said numbers were the common members of *all sets* z such that $0 \epsilon z$ and (y) (if $y \epsilon z$ then y's successor ϵz).[11]

To say that a given collection has n members we speak of the collection as being equinumerous with suitable other sets.

And to cap everything, it has been found that if we quantify over sets, there is no need to quantify over numbers as distinct entities at all! That is, the whole of the doctrine of number can be expressed as quantifying over sets, and sets alone. To express it technically, number theory can be modeled in set theory.

There are in fact various ways of doing this. Frege was the first, and following him Russell showed independently a virtually equivalent result. Russell at the turn of the century identified the number n with the set of all n-numbered sets. The number 2, for example, has not just two members, but all the indefinitely many pairs. If we have as objects a, b, c, d, e, and so on, then

$$2 = \{\ \{a,b\}\ ,\{a,c\}\ ,\{a,d\}\ ,\{a,e\}\ ,\{b,c\}\ ,\{b,d\}\ ,\ldots\}.$$

The arithmetic operations of addition and so forth are redefined as suitable *set-theoretic* operations.

---

10. See, for example, Quine, *Set Theory*.
11. 'ϵ' is the sign for set membership. '$x \epsilon y$' means that x is a member of the set y.

In 1908, Zermelo went further and showed how number theory could be modeled in a set theory which clearly required no objects whatever besides sets themselves. Zero he identified with the null set $\wedge$, and 1 has the null set as its sole member, while 2 has 1 as its sole member, and so forth. The number sequence looks like this:

$$0, \quad 1, \quad 2, \quad 3, \quad \ldots$$
$$\wedge \quad \{\wedge\} \quad \{\{\wedge\}\} \quad \{\{\{\wedge\}\}\}$$

And von Neumann proposed in 1923 what is in one respect the most suitable scheme, in which every number contains all and only its predecessors. Each number n is a set containing just n members:

$$0, \quad 1, \quad 2, \quad 3, \quad \ldots$$
$$\wedge \quad \{\wedge\} \quad \{\wedge,\{\wedge\}\} \quad \{\wedge,\{\wedge\},\{\wedge,\{\wedge\}\}\}$$

Since both Zermelo's scheme and von Neumann's rest on the null set alone, number theory requires nothing beyond itself, nothing but sets whose members, if any, are sets.

Unless we recognize sets, we have no coherent account of the nature of number. And unless we can take mathematics in full seriousness, our physics and our whole science will be hopelessly crippled. Like them or not, sets are indispensable to our whole investigation of our world. They are crucial for our metaphysics. To cut ourselves off from the assistance of mathematics on the basis of qualms about sets would be irresponsibly quixotic. For categories as for anything, by their fruits shall ye know them. On that test, sets are triumphant. They earn a place in our ontology by what they can do for mathematics. Such is Quine's position, and he has felt qualms about sets as strongly as anyone.[12]

The Scandal of Sets. We saw above that there is something fishy about sets. Uncollected collections, especially of one or of no objects, rightly rouse our suspicions. But fishiness is not of itself sufficient objection to set against the manifest utility of sets in the mathematical field. Yet perhaps more substantial objections can be raised. Nelson Goodman is the most persistent raiser of such objections.

The Ontic Prodigality of Set Theory No one who believes in sets can take one thing at a time. As Russell noticed, when there is a cow in the field there is not just the cow, but the set containing the cow, and the set containing the cow and the null set, and so forth:

$$\text{cow}, \quad \{\text{cow}\}, \quad \{\wedge, \text{cow}\}, \quad \{\wedge,\{\text{cow}\}\},$$
$$\{\{\text{cow}\}\}, \quad \{\{\text{cow}\},\{\text{cow}\}\}, \ldots$$

As Zermelo's and van Neumann's constructions of the natural numbers showed,

---

12. N. Goodman and Quine, "Steps Toward a Constructive Nominalism."

this sort of ramification is endless. There are *indefinitely many* sets all built on the basis of just this one cow.

Goodman is an uncompromising Occamite. He resists multiplying entities. And here is multiplication gone berserk. For every new individual I recognize, I am bound to admit a new infinity of distinct objects. Such a multiplication of entities is altogether excessive.

And it is suicidal to insist that only things that are *not* sets can be members of sets. That will certainly stop the infite ramifications of sets of sets of sets of cows. But it will also ruin set theory as the basis of mathematics.

The Utah or Combinations Problem Consider Utah. It is composed of counties. It is also composed of acres. The set of counties makes up Utah. The set of acres makes up Utah, or so we should suppose. But the set of counties of Utah has one number of members (all of them counties), and the set of acres has a much larger number of members (none of them counties). The two sets are utterly different. They have no single member in common.

Goodman views this situation and issues a challenge: *How* can two items with identical content (the territory of Utah) be different things? There is no doubt that according to set theory the set of counties of Utah is a different object from the set of acres of Utah. But if one of them is Utah, why isn't the other? Taken as parts of a whole, the acres and the counties amount to the same whole, and all is plain sailing. What other way is there to take then?

This scandal can be generalized. Take four items a, b, c, d. Then according to set theory, $\{a, b, c, d\}$ is different from $\{\{a, b,\},\{c, d\}\}$ and from $\{\{a, c\},\{b, d\}\}$ and from $\{\{a\},\{b\},\{c\},\{d\}\}$, and so on. Yet if a, b, c, and d are to be "taken together" in forming sets, then all these sets, which consist precisely of a, b, c, and d taken together, should be identical.

This is not, of course, a knock-down argument. But it is designed to suggest, very strongly, that the "difference" between these different sets is in some way a manufactured, fictitious difference, an unreal differentiation.

The Null Set and the "Necessity" of Sets Set theorists, with the null set, are the only people who have succeeded in creating something from nothing. In this case even the talk about "collecting" or "considering together" has no application. The null set is only acceptable as an extension of what holds for more normal sets with members. But even normal sets are odd. They seem to exist by some strange necessity. If there are Tweedledum and Tweedledee, how can there *not* be the set {Tweedledum, Tweedledee}? To put it dramatically, how could God avoid creating sets when he created other things? And if he couldn't avoid it, is this not some aspersion on his omnipotence? Especially as the set is supposed to be something *distinct* from its members? And what about the null set? How could God avoid creating *that?* If He creates nothing, there is the null set just the same. Indeed the null set is uncannily like God, who is supposed to be, in the fullness of his being, the diametric opposite of such negations as the null set. Yet the null set is eternal, uncreatable (there is no creating to do), undestroyable, eternal. If anything exists, the null set does. At every time and every place, the null set is the same and unchanging. The null set is a necessary being, and there cannot be more than one of them. Where none of us are gathered together, there is it in our midst . . . .

Here again is no knock-down argument, but rather the challenge: Can you believe such a thing exists?

Avoiding Sets. Some progress can be made in the philosophy of mathematics without any serious commitment to sets. In certain contexts, quantification over sets can be eliminated in favor of quantification over the members of the set. Where this is possible we have what is known as the *virtual theory of sets*. The virtual theory is ontically innocent, involving its user in no additional commitment beyond the members of the sets. "Steps Towards a Constructive Nominalism" used the devices of set avoidance in attempting to provide a foundation for mathematics. This attempt came to grief fairly early on—there is no known way of avoiding quantification over sets in the definition of the ancestral of the successor relation—and Quine subsequently accepted the full realistic set theory. Goodman insists that it is still not established that arithmetic without sets is impossible, and he urges further effort in this direction, using part and whole, for example, in place of member and set.

It seems likely to me, however, that full classical mathematics does require ineliminable quantification over sets. If that is the case, we are in a dilemma. Can we perhaps take the virtual theory of classes as the literal (but eliminable) truth, and the remainder, the really useful bit, as a convenient fiction, in which we *talk* of null sets, unit sets, infinite sets, sets of sets of sets, and so forth, to help us along with physical calculation? If that were possible, we could enjoy the best of both worlds, the mathematical world of useful ideas and the metaphysical world of economical theory.

But this tempting line of approach is open to a great objection. Quine above all has taught us the frivolity of using certain theoretical elements while at the same time claiming no reality corresponds to the theory. If a coherent body of theory involves quantification over a certain category of item, and if that body of theory contains sentences which we hold to be true and for which we have no reductive paraphrase, then on Quine's doctrine of ontic commitment we are committed to the existence of items from that category. And there is no way of getting around it, of fudging or evading or hoping for the best.

Yet if we abandon Quine's criterion of ontic commitment, we have nothing to put in its place. The empiricist dogma that only what is perceptible exists is thoroughly discredited. The rationalist dogma that only what recommends itself to the natural light as necessary exists is in no better condition. Being essential in good theory is the best guide we have to being. And embarrassingly, sets pass that test.

To avoid commitment to sets, we must either show how quantification over sets can be eliminated, or we must provide a convincing alternative test of reality to put in place of indispensability in good theory. Anything else is whistling in the dark.

I do not say either alternative is impossible. Only that it will not be easy.

14 Universals and Tropes

Our schedule of categories is beginning to lengthen. We have already encountered concrete particulars, events, and sets. In this chapter we consider yet more candidate categories, those involved in the idea of a *property* which one or more items may have.

THE PROBLEM OF ONE OVER MANY

We customarily group objects, especially concrete particulars, into sorts according to what they are like. Thus we think two white dogs belong more closely together than a white dog and a black, and that in turn all dogs go together in contrast to cats, cows, and geese. We assume there is something the same about all things which are alike, something which they and only they have. What is this something? In our first example of the two white dogs, the something is their color—to be specific, whiteness.

In our everyday and scientific thought and speech this way of treating *kinds* and *species* of things seems natural and unproblematic. Yet it lies at the heart of one of philosophy's classic problems, the problem of universals: What is the link among several items which all deserve a common description?

Take two white things again. They deserve a common description, namely, "white." What is the link between them which underlies this linguistic fact? We said above that they *have something in common* which provides the link.

Now by Quine's rule for ontic commitment, this answer introduces some new items, for it is an affirmative existential quantification.

a and *b* have something in common

UNIVERSALS AND TROPES

has the paraphrase—allowing singular terms for the moment—

(∃ x) (a has x. b has x).

What is the something in common? In the traditional reply it is, in the case of our example, whiteness, a color, and to speak in general terms of every case, it is a *property* or *universal*.

If there are such things as properties or universals, they constitute a new category. For unlike any members of the other categories (except perhaps *sets*), properties are the very same thing, completely present, at many different places at once. The problem of one over many, of unity in plurality, is the problem of whether there are properties like whiteness or doghood, simultaneously completely present in indefinitely many different locations. And if there are, what are these properties, how do they manage their characteristic unity in plurality, and how can they be fully present at more than one place?

That some things are like one another and unlike all other things seems the most obvious and natural fact in the world. When we try to explain that fact, we slip into talk of what some groups of things have in common, something not shared by outsiders. And when we take this explanation seriously, as philosophers should, we find that we have postulated the existence of a new category, that of properties, which have the anomalous and indeed astonishing feature of identity across indefinitely many places and times.

This result has quite properly raised doubts. Everything that is real, according to a venerable philosophical tradition, is particular—whereas properties are universal. Worse, the relationship between a property and the object which possesses it has defied satisfactory formulation. But if there are no such things as properties, what *is* the link between all and only white things, all and only dogs, and so forth? This dilemma is the classic problem of universals.

QUINE'S POSITION: QUASI-NOMINALISM

Quine repudiates properties. He holds, first, that the basic claim-making mechanism of predication does not involve the existence of any items beyond concrete particulars. In

This stone is white,

the subject expression 'this stone' refers to a concrete particular, while the predicate 'is white' does not name the property of whiteness possessed by the stone, but is directly true of the stone itself.

And he claims, second, that the problem of a common link between several white items can be dealt with by appeal to sets rather than properties. Sets are different from properties in at least this way, that 'two' sets with exactly the same members are the same set, whereas two different properties, perhaps *being bald and bespectacled* and *being an absent-minded professor*, can belong to exactly the same objects.

The link among all and only red things, in Quine's view, is not that they all have or participate in or instantiate the property redness. It is that they, and only they, belong to the set of red things. What do a and b, which are both F, share? They are both F. That is, they share membership in the extension of 'F,' which is $\{x: Fx\}$, the set of Fs.

We could dub this doctrine *quasi-nominalism*. It shares with medieval nominalism the rejection of properties. But it does not go so far in the direction of absolute concrete particularism as the medieval view, which held that all that Fs have in common is joint description by the word 'F.' Quine's view admits sets, which are abstract entities, and does not restrict what is common among Fs to a mere name. They also have in common their membership in a set.

But as Quine recognizes, we must distinguish different sorts of set to make this view attractive. There can be *arbitrary* sets—any random collection of objects—and *kinds*— sets whose members are all somehow related to each other. Only kinds are involved in a Quinean account of ordinary general terms.

To put this rather more fully, there can be arbitrary sets, collected higgledy-piggledy from the most heterogeneous items, say Sydney Opera House, Napoleon's head, the number four, the North Pole, and Beethoven's Fifth Symphony. The members of such a collection, we would ordinarily insist, have nothing in common. Yet they form a perfectly proper set, and we can introduce a predicate true of them all with no difficulty. We just define the predicate 'G' thus:

Gx = df, x = Sydney Opera House v x = Napoleon's head v x = 4 v x = North Pole v x = Beethoven's Fifth Symphony.

This predicate 'G' is true of all and only the members of our arbitrary set.

But this predicate is just an artificial device. No real likeness corresponds to such a predicate. By contrast, the members of some other sets are united by some real likeness of character (such as all squares) or of functions (such as all chairs) or of mode of production (like all cakes). These sets are kinds.

The predicates involved here are not specially manufactured ones like 'G'. Where we meet a previously unencountered item we are in some position to judge whether or not it is a square, a chair, or a cake. But with 'G' either it is explicitly restricted in application to the items already listed, or we have no idea whether or not to apply it to a new item. In technical terms, predicates such as 'square' and 'chair' can be *projected*, whereas 'G' cannot.

Now Quine holds that a kind can be recognized because it is a set of objects related by similarities. There is a group of typical examples of, say, rabbits, and these rabbits can be singled out as *paradigm* members of the rabbit kind. Then there is another set of objects, the *foils*, which are just too different from the paradigms to count as rabbits. Then anything is a rabbit which is more like the paradigms than any of the foils is.[1]

---

1. See "Natural Kinds" in W.V. Quine, *Ontological Relativity*.

Quine's treatment of the problem of universals, then, appeals to sets and then to a special type of set, the kind. And kinds are defined by way of similarities. But the trouble is that there is no accepted way of explaining *similarity* between *a* and *b* which does not fall back on the idea that *a* and *b* share a common property. How could *a* and *b* be similar unless they matched in some quality or characteristic?

The problem of universals would be solved if we could offer a convincing analysis of what it is for one thing to resemble another. For then we *could* explain how it is that different things deserve a common description. But the problem of universals is not solved, but merely postponed, if we appeal just to resemblance or similarity as an unanalyzed idea.[2]

PUTNAM'S ARGUMENT

H. Putnam has recently argued that in the sciences we regularly do quantify over properties and that there is no known way to avoid this.[3] That something is essential to the scientific enterprise provides the best of reasons in its favor. And by Quine's rule for ontic commitment, which Putnam accepts, this involves the acceptance of properties as one kind of being—in our terminology, as a new category.

One arm of Putnam's argument concerns physical magnitudes such as temperature, mass, volume, degree of acidity, and so forth. We do quantify over such magnitudes when we say, for example,

> Temperature is the same property as mean molecular kinetic energy,

or

> Surface tension is one of the phenomena in which molecular attraction is manifested.

We can generalize this point; not only identity claims but general causal claims are typically cast in a way which quantifies over properties. Characteristic examples are

> Excessive salinity in water causes crop failure,

or

> Radioactivity increases the temperature of rocks.

---

2. The use of *similarity* in tackling the problem of universals is further discussed below, in the section "Tropes and Universals."
3. H. Putnam, "On Properties."

A second arm of Putnam's case points out that we speak in general terms of such magnitudes, asking for example how many there are, whether there are any as yet undiscovered, and whether they all reduce to some small set of fundamentals. In these cases, no particular magnitudes are specifically mentioned. So there is no prospect of finding ways to answer these questions in which all we do is describe concrete particulars using specific general terms for the magnitudes in question. And that being so, we cannot avoid quantifying over properties.

Yet a third line of thought in Putnam's paper concerns functional descriptions. To get a better picture of this, suppose we encounter a spaceman. He climbs down from his saucer wearing no helmet, apparently breathing, showing no signs of distress, and tells us how pleased he is to find another planet with air. We, who are absolutely in the dark as to the physiological arrangements of spaceman life, cannot of course say what his "lungs" or "gills" or whatever are made of, nor how they work. But we can report that the spaceman's respiratory system functions in the earth's atmosphere. Here we describe a part of his body by its function: respiratory system. But a respiratory system is some arrangement or other which *has the property* of supplying the organism with oxygen.

Functional descriptions are exceedingly common: condenser, resistor, valve, filter, compressor, solvent, generator, skin, insulator, analgesic, homogenizer, purifier, thermostat, stabilizer, contraceptive, . . . From every branch of science a dozen examples can immediately be found. But functional descriptions, according to Putnam, attribute a property (of producing this or that result in this or that circumstance). And because we may well be in ignorance of the inner mechanism by which the result is produced, we cannot replace functional terms with predicates which describe the mechanism directly, and make no reference to the functional property.[4]

A fourth and closely related point concerns conditions, such as diseases, which are known only causally. That is, some diseases can be identified not directly but only through their causes or their effects. Multiple sclerosis, for example, is known to us only as *that condition* which results in a certain set of symptoms. And radiation sickness is *that condition*, whatever its details may be, which results from exposure to radioactivity.

Putnam's case is a formidable one; to my knowledge, no nominalist or quasi-nominalist has set about replying to it point by point.

WHY NOT ACCEPT THE EXISTENCE OF PROPERTIES?

The problem of universals requires some solution, and we have urged that quasi-nominalism, and a fortiori strict nominalism, are unsatisfactory. The ontic implications of our best science deserve respect, and Putnam's case for properties in this connection is a powerful one.

---

4. Functional descriptions are rather like the dispositional predicates discussed in chapter 11. And perhaps a philosopher who wished to avoid this part of Putnam's argument could claim that functional descriptions only do duty to cover our ignorance of inner mechanisms, and that they can eventually be superseded.

In the light of these considerations, why not just accept properties as one more category in our ontological inventory? There are three great stumbling blocks. First, there is the *mysteriousness* of such entities. We have already mentioned this. Properties, as universals, are supposed to be completely present wherever there is anything which "has" them. But what kind of being is it which is not increased by giving it a million more locations or diminished by destroying a million of its instances? How can anything be multiply located in this way?[5] God is sometimes spoken of in something like these terms, but universals are not supposed to be divinities.

There are two traditions among philosophers who have accepted the reality of universals, the Platonic and the Aristotelian. The Platonic holds that whiteness, for example, is an independently existing form, and that those things are white which stand in a special relation to this form. It is not, strictly speaking, whiteness itself present in all white things. So Platonists avoid the difficulty of multiple presence. But for this advantage they pay the price of filling the notorious Platonic heaven with eternal and immutable essences or forms distinct from (and superior to) the particular world of change and decay which we inhabit.

The second, Aristotelian, tradition holds that the universals are not distinct from and prior to their particular instances, but are rather coeval with, and exist in and only in, their instances. If there are no instances of witchhood, then there is no universal witchhood. Universals are not distinct heavenly forms, but in some sense the very constituents of this our familiar world. This sounds much more reassuring and down to earth. But now just exactly what these universals (properties) are remains a mystery. We are back with these anomalous entities which are not increased by being multiplied a million times.

The second stumbling block concerns the relation between a universal such as whiteness and the particular white things which "have" it. If whiteness is an independently existing form, then particular white things "participate" in it, or "imitate" it (both metaphorical expressions), or "instantiate" it (a jargon term whose meaning is exactly what needs to be explained). Attempts to state the relations of form to particular exactly and literally have so far proved unsuccessful.[6]

On the other hand, if whiteness exists in white things as some kind of constituent, what kind of constituent? How does it attach to the white thing? How can something fully present in the snow at the North Pole be part of, or belong to, or be found in, the snow at the South Pole?

The third stumbling block is the one that counts with Quine. It has (so far) proved impossible to state in an extensional language the conditions under which 'two' properties are really the same, and conversely the conditions under which they are different—the *identity conditions* for properties.

If two properties are to be found in different sets of objects there is no prob-

---

5. See Plato's dialogue *Parmenides*.
6. See D.M. Armstrong, *Universals and Scientific Realism*.

lem; they are different properties. Being *wholly blue* and being *red and white striped* would be different properties on this basis. The trouble arises with properties which are always found together, like *being bald and bespectacled* and *being an absent-minded professor* (according to legend), or *being a descendant of a* Bounty *mutineer* and *being born on Pitcairn Island* (these coincided for a while).

If two predicates *F* and *G* are true of exactly the same objects, then we cannot say, in extensional terms, what distinguishes the property picked out by *F* from the one picked out by *G*.

So if we are confined to an extensional language, we are in an intolerable situation. The slogan covering the case is: No entity without identity. In other words, never admit in your ontology putative entities for which no identity conditions can be supplied. For in that case, you will literally not know what you are talking about. Properties are to be banished on this ground if on no other.[7]

In view of the deficiencies of nominalism and the stumbling blocks to realism, properties seem to be on the one hand indispensable and on the other unacceptable. Is there any way out of this dilemma?

ABSTRACT PARTICULARS OR TROPES

A different approach to this tangle of questions is advocated by D.C. Williams.[8] Consider, he says, the instance of a property (as we might call it) in some concrete particular, say the particular shape that this very lollipop has, or its specific color, the particular case of color that is present here, in this place at this time. Or this specimen of flavor which it has. This case of shape, this specimen of color, this instance of flavor can and should be taken as beings in their own right. They are, indeed the elements of being.

They are particulars; that is, they exist at one definite place in space at any one time. They are not multiple like universals. They are not fully present in indefinitely many locations, but precisely one. The (instance of) color in one lollipop is a different item from the (instance of) color in a second lollipop, even if the lollipops are just the same shade of red. And this numerical difference is the characteristic mark of a particular. These particulars are clearly not ordinary things like shoes and ships. We can get them "before the mind" by taking a concrete particular like a lollipop and ignoring or thinking away every feature it has except one, its shape, say, or its color. This process of mentally separating one quality of a thing is called *abstraction*. Any particulars isolated in this way are properly called *abstract particulars*. For convenience, Williams labels them *tropes*.

---

7. This is a difficult business. It is not clear how much an extensional language can be made to do, nor how crucial identity conditions are. But there is enough of a problem here to make us pause over admitting properties into an ontology.

8. D.C. Williams, "The Elements of Being," in *Principles of Empirical Realism*.

UNIVERSALS AND TROPES 213

Tropes are each of them absolutely specific, of course. The *color* red includes various different hues, tones, and shades, varying from vermilion to scarlet and in other directions too. But a trope is a particular. It is the very redness of this lollipop. It embraces no variety at all. Should the color of the lollipop change, then the original trope exists no longer. The original trope has been replaced by another which is in turn quite specific.

Not all tropes are on the same footing, and not all are independent of one another. Some tropes are primitive and others are derived from them. This situation is just a reinterpretation of what is already discovered in the field of reduction: the temperature trope of a body of gas, for example, derives from the mean kinetic energy tropes of constituent molecules.

Now an ontology resting on tropes as the fundamental category has some powerful attractions.

TROPES AND CONCRETE PARTICULARS

Tropes can be grouped in two basic ways. If they are grouped according to similarity with one another, the resulting group will be, in our former way of speaking, all the instances of some universal—all the cases of redness, for example. But if tropes are grouped by their common location, the result will be an ordinary thing, a concrete particular.

More exactly, tropes, unlike solids, do not exclude one another from the same place. A shape, a size, a color, a flavor, a sweetness, a chemical composition, a temperature, a hardness, and indefinitely many more tropes can all be at the same place at the same time—the place which we would call in ordinary terms the place where the lollipop is. Let *compresence* be the relation between any two tropes with the same location.

We can consider the abstract particulars, tropes, singly. Or in compresent pairs or trios. We can build up from the "thin" trope "thicker" items, groups of compresent tropes. Taking this process to its limit, and taking all the compresent tropes, we have the fully *concrete* particular, the familiar shoe or ship or lump of sealing wax.

On this view of the world, it is a matter of fact, something that is so but did not have to be so, that tropes come in clumps, or at any rate that they do for the most part. These clumps cannot ordinarily be separated off by manipulation. We cannot, for example, extract the hardness from a lollipop and set it aside on its own. Clumps of tropes, of course, are familiar material objects. Tropes come in clumps so often that concrete particulars have often been taken as unitary items and indeed the basic units of the world.

That tropes come in clumps is a great boon for us. We get the waterproof trope onto the roof by getting the size, shape, and solidity up there. To have the house's color at one place, solidity at another, and resistance to fire at yet a third would make life a nightmare if it were possible at all. If our own solidity did not keep company with our shape and size we could have some entertaining times, but the problems in wielding tools or even gathering food (or eating it) defy the imagination.

So, many have thought that there was some necessity about the grouping of tropes into concrete particulars and thus have claimed that an isolated trope is an impossibility. You can't just have an instance of color, free floating in the cosmos. It must be the color of *some thing*. But what about the blue of the sky and the colors of the rainbow? You can't just have a shape; it has to be the shape of something, some concrete particular. But what about the orbit of a comet? Isn't it possible that there be sounds which are not the sounds of anything? You can't just have a grin; it has to be the grin on a face. The Cheshire cat is a joke. But that is because a grin is an arrangement of a face. Does a face have to be the face of something? The Cheshire cat reminds us that some tropes do depend on others. And in those cases the tropes are compresent of natural necessity. No solidity without mutual exclusion. No acid tropes without free hydrogen ion tropes. Where scientific knowledge points to the dependence of tropes on one another, we do have a situation requiring compresence. But independent tropes are commonly clumped, in our world, to a degree which is highly convenient but not necessary.

A concrete particular is a clump of all the compresent tropes at a place. We do not need both categories, tropes and concrete particulars, in our ontology.

THE PROBLEM OF INDIVIDUALS

The attempt to get a clear understanding of the nature of basic concrete particulars (individuals) has uncovered a problem which is in many ways the mirror image of the problem of universals. We can express the problem of universals thus: How is it possible for many particulars to be instances of the same one universal? The problem of individuals is: How is it possible for many different properties (universals) to all be properties of the same one individual? What binds the properties together and makes them all properties of the same thing? In traditional metaphysics we find an oscillation between two answers to this question.[9] There is Locke's answer, that underlying all the properties, binding them together and giving unity to individuals, is a *substratum*. This is a special entity which gives thinghood to things; properties, which are not capable of independent existence, can "inhere" in a substratum. This answer has never been popular. The substratum has, itself, no properties—properties inhere *in* it, but they are properties *of* the whole concrete particular or thing, not its substratum. So the substratum is invisible, intangible, without taste, silent, of no composition; it is not radioactive, acidic, rusty, metallic, solid, or liquid. It must totally defy investigation. "And how different this is from nothing at all," remarked Berkeley testily, "I should be glad to be informed."

---

9. See, for example, A. Quinton, *The Nature of Things*, Part I.

But if we abandon the substratum, the only alternative seems to be the view that an individual is a bundle of qualities, that is, universals. A particular is the union of all its constituent universals. The great difficulty with this conception is that it is unable to distinguish *two* individuals with exactly the same qualities. For if the individual is just the union of constituent qualities, the union of the same qualities is the same individual. So this conception involves that contentious doctrine, the *identity of indiscernibles*.

The identity of indiscernibles may be true. But if so, that is just a matter of luck. And we do not know it. Take, for example, the concertina world. In this cosmology, the universe passes through successive cycles, from the great ur-atom or world egg containing all matter and energy, through the big bang and the expanding universe to a maximum, on through a period of diminishing and gravitational collapse to another ur-atom, another big bang, and so on. Now suppose that each cycle exactly reproduces its predecessor, and *its* predecessor. There will be, in each cycle, a frog on a lilypad, say. And this frog will have all and only the qualities of its counterpart in every other cycle. But if the frog is nothing but its qualities, every frog will be, contrary to our hypothesis, the very same frog. These days we do not think abstract metaphysical considerations concerning the constitution of individuals can disprove a cosmology like the concertina world. Nothing can give the principle of the identity of indiscernibles sufficient authority to rule out the concertina world as impossible.

You have been wanting to protest that *location* in space-time distinguishes the frogs. If the cycles of the concertina world are without beginning and without end, it may prove difficult to distinguish the space-time locations of frog 23 and frog 24, but let the problem of distinguishing them pass.[10]

There is a dilemma here. Either locations are universals or they are not. If they are, if, that is, they are repeatable items, then space-time must have a *relational* status, positions must be specifiable only by describing relations among things, and in that case frog 23's locational description will be exactly the same as frog 24's. And then location will not distinguish frog 23 from frog 24 as it was designed to do. Contrary to hypothesis, frog 23 and frog 24 will once more turn out identical.

If, on the other hand, locations are not universals, then to introduce locations is to start talking about the *instances* of greenness, frogginess, and lilypaditude *at a place*. When we think of universals at a place, we are thinking of particular instances of universals. In short, we are dealing with tropes.

The 'bundle' theory of the individual, the idea that it is a bundle of universals, commits us to the dubious doctrine of the identity of indiscernibles unless locations are taken to be something special, distinct from universals. Then the bundle of universals-at-a-place is a bundle of tropes.

If an individual is thought of as the union not of its qualities but of its *tropes*, we avoid both the difficulties of the alleged substratum and the problem of the identity of indiscernibles. For the tropes of frog 23 are entirely different from the

---

10. I think it would be impossible unless space-time were in some way absolute.

tropes of frog 24. So far from being indiscernible, our frogs have quite separate constituents and so can be distinct.

So far as I can see, only an ontology of tropes provides a satisfactory solution to the problem of the constitution of concrete particulars. The category of concrete particulars is derivative from the category of tropes.

TROPES AND UNIVERSALS

Tropes are well behaved. They exist at one definite location. They are not multiple. They generate no problem of one over many. The whiteness (trope) of the snow at the North Pole is different from the whiteness (trope) of the South Pole's snow. The North Pole's whiteness does not have to be at the South Pole too. So far so good.

Williams suggests that the universal whiteness is just the similarity grouping of white tropes. It would be splendid if this were so, for whiteness would no longer be simultaneously fully present at indefinitely many places. Different members of the similarity set of white tropes would be at the different places.

Carnap and Goodman have explored the possibility of construing universals as similarity groupings of concrete particulars,[11] but these proposals have all come to grief because two things may resemble each other in color while a third resemble the second in, say, shape but not color. This introduces a "foreigner" into the similarity set, and it seems that the problem can only be overcome by insisting that the similarity in question must be a similarity in (say) *color*, which reintroduces the quality universal we were trying to do without.

This difficulty does not affect groups of tropes, which, precisely because they are not concrete particulars, do not have many qualities. If any two tropes resemble each other, they resemble each other in the same respect.[12] So one hurdle can be cleared in the project of displaying universals as a category which, like that of the concrete particular, derives from tropes as basic.[13]

But the situation is far from clear. The problem of universals springs from our conviction that some groups of particulars deserve to be classed together on the basis of something they have in common. Is this not the case with tropes also? Can't we ask about two white tropes, no less than about two white things, what it is that gives them their resemblance? Perhaps we can answer legitimately just that they resemble each other because of what they are or are like, or because of their character or nature. Perhaps if we quantify over tropes we will have no

---

11. See N. Goodman, *The Structure of Appearance*, part 2.
12. This oversimplifies the position. A color trope has only its color as a quality of the kind we credit concrete particulars with. But tropes can be, in their turn, brilliant, or constant, or delightful. And if two different tropes are both brilliant, does this not just reproduce the problem of universals which arises over two different things which are both scarlet? Or can there be tropes of tropes?
13. Goodman calls the problem of the foreign concrete particular the "problem of imperfect community."

UNIVERSALS AND TROPES

cause to quantify over universals as well. But I for one have no confidence one way or the other.

TROPES AND THE OTHER CATEGORIES

An ontology which begins with Quine's concrete particulars (including epochs) and sets, comes under pressure to extend its inventory, as we have seen. Events and processes, properties and tropes all have claims to be included, and the result is neither economical nor beautiful in symmetry and interconnection.

If we rest on tropes as the basic ontological category, we find that concrete particulars can be seen as groups of compresent tropes. And perhaps universals are groups of similar tropes. Our ontology begins to show some order.

Furthermore, *events* and *processes* fit the scheme neatly. An orderly succession of tropes is a process. The cutoff point where one trope succeeds another is an event. Tropes do not exclude one another; there can be many tropes at the same location, just as there can be many events or processes at the one place simultaneously. Just as a concrete particular is a stable clump of tropes, a process is an unstable one. We can understand now the interdependence and interrelation of things and processes, which is left incomprehensible in an ontology which takes concrete particulars as basic.

An epoch is an unusually comprehensive clump of tropes. Epochs are no more problem to a trope ontology than any other.

When we see how much tropes can do in giving unity and economy to ontology, we are encouraged to venture that perhaps the *one* basic category is the trope, and all others can be displayed as derivative from it.

Sets are the stumbling block. A trope is not a set. Sets of tropes, like sets of anything else, much be considered as distinct from their members if orthodox set theory is to be retained. But even here there is some prospect of advance. One scandal of sets, the Utah or combinations problem, evaporates. That problem, you recall, was the unpalatable conclusion that the set of acres of Utah is something different from the set of counties of Utah, although they seem to consist in just the same item, Utah itself. But a particular like Utah consists in indefinitely many tropes at once. If we allow the artificial tropes acrehood and countyhood (and why not?), then Utah can have at once the different combination-tropes *all the acres* and *all the counties*. Our wish to identify these sprang from an ontology of concrete particulars, according to which Utah is one unitary thing (so the acres and the counties must combine into the *same* thing). If Utah is a complex of many tropes, *that* difficulty can be overcome. The acres make up the *all the acres* trope. The counties make up *all the counties*. Utah is both these distinct tropes, and many others as well.

I see no way to overcome the scandal of the infinite ramifications of set theory by appeal to tropes. If we wish to avoid sets, we must find some account of counting and measuring and calculating in terms of particulars and complex scattered particulars. In the meantime, tropes and sets comprise the best categorial ontology I know.

218   A FIRST SURVEY OF ONTOLOGY

QUANTIFYING OVER TROPES

If we quantify over tropes there is no problem with our many attempts to describe not simply objects but the qualities of objects. We can say quite straightforwardly that the color of an opal is brilliant,

$(\exists x)$ (x is a trope of an opal . x is a color. x is brilliant),

or that the salinity of a river is constant, and so forth.

And because so much of our description of the world is of concrete particulars, we allow the variables of quantification to range over tropes both singly and in clumps.[14] Generally speaking, our adjectives apply directly to tropes, and our nouns and verbs to clumps of tropes.

There are green frogs,

for example, is not true of any trope, for no trope is a frog. Only clumps of tropes are frogs. If we let our variables range over either tropes or clumps, we can paraphrase this sentence as before:

$(\exists x)$ $(Fx . Gx)$.

But we now have to understand this as making a claim either about tropes or about trope complexes. We must read it, in general, as

Something is a trope or trope complex which is or includes F and is or includes G.

And in this particular case, it comes out as

Something is a trope complex *frog* which includes a trope *green*.

TROPES IN COSMOLOGY

To take tropes as basic has some salutary effects in cosmology. Here I just mention two from which speculation can develop. First, we take the *regularity of causes* too much for granted. By thinking of general causal connections as involving the same *properties* on all occasions, we prejudge the question of whether the same cause will always have the same effect. But if not salinity (the universal), but the salinity of this river (the trope), is responsible not for crop failure in general, but for the failure of this crop, then we can be properly

---

14. Recall that in chapter 12, we found it advantageous to allow variables to range over both fundamental particles and clumps of them. Here we extend that license.

astonished that the salinity of another river (a different trope, so in one sense a different cause) has a like effect on a different crop.

Another example of how trope thinking can release the imagination: When we think about minds and their relation to brains in terms of concrete particulars, we seem to face the choice of claiming the mind is the same thing as the brain, or that it is a different (and elusive and mysterious) thing. So a naturalism which takes evolution and physiology seriously is impelled towards materialism and attempts to reduce all psychology to physics.

But if we think in terms of tropes, the physical tropes and the mental tropes of people can comprise two subsets of the tropes making up one concrete particular. And we can investigate connections and identities among these tropes without the same compulsion to fit them all into the material box. A naturalism of tropes has more options comfortably open to it than a naturalism of concrete particulars.

For the economy and system that tropes promise in ontology, and the flexibility they offer in cosmology, work on developing and elaborating the metaphysic of tropes will be effort well spent.

THE ONTOLOGY OF LOGIC

In this survey of ontology and the categories there is a great omission. We have not, and will not, consider the question of what entities are required by logical theory. But the question is unavoidable in any truly comprehensive inquiry.

What is the subject matter of logic? What must there be in order for sentences to be meaningful? in order for them to be true? in order for some to imply others?

Many philosophers consider that the possibility of thinking meaningfully, stating truly, and arguing justly rests on the existence of special categories whose reality does not emerge from a study of the natural sciences. They claim we must recognize the existence of *concepts* as meanings for terms, *propositions* as meanings for sentences, *facts* as truthmakers, and *possibilities* and *probabilities* as the underpinning of reasoning.

Here is material for a whole new inquiry. But in one book, enough is enough.

Glossary

A POSTERIORI   An a posteriori claim is one which, if known at all, is known by way of experience, and can be overturned by experiment or perception. What is not a posteriori is a priori (q.v.).

A PRIORI   Something is known a priori if it is known independently of any perceptual or experimental or hypothetical inquiry. Anything known in this way cannot be overturned by any course of experience. See also A POSTERIORI.

ABSTRACT PARTICULAR   See TROPE.

ABSTRACT SUBJECT   Singular term purporting to refer to an abstraction (q.v.).

ABSTRACTION   Unsatisfactorily vague term for anything which is not definite, complete, concrete, or material. Numbers, angels, thoughts, propositions, and classes have all been described as abstractions for this sort of reason.

ACCIDENT   Property, especially nonessential property, of a substance or concrete particular (q.v.). See UNIVERSAL.

ACTIVE   Capable of spontaneous, self-induced change. Characteristic of mind rather than matter in the thought of Leibniz and Berkeley.

ANALYSIS   In philosophy, the process of distinguishing and identifying the component elements in sentences or in concepts. Also, sometimes, the business of identifying the truth conditions for claims of a certain type.

GLOSSARY 221

ANALYTIC   A truth is analytic if its truth depends on logic and definitions alone. Otherwise, it is synthetic (q.v.).

ANTECEDENT   See CONDITIONAL.

APPEARANCE   What seems to be the case and, while not being what truly is, yet has its foundation in real facts. Contrasted on one side with reality, on the other with illusion.

APPETITION   In Leibniz's system, a primitive form of intention or desire characteristic of monads (q.v.).

ASSIGNMENT   Temporary settlement of definite reference of an individual variable (q.v.) to a particular item in the domain (q.v.).

ATOMISM   The theory that the material world consists of nothing but combinations of tiny material bodies (atoms), which are the theory's basic particulars (q.v.). Variant: the material world consists of space, time, and atoms in space and time. In the seventeenth century, Gassendi, Locke, Boyle, and (with reservations) Newton gave atomism its modern impetus.

AXIOM   Fundamental, unproved expression which forms a basis for reasoning in developing a deductive theory. See also INTERPRETATION OF AXIOMS.

BASIC PARTICULAR   Fundamental, independent, nonderivative concrete particular (q.v.). One of the meanings of *substance*.

BOUND VARIABLE   See INDIVIDUAL VARIABLE.

CANONICAL NOTATION   Simplified, purified, clarified standard language.

CATEGORY   Basic division of reality. Concrete particulars, universals, tropes (q.q.v.), events are possible examples.

CAUSA SUI   In Spinoza's philosophy, the characteristic of being self-contained, furnishing one's own basis for existence and nature, distinctive of substances.

CLOSED SENTENCE   Complete generalization (q.v.) in a canonical notation (q.v.). See also OPEN SENTENCE.

COMPLETE NOTION   In Leibniz's philosophy, the divine thought or impersonal specification of the entire set of properties of an object.

GLOSSARY

COMPRESENCE   Relation between two tropes (q.v.) which are at the same place in space and time.

CONCRETE PARTICULAR   Complete and apparently independent thing. A dog or poker chip are typical examples. See also BASIC PARTICULAR, DERIVATIVE PARTICULAR.

CONDITIONAL   An 'if (antecedent)-then(consequent)' sentence. The *material* conditional claims merely that it is not the case that the antecedent is true and the consequent false. The *strong* conditional claims further that there is a connection between antecedent and consequent.

CONSEQUENT   See CONDITIONAL.

CONTEXTUAL DEFINITION   Paraphrasing technique for an incomplete symbol (q.v.).

CONTINGENT   A truth is contingent if it is so, but is not so of necessity. Its negation cannot be a self-contradiction, and so *it* is a contingent falsehood. If a sentence is not contingent, it is either necessary or impossible.

COPULA   In Aristotelian logic, a joining particle which unites two terms into a sentence.

CORPORA SIMPLICISSIMA   The simplest bodies. The nearest things to atoms in Spinoza's metaphysics.

CORPUSCULARIANISM   See ATOMISM.

COSMOLOGY   The study or science of the general features of the reality underlying what appears as the space-time world.

COUNTERFACTUAL   Strong conditional (q.v.) with unfulfilled antecedent.

CRITERION   Rule or standard of judgment by use of which a question can be decided with finality.

CROSS-REFERENCE   Relationship among variables and quantifiers, or pronouns and antecedents, fixing the precise claim made by a complex sentence.

DEFINITE DESCRIPTION   Noun phrase, beginning with 'the', standing in subject position in a sentence or clause, used to refer to one object, e.g., 'the man in white boots'.

GLOSSARY

DEMONSTRATIVE   Expression, such as 'this' or 'that', whose reference needs to be fixed by gesture and context.

DERIVATIVE PARTICULAR   Any concrete particular which is not independent of other particulars, so is not basic. A derivative particular reduces to some combination or part of a basic particular.

DEUS-SIVE-NATURA   God-or-Nature. Spinoza's term for the all-embracing totality of being which, for him, constituted the only basic particular (q.v.) or substance.

DISCERNIBILITY OF DIVERSES   See IDENTITY OF INDISCERNIBLES.

DISPOSITIONAL   Sentence claiming a disposition.

DOMAIN   World, or part of world, concerning which a language makes claims.

EGOCENTRIC PARTICULAR   Indicator (q.v.).

EMPIRICISM   The thesis in philosophy that mankind's only mode of establishing synthetic truths (q.v.) is by the direct or indirect use of perception. Locke, Berkeley, Hume, Mill, Russell, Ayer, and Carnap are notable empiricists. See also LOGICAL EMPIRICISM.

EPOCH   In Quine's work, temporal slice across entire spatial world, perpendicular to the time axis.

EQUIVALENCE   See MATERIAL EQUIVALENCE.

EPISTEMIC   Concerning knowledge. See also EPISTEMOLOGY.

EPISTEMOLOGY   The science or study of human knowledge: its foundation, constitution, extent, and validation.

ESSENCE   Those qualities essential to an object, that is, those qualities without which it would not be the kind of thing it is. See also NOMINAL ESSENCE.

EXISTENTIAL QUANTIFIER   See QUANTIFIER.

EXPLICATIVE   Concerning the unfolding of a concept, the explaining of the meaning contained in a word or expression.

EXTENSION: 1. In Cosmology   Volume.

EXTENSION: 2. In Logic   The extension of a general term (or predicate) is the class of all objects to which that term applies. The extension of 'dog' is the class of all dogs.

EXTENSIONAL   Linguistic expressions can be divided into two classes, the extensional and the intensional (q.v.). In an extensional sentence, a singular term (q.v.) can be substituted for another which refers to the same thing, without disturbing the sentence's truth value (salva veritate). And a general term (q.v.) can be similarly substituted for another with the same extension (q.v.). So, for example,

> Oliver Cromwell was a general

is extensional, since its truth value is not disturbed by the substitution of 'the Protector' for 'Oliver Cromwell', or 'commanded an army' for 'was a general'.

EXTERNAL NEGATION   See NEGATION.

FEATURE-PLACING SENTENCE   Simple sentence claiming the presence of a quality, characteristic, or item.

FIGURE   Shape.

FINITE MODE   In Spinoza's system, a partial, limited element of Deus-sive-Natura (q.v.), the sole genuine substance.

FIRST-ORDER PREDICATE LOGIC   Logical system permitting quantification over individual variables, but not over predicates, all of which are constants.

FORM: 1. In Ontology   Platonic universal (q.v.) held to enjoy an eternal and perfect existence in a world beyond space, time, and change.

FORM: 2. In Logic   Structure of a sentence considered in abstraction from its subject matter.

FREE VARIABLE   See INDIVIDUAL VARIABLE.

GENERAL TERM   Any expression used to apply descriptively to any number of distinct objects. Adjectives, nouns, verbs are general terms. General terms provide the chief material in predicates (q.v.).

GLOSSARY

GENERALIZATION   Sentence making a claim not about any particular object, but about some or all members of some kind of object.

GEOCENTRIC   Earlier, earth-centered theory of the solar system, most fully developed by Ptolemy in Alexandria (second century). Replaced by heliocentric theory (q.v.).

HELIOCENTRIC   Modern, sun-centered theory of the solar system, presented by Copernicus, Kepler, Galileo, and others. Contrasted with geocentric (q.v.).

IDEALISM   The doctrine that reality is mental in character. In particular, that perceptual experience is experience of states of mind. Berkeley, Hume, Kant are famous idealists.

IDENTIFYING PROPERTIES   Features of an object in virtue of which it is the very thing it is.

IDENTITY OF INDISCERNIBLES   Purported principle of metaphysics according to which any 'two' items with exactly the same properties ('two' indiscernibles) are in fact but one and the same thing (identical). It can be stated the other way, that any genuine two items have at least one difference in their properties (the discernibility of diverses).

IDEOLOGY   In Quine's work, the stock of predicates, and so the range of ideas, available within a theory.

IMMANENT   Residing within or under. Pantheism holds that God is immanent; Islam has the purest transcendent (q.v.) conception of Deity.

IMMATERIALISM   Cosmology holding that matter belongs to appearance but is no constituent of reality. Berkeley and Leibniz advanced such a view. See also MATERIALISM.

INCOMPLETE SYMBOL   Part of a sentence not given semantic interpretation in its own right. The entire sentence containing an incomplete symbol as a part is given a paraphrase (q.v.) in which the incomplete symbol disappears.

INDEFINITE SINGULAR TERM   Term in subject position in a sentence but involving the ideas of some, all, or none, and so in fact introducing a generalization (q.v.).

INDICATOR   Term whose reference is determined by the situation of the speaker, such as 'you', 'here', etc.

GLOSSARY

INDIVIDUAL   Concrete particular. Often, basic concrete particular.

INDIVIDUAL VARIABLE   Linguistic element, written 'x', 'y', . . . , used to apply to particulars in the generalizations of several canonical notations (q.v.). Individual variables can be *free* (unattached to any quantifier) or *bound* (governed by a quantifier). If, but only if, all variables are bound, the sentence is closed.

INTENSIONAL   A linguistic expression is intensional rather than extensional (q.v.) if substitution within it of singular terms with the same reference or general terms with the same extension can disturb the expression's truth value, extension, or reference. Thus, for example,

   Peter was looking forward to the eclipse

is intensional, since we may disturb its truth value by substituting for 'the eclipse' the term with the same reference 'the event which blinded him'. An intensional context is sometimes said to be *referentially opaque*.

INTERACTION PATTERN   Pattern of causes and effects distinctive of objects with a primary quality (q.v.).

INTERNAL NEGATION   See NEGATION.

INTERPRETATION OF AXIOMS   A set of axioms (q.v.) can be considered purely formally as merely a set of marks from which other sets of marks can be reached by logical manipulation, or they can be treated as sentences, containing predicates, which have definite extensions (q.v.). To treat them in this way, to make them say something about a particular subject matter, is to give the axioms an interpretation.

LEMMA   An intermediate theorem required for completing a complex proof and sufficiently important to be separately distinguished. Plural: lemmata.

LOGIC   Study of the formal structure of sentences and justifiable inferences of one sentence from another. Mathematical or symbolic logic (q.v.) established the scope and limits of inferences in which the truth of the premises is sufficient to guarantee the truth of correctly drawn conclusions.

LOGICAL ATOMISM   Doctrine of Wittgenstein and Russell, according to which everything reduces to simple atomic facts or basic structures of relationship among simple elements. Called *logical* atomism because it proceeds by analysis of sentences rather than material bodies.

LOGICAL CONSTRUCTION X is a logical construction out of Ys if every true statement about Xs can be replaced by other statements which are about Ys only. If X is a logical construction out of Ys, then Xs can be *reduced* to Ys.

LOGICAL EMPIRICISM   Doctrine of Carnap and the Vienna Circle in the twentieth century. A variety of empiricism (q.v.) according to which the content of concepts and the meaning of sentences are determined by the relevant perceptual experiences. Also called logical positivism or positivism.

LOGICAL PARTICLE   Element of a sentence which, lacking special material meaning, serves to relate linguistic elements by fixing a sentence's form. Examples: 'not', 'and'.

LOGICAL POSITIVISM   See LOGICAL EMPIRICISM.

LOGICALLY PROPER NAME   Proper name which it is guaranteed refers to exactly one object, and which contains no discriptive elements.

MACROPROPERTY   Literally a 'large scale' property. Property of objects of large scale, hence of complex objects in atomistic cosmologies. Largeness is relative; a grain of sand is large compared with an atom, and properties of grains of sand are macroproperties. See also MICROPROPERTY.

MANIFEST IMAGE   The world as conceived and understood by common perception and common sense. The appearance of space, time, and matter. See also SCIENTIFIC IMAGE.

MATERIAL CONDITIONAL   See CONDITIONAL.

MATERIAL EQUIVALENCE   Two sentences are material equivalents if and only if they have the same truth value (both true or both false).

MATERIAL POINT   Basic particular in Boscovich's system. A material object with position but no volume.

MATERIALISM   Metaphysical thesis according to which nothing exists except what is exclusively material in nature. Hobbes was a materialist, and in our own time D.M. Armstrong and J.J.C. Smart.

MECHANISM   Doctrine that all changes in the material world are brought about according to law without intent, desire, or striving. See also TELEOLOGICAL.

METALANGUAGE   Language used to describe a (different) language or canonical notation.

MICROPROPERTY   Property of the tiny. In atomistic cosmologies, properties of the smallest, and hence most basic, particulars. See also MACROPROPERTY.

MODAL CONSTRUCTION   Sentence involving a modality, viz. necessary, possible, or impossible.

MONAD   In Leibniz's philosophy, a monad is a basic particular (q.v.) or substance. It is a simple, single, partless, independent object, a primitive mind.

MONISM   Doctrine that everything is ultimately one, denying the fundamental status of division and differentiation. Spinoza was a monist. See also PLURALISM.

NATURAL KIND   In Quine's use of the term, a set all of whose members resemble one another in this way: any member is more like one of the paradigms (typical members) than it is like any of the foils (objects just too different to belong to the set).

NATURALISM   Thesis that reality is exhausted by the natural world. Denial of the reality of the supernatural.

NEGATION   The negation of a sentence asserts that matters are not as stated in that sentence. The *external* negation of 'S is P' is 'It is not the case that S is P'. The *internal* negation is 'S is non-P'

NOMINAL ESSENCE   The ideas composing a complex conception. To give the nominal essence of X is to provide a definition of X. See also ESSENCE.

NOMINALISM   Any theory of the meaning and function of general terms which avoids appeal to universals (q.v.) or any other abstraction (q.v.). See also QUASI-NOMINALISM.

NOMOLOGICAL   Concerning natural law.

NONCONTRADICTION, PRINCIPLE OF   The principle that it can never be that both a sentence and its negation are true at once.

NOUMENON   Kant's term for something belonging not to appearance but to reality.

GLOSSARY

NULL SET The set with no members.

OBJECTIVE CORRELATE Physical state of affairs forming the basis for perception of a secondary quality (q.v.).

OBJECTUAL QUANTIFICATION See QUANTIFICATION.

ONTIC See ONTOLOGY.

ONTIC COMMITMENT The being or ontology to which a theory is committed; i.e., what must exist in order for the theory to be true.

ONTOLOGY The study or science of the general structure of being or reality. 'Ontological' is used to mean 'pertaining to the study of being', and 'ontic' to mean 'pertaining to being or reality'.

OPAQUE CONSTRUCTION See INTENSIONAL.

OPEN SENTENCE A fragment of a sentence formed by joining a predicate with appropriate individual variables (q.v.). Closed, to make a sentence, be addition of appropriate quantifiers (q.v.).

ORDERED SET Set of objects considered in one particular order. The set $\{a,b\}$ is the same as the set $\{b,a\}$, but the ordered pair $\langle a,b \rangle$ is distinct from the ordered pair $\langle b,a \rangle$.

PANTHEISM Cosmology (q.v.) according to which appearance all reduces to one reality, God. Characteristic of monisms (q.v.) such as Spinoza's.

PARAPHRASE Canonical alternative to sentence of natural language.

PARTICULARISM Any doctrine whose basic items are particulars. In cosmology, a theory of spatiotemporal being based on individual things. In ontology, the attempt to dispense with universals.

PERDURATION The characteristic of remaining the same item (preserving identity) through a change involving the properties of something. A knife perdures in the process of sharpening it; it remains the same knife, although not of course a blunt one.

PERFECT LANGUAGE Ideal language with perfect clarity and perfect expression of truth, whose structure perfectly mirrors the world's constitution. Perhaps not attainable.

PHENOMENA What are manifest to the senses. In Kant's usage, what belongs to appearance, whether sensory or scientific.

PHENOMENALISM   The doctrine that all reality can be reduced to phenomena (q.v.). An extreme variety of empiricism (q.v.).

PLENIST   One who affirms that the world is a plenum, who denies the existence of the void (q.v.).

PLURALISM   Doctrine that the world is ultimately many, distinguished into several distinct and irreducible realities. Leibniz was a pluralist. See also MONISM.

POSITIVISM   See LOGICAL EMPIRICISM.

POWER   Capacity to produce effects.

PREDICATE   An expression, applying to or *true of* objects, which makes a complete declarative sentence when conjoined with one or more singular terms.

PREDICATE SCHEMA   Dummy predicate, written 'F', 'G' ... , used in discussing the formal characteristics of a canonical notation.

PREESTABLISHED HARMONY   In Leibniz's metaphysics, the divine arrangement which ensures that monads (q.v.), independent of one another, nevertheless develop in a coherent and mutually accommodating way.

PRIMARY QUALITY   Quality of a material body which it has independently of any manner in which it might be perceived or detected by an observer. Example: shape. See also SECONDARY QUALITY.

PROPERTY   See UNIVERSAL.

PROPOSITIONAL ATTITUDE   A verb of propositional attitude occurs in a psychological sentence claiming that someone believes, hopes, fears, wonders whether, ... something or other.

QUANTIFICATION   1. Objectual quantification. Interpretation of closed canonical generalizations relating variables to items in the domain. 2. Substitutional quantification. Interpretation of quantified sentences relating individual variables to definite singular terms.

QUANTIFIER   Technical, canonical version of the indefinite singular term (q.v.). The *universal* quantifier corresponds to 'all', and the *existential* quantifier to 'some'

GLOSSARY

QUASI-MATERIAL EQUIVALENCE   Relation between natural sentence and canonical sentence where the canonical sentence has the same truth value as the natural sentence if that natural sentence does have one, definite, truth value.

QUASI-NOMINALISM   A theory of universals (q.v.) which treats them as a special type of set, viz. a natural kind (q.v.). This view is associated with Quine.

RATIONALISM   That approach to philosophy which bases as much as possible on proof by purely rational methods from the principle of non-contradiction (q.v.). Descartes, Spinoza, Leibniz, and Hobbes were rationalists.

REAL PART   Part of a concrete particular which is itself in turn a concrete particular.

REALISM   Thesis that objects, including particularly objects in perception, have a reality independent of experiences, knowledge, or thought about them. Contrasted with subjective idealism or phenomenalism (q.v.).

REDUCTION   A demonstration that Xs are in fact nothing more than, nothing over and above, certain combinations of Ys is a reduction of Xs to Ys. See also LOGICAL CONSTRUCTION.

REFERENCE   Relation of singular term, or variable under assignment, to element in the domain, by means of which sentences have a subject matter.

REFERENTIAL OPACITY   See INTENSIONAL.

REGIMENTATION   Process of specifying paraphrases (q.v.).

RELATION   Predicate (q.v.) true of objects taken not singly, but in pairs, triads, or, in general, n-membered ordered sets (q.v.). Sometimes the term 'relation' is applied to the characteristic of objects which an n-termed predicate speaks of. It is then a special kind of property rather than a special kind of predicate.

RELATIONAL   A theory is relational if it maintains that some subject matter can be reduced to a set of relations among objects. Relational theories of space are important and influential.

SALVA VERITATE   Preserving truth value.

SCIENTIFIC IMAGE   The world as conceived and described by a general scientific theory of the world of space, time, and what they contain. See also MANIFEST IMAGE.

SCHOLASTICS   Medieval philosophers influenced by Aristotle.

SCIENTIFIC REALISM   Cosmology according to which all and only those entities recognized in scientific theory are real.

SCOPE   Of a quantifier. That fragment of text in which the quantifier (q.v.) binds the appropriate variable (q.v.).

SECONDARY QUALITY   Quality of a material body which it has in virtue of the specifically human manner in which we perceive or detect objects. Possible example: color. See also PRIMARY QUALITY.

SEMANTICS   Statement of relations between (elements of) a language and the subject matter in the world of which it treats.

SENSATION   Conscious experience in sensory perception.

SENSE DATA   The immediate objects of perception. Conceived of in phenomenalism (q.v.) as independent items (sights, smells, sounds, . . .) to which familiar material objects must be reduced.

SET THEORY   That branch of mathematics (or logic) which explores and establishes the properties of sets or classes or collections of objects of any kind.

SINGULAR TERM   Any expression which is treated, by those who use it, as referring to just one object. Proper names and definite descriptions (q.v.) are the most familiar singular terms.

STRONG CONDITIONAL   See CONDITIONAL.

SUBJECT   In logic, a singular term used in a sentence to refer to some particular object about which the sentence makes a claim. In epistemology, the knowing mind as contrasted with what is known.

SUBSTANCE   See BASIC PARTICULAR.

SUBSTITUTIONAL QUANTIFICATION   See QUANTIFICATION.

SUBSTRATUM   Being which, underlying a thing's qualities, unites them all into one unitary particular. A feature of Locke's account of individuals (q.v.).

GLOSSARY 233

SYMBOLIC LOGIC   Unnecessarily frightening title for logic (q.v.) which achieves flexibility, accuracy, and power of expression by using specially invented symbols. Developed principally by Frege, Russell, and Whitehead.

SYNTAX   Statement of relations among linguistic elements of sentences.

SYNTHETIC   A truth is synthetic if its truth depends not just on logic and definition, but also on how the facts actually are. What is not synthetic is analytic (q.v.).

TELEOLOGICAL   Concerning ends or aims to be attained. In teleological causation, what is intended or desired helps determine what happens.

TIMELESS PRESENT   Present tense, used in canonical notation in abstraction from considerations of time, as in mathematics.

TOKEN-REFLEXIVE TERM   Indicator (q.v.).

TRANSCENDENT   Standing behind or beyond. Usually, behind or beyond the spatiotemporal world. In epistemology, behind or beyond experience. See also IMMANENT.

TROPE   A trope, or *abstract particular*, is the instance of a quality occurring at a particular place and time. Not squareness in general, but the squareness of this particular tile here now, is a trope.

TRUTH CONDITIONS   Of a sentence, the set of circumstances any one of which, if it obtains, renders the sentence true.

TRUTH VALUE   Truth or falsity (in two-valued logic). In many-valued logics, truth, falsity, or some other related characteristic.

TRUTH-VALUE GAP   A sentence suffers from truth-value gap if its truth conditions (q.v.) and falsity conditions do not exhaust all possibilities, so that in some circumstances it is neither true nor false.

UNIVERSAL   An entity which is not particular, and so not restricted to occurrence at specific places and times. Universals can be multiply present as the qualities, characteristics, or features of indefinitely many things. 'Squareness' is a typical example.

UNIVERSAL QUANTIFIER   See QUANTIFIER.

UNIVERSE OF DISCOURSE   See DOMAIN.

VERIFICATION PRINCIPLE   Thesis that for contingent truths, the content and legitimacy of concepts and claims is established by specifying rules for application in experience. The central doctrine of logical empiricism (q.v.).

VIRTUAL THEORY OF SETS   That fragment of set theory (q.v.) which can be replaced by statements about the members of the sets involved.

VITALISM   Doctrine that living organisms operate, at least in part, according to special laws not governing merely inanimate matter. Such laws are often held to be teleological (q.v.) rather than mechanical in character.

VOID   Empty space, that is, a volume which is not a volume of anything except space. If there is no void, the space-time world is a plenum.

Bibliography

This selective list of references is confined, with a few exceptions, to works mentioned in the text. It is arranged in sections corresponding to divisions of the book, to make it more serviceable as a guide for further reading. One consequence of this is that several titles occur more than once.

ABBREVIATIONS USED:

AJP	Australasian Journal of Philosophy
Canadian J. Phil.	Canadian Journal of Philosophy
J. Phil.	Journal of Philosophy
JSL	Journal of Symbolic Logic
PAS	Proceedings of the Aristotelian Society
Rev. Met.	The Review of Metaphysics

PART ONE: A SKETCH OF THE BACKGROUND

Aristotle *The Works of Aristotle*. Translated into English under the editorship of W.D. Ross. Oxford: Oxford University Press, 1928. Particularly Vol. 1, Categoriae.

Ayer, Alfred J. *Language, Truth, and Logic*. 2d ed. London: Gollancz, 1946.

Descartes, Rene *Discourse on Method*. Many editions in English.

Carnap, Rudolpf "Empiricism, Semantics, and Ontology." In *Meaning and Necessity*. 2d ed. Chicago: University of Chicago Press, 1956.

Feyerabend, Paul K. "Problems of Empiricism." In R.G. Colodny (ed.), *Beyond the Edge of Certainty*. Englewood Cliffs: Prentice-Hall, 1965.

235

Frege, Gottlob *Begriffsschrift.* Halle, 1879. English version in J. van Heijenoort (ed.), *From Frege to Godel.* Cambridge, Mass.: Harvard University Press, 1967.

Hobbes, Thomas *Elements of Philosophy, The First Section Concerning Body.* This is an anonymous translation of *De Corpore,* first appearing in 1656. Parts of it are reprinted in Mary Calkins (ed.), *The Metaphysical System of Hobbes.* 2d ed. Chicago: Open Court, 1913. Chapter 6 discusses method.

Hume, David *An Enquiry Concerning the Human Understanding.* Many editions since its first appearance in 1748.
A Treatise of Human Nature. Many editions since its first appearance in 1739.

Kant, Immanuel *Critique of Pure Reason.* Trans. N. Kemp Smith. London: Macmillan, 1929.

Kuhn, T.S. *The Structure of Scientific Revolutions.* Chicago: University of Chicago Press, 1962.

Lazerowitz, Morris *The Structure of Metaphysics.* London: Routledge and Kegan Paul, 1955.

Plato *The Republic.* Many translations.

Quine, W.V. *The Ways of Paradox.* New York: Random House, 1966.

Russell, Bertrand *Logical Atomism.* ed. D. Pears. London, 1972.

Smart, J.J.C. *Between Science and Philosophy.* New York: Random House, 1968.

Spinoza, Benedict *Ethica, Ordine Geometrico Demonstrata.* Several translations.

Whitehead, A.N., & Russell, B. *Principia Mathematica.* Cambridge: Cambridge University Press, 1910.

Williams, Donald C. *Principles of Empirical Realism.* Springfield, Ill.: Thomas, 1966.

Wisdom, John *Philosophy and Psychoanalysis.* Oxford: Blackwell, 1957.

Wittgenstein, Ludwig *Philosophical Investigations,* 2d ed. Trans. G.E.M. Anscombe. Oxford: Blackwell, 1958.
Tractatus Logico-Philosophicus. Trans. D. Pears and B. McGuinness. London: Routledge and Kegan Paul, 1961.

PART TWO: THE PHILOSOPHY OF MATTER
Chapter 3: *The Framework of Concrete Particularism.*

Aristotle *Metaphysica.* Trans. W.D. Ross. Oxford: Oxford University Press, 1908.

Austin, J.L. *Sense and Sensibilia*. Oxford: Oxford University Press, 1962.

Berkeley, George *Of the Principles of Human Knowledge*. In, for example, *A New Theory of Vision and Other Writings*. London: Dent, 1910.

Einstein, Albert *Relativity . . . A Popular Exposition*. Trans. R.W. Lawson. London, 1920.

Leibniz, Gottfried Wilhelm *Monadology*. In *Philosophical Writings*. Trans. Mary Morris. London: Dent, 1934.

Quine, W.V. *The Ways of Paradox*. New York: Random House, 1966.

Sellars, Wilfred *Science, Perception, and Reality*. London: Routledge and Kegan Paul, 1963.

Spinoza, Benedict *Ethics*. ed. J. Guttman. New York: Hafner, 1949.

Strawson, P.F. *Individuals*. London: Methuen, 1959.

Whitehead, A.N. *Process and Reality*. Cambridge: Cambridge University Press, 1929.

Williams, Donald C. "Realism as an Inductive Hypothesis." In *Principles of Empirical Realism*. Springfield, Ill.: Thomas, 1966.

Chapter 4: Classical Atomism

Boyle, Robert *New Experiments Physico-Mechanicall, Touching the Spring of the Air*. 2d ed. Oxford, 1662. The first edition, 1660, does not give Boyle's law.
Origin of Forms and Qualities, According to the Corpuscular Philosophy. In *Works*. London, 1744. Vol. 2.

Descartes, Rene *Principles of Philosophy*. Many editions in English.

Galilei, Galileo *Dialogue Concerning the Two Chief World Systems*. Trans. S. Drake. 2d ed. Berkeley: California University Press, 1967.
Dialogues Concerning Two New Sciences. Trans. H. Crew and A. de Salvio. New York: Macmillan, 1914.

Gassendi, Pierre *Syntagma Philosophicum, Pars Secunda*. In *Opera*. Lyons, 1658. Vol. 1.

Harré, R. *Matter and Method*. London: Macmillan, 1964.

Kuhn, T.S. *The Copernican Revolution*. New York: Random House, 1959.

Leclerc, Ivor *The Nature of Physical Existence*. London: Allen and Unwin, 1972.

Leibniz, Gottfried Wilhelm *Correspondence with Clarke*. In *Philosophical Writings*. Trans. Mary Morris. London: Dent, 1934.

Locke, John *Elements of Natural Philosophy.* In Locke's *Collected Works.* For example, the 8th ed. of 1777 or the "New" ed. of 1832.
Essay Concerning Human Understanding. Numerous editions since its first appearance in 1690.

Lomonsov, Mikhail *On the Corpuscular Theory.* Trans. H.M. Leicester. Cambridge, Mass: Harvard University Press, 1970.

Lucretius *De Rerum Natura. (On the Nature of Things).* Many translations.

Priestley, Joseph *Writings on Philosophy, Science, and Politics.* ed. J.A. Passmore. New York: Collier, 1965.

Newton, Isaac *Philosophiae Naturalis Principia Mathematica. (Mathematical Principles of Natural Philosophy).* Trans. A. Motte, revised F. Cajori. Berkeley: University of California Press, 1960.

Toulmin, S., & Goodfield, J. *The Architecture of Matter.* London: Hutchinson, 1962.
The Fabric of the Heavens. London: Hutchinson, 1961.

Whyte, L. *Essay on Atomism.* New York: Harper, 1963.

Chapter 5: Primary and Secondary Qualities

Amoore, J.E. "The Stereo-chemical Theory of Odor." *Scientific American,* February 1964.

Armstrong, D.M. "The Secondary Qualities." *AJP* 46 (1968): 225–241.

Campbell, Keith "Colours." In W. Brown and C.D. Rollins (eds.), *Contemporary Philosophy in Australia.* London: Allen and Unwin, 1969.
"Primary and Secondary Qualities." *Canadian J. Phil.* 2 (1972): 219–232.

Eddington, Arthur S. *The Nature of the Physical World.* Cambridge: Cambridge University Press, 1929.

Locke, John *An Essay Concerning Human Understanding.* Many editions.

Smart, J.J.C. *Philosophy and Scientific Realism.* London: Routledge and Kegan Paul, 1963.

Stebbing, Susan *Philosophy and the Physicists.* Harmondsworth: Penguin, 1944.

Stout, G.F. "Primary and Secondary Qualities." *PAS* 4 (1903–04): 141–160.

Williams, Donald C. *The Principles of Empirical Realism.* Springfield, Ill.: Thomas, 1966.

BIBLIOGRAPHY

Chapter 6: Alternative Particularist Systems

Berkeley, George *Of the Principles of Human Knowledge*. In, for example, *A New Theory of Vision and Other Writings*. London: Dent, 1910.

Boscovich, Roger J. *Theoria Philosophiae Naturalis*. Venice, 1763. *(A Theory of Natural Philosophy)* Trans. J.M. Child. New York, 1922. Paperback edition: M.I.T. Press, 1966.

Descartes, René *Principles of Philosophy*. Many editions in English.

Leibniz, Gottfried Wilhelm *Monadology*. In *Philosophical Writings*. Trans. Mary Morris. London: Dent, 1934.
Correspondence with Clarke. In *Philosophical Writings*. Trans. Mary Morris. London: Dent, 1934.
Principles of Nature and Grace, Founded On Reason. In *Philosophical Writings*. Trans. Mary Morris. London: Dent, 1934.
Exposition and Defence of the New System. In *Philosophical Writings*. Trans. Mary Morris. London: Dent, 1934.

Priestley, Joseph *Writings on Philosophy, Science, and Politics*. ed. J.A. Passmore. New York: Collier, 1965.

Rescher, Nicholas *The Philosophy of Leibniz*. Englewood Cliffs: Prentice-Hall, 1967.

Spinoza, Benedict *Ethics*. ed. J. Gutmann. New York: Hafner, 1949.

Whyte, L.L. (ed.) *Roger Joseph Boscovich. Studies of his Life and Work on the 250th Anniversary of his Birth*. London: Allen and Unwin, 1961.

Chapter 7: Atomism and Modern Physics

Berkson, William *Fields of Force: The Development of a World View from Faraday to Einstein*. London: Routledge and Kegan Paul, 1974.

Campbell, Keith *Body and Mind*. New York: Doubleday, 1970.

De Broglie, L. *Nature*. 118 (1926): 441−442.

Einstein, Albert *Annalen der Physik* 17 (1905).
The Evolution of Physics. 2d ed. Cambridge: Cambridge University Press, 1961.

Gamow, George *Biography of Physics*. New York: Harper, 1961.
Thirty Years that Shook Physics: The Story of Quantum Theory. London: Heinemann, 1966.

Heisenberg, Werner *Quantenmechanik*. Naturwissenschaften, 14 Jahrgang, Heft 45.

Misner, Thorne, & Wheeler *Gravitation*. San Francisco: Freeman, 1973.

Hund, Friedrich *The History of Quantum Theory*. Trans. G. Reece. London: Harrap, 1974.

Russell, Bertrand *The Analysis of Matter*. London: Allen and Unwin, 1927.

Toulmin, S., & Goodfield, J. *The Architecture of Matter*. London: Hutchinson, 1962.

Wheeler, J.A. *Geometrodynamics*. New York: Academic Press, 1962.

PART THREE: A SURVEY OF ONTOLOGY
Chapters 8–11: Canonical Notation

Dennett, D.C. *Content and Consciousness*. London: Routledge and Kegan Paul, 1969.

Donellan, Keith "Proper Names and Identity Descriptions." *Synthese* 21 (1970).

Frege, Gottlob *Philosophical Writings*. ed. Geach and Black. 2d ed. Oxford: Blackwell, 1960.

Hilbert, D., & Bernays, P. *Grundlagen der Mathematik*. Vol 1, 2d ed. Berlin: Springer, 1968.

Hughes, G., & Cresswell, M. *An Introduction to Modal Logic*. London: Methuen, 1968.

Lacey, Hugh "Quine on the Logic and Ontology of Time." *AJP* 49 (1971): 47–67.

Lewis, David *Counterfactuals*. Oxford: Blackwell, 1973.

Linsky, L. (ed.) *Reference and Modality*. London: Oxford University Press, 1971.

Mackie, J.L. *Truth, Probability, and Paradox*. Oxford: Oxford University Press, 1973.

Marcus, Ruth Barcan "Quantification and Ontology." *Nous* 6 (1972): 240–250.

Nagel, Ernest *The Structure of Science*. London: Routledge and Kegan Paul, 1961.

Plato *Republic*. Many translations.

Quine, W.V. *Methods of Logic*. 2d ed. New York: Holt, Rinehart, and Winston, 1962.
Ontological Relativity. New York: Columbia University Press, 1969.
The Ways of Paradox. New York: Random House, 1966.
Word and Object. New York: M.I.T. and Wiley, 1963.

Russell, Bertrand *Logical Atomism*. ed. David Pears. London, 1972. Contains *The Philosophy of Logical Atomism* (1918) and *Logical Atomism* (1924).
"On Denoting." *Mind* 14 (1905): 479–493. Reprinted in *Logic and Knowledge*.

Ryle, Gilbert *The Concept of Mind.* London: Hutchinson, 1949.

Strawson, P.F. *Introduction to Logical Theory.* New York: Wiley, 1952.
"On Referring." *Mind* 59: (1950).
"Singular Terms, Ontology, and Identity." *Mind* 65 (1956): 433–454.

Williams, Donald C. *Principles of Empirical Realism.* Springfield, Ill.: Thomas, 1966.

Wittgenstein, Ludwig *Philosophical Investigations.* Trans. G.E.M. Anscombe. Oxford: Blackwell, 1953.
Tractatus Logico-Philosophicus. Trans. Pears and McGuinness. London: Routledge and Kegan Paul, 1961.

Chapters 12–14: Ontology

Allen, R.G.D. *Basic Mathematics.* London: Macmillan, 1962.

Armstrong, D.M. *Universals and Scientific Realism.* Forthcoming.

Black, Max "The Elusiveness of Sets." *Rev. Met.* 24 (1971): 614–636.

Cantor, Georg *Gesammelte Abhandlungen.* Hildesheim: Olms, 1962.

Cartwright, R.L. "Ontology and the Theory of Meaning." *Philosophy of Science* 21 (1954): 316–325.

Davidson, Donald "Causal Relations." *J. Phil.* 64 (1967): 691–703.
"The Logical Form of Action Statements." In N. Rescher (ed.), *Logic of Decision and Action.* Pittsburgh: Pittsburgh University Press, 1966.
"Theories of Meaning and Learnable Languages." In Y. Bar-Hillel (ed.), *Logic, Methodology and Philosophy of Science, Proceedings of the 1964 International Congress.* Amsterdam: North Holland, 1965.

Goodman, Nelson *The Structure of Appearance.* 2d ed. New York: Bobbs-Merrill, 1966.
"A World of Individuals." In *The Problem of Universals.* Notre Dame, 1956.

Goodman, N. &, Quine, W.V. "Steps Toward a Constructive Nominalism." *JSL* 12 (1947): 105–122.

Lewis, David & Stephanie "Holes." *AJP* 48 (1970): 206–212.

Mackie, J.L. *Truth, Probability, and Paradox.* Oxford: Oxford University Press, 1973.

Plato *Parmenides.* Many translations.

Putnam, Hilary "On Properties." In N. Rescher (ed.), *Essays in Honour of Carl G. Hempel.* Dordrecht: Reidel, 1969.

Quine, W.V. *From a Logical Point of View*. 2d ed. Cambridge, Mass.: Harvard University Press, 1961.
Ontological Relativity. New York: Columbia University Press, 1969.
Set Theory and Its Logic. Cambridge, Mass.: Belknap, 1963.
The Ways of Paradox. New York: Random House, 1966.

Quinton, Anthony *The Nature of Things*. London: Routledge and Kegan Paul, 1973.

Whitehead, A.N. *Process and Reality*. Cambridge: Cambridge University Press, 1929.

Williams, Donald C. *Principles of Empirical Realism*. Springfield, Ill : Thomas, 1966.

Index

A posteriori, 7−8
A priori, 7−8, 10
Abstract particulars. *See* Tropes
Abstractions, 32, 110, 115−116
Accident, 57
Activity, 82, 84
Adverbial constructions, 194−198
Allen, R. G. D., 200
Ambiguity, 120−121, 159−160
Amoore, J. E., 64, 68
Analytic truth, 8−9, 9−10
   appearance and, 2−5, 9−10, 11, 27, 41, 82
Appetition, 86
Aquinas, St. Thomas, 2, 9
Aristotle, 2
   on atomism, 45
   on concrete particulars, 29
   on method, 5, 13
   on physics, 44, 46
   on properties, 211
Armstrong, D. M., 67, 211 fn.
Assignment, 131−132, 133
Astronomy, 44−45
Atomic physics, 52−53, 98, 100−101
Atomism. *See also* Atoms
   basic particulars and, 31, 38−39
   Boscovich and, 86−88
   chemistry and, 95−96
   in Democritus, 3−4
   derivative particulars and, 37
   Leibniz and, 85−86
   materialism and, 57−58
   in physical theory, 44−48, 98−99, 100−101
   primary qualities and, 48−52, 68−69, 70
   qualitative differences and, 55−56
   reduction and, 52−55, 64, 66−67
   solidity and, 70, 89
   Spinoza and, 78−79
   the void and, 56−57
Atoms. *See also* Atomism

   in chemistry, 95−96
   cohesion of, 85−86
   in Locke, 48, 49−50
   properties of, 48−52, 53−55
   reduction and, 41, 53−55
   in Russell, 4
   as simple, 31, 83, 85−86
Austin, John L., 27
Axiomatization
   of logic, 135
   of set theory, 201−202
Ayer, Sir Alfred J., 14 fn., 41

Berkeley, George
   on atomism, 58, 75 fn.
   on cause, 40
   on God, 40
   on nature of matter, 32, 40, 71 fn.
   on nature of mind, 40
   on reality of bodies and minds, 4, 40, 71
Bernays, Paul, 115 fn.
Biology, 104−105
Black, Max, 201
Boscovich, Roger J.
   on atomism, 57−58, 75
   on collision, 88
   fields and, 99−100
   on material points, 55, 86−87, 93−94
   on physical theory and, 86−87, 88−89, 92
   on primary qualities, 69, 92
   on solidity, 89−90, 91
Boyle, Robert, 52, 53, 56
Brown, W., 64 fn.
Bulk. *See* Solidity

Campbell, Keith, 61 fn., 64, 105 fn.
Canonical notations
   Aristotelian, 122−123
   idealist, 123
   logical atomist, 124

244 INDEX

ontic commitment and, 174–176
Quine's
  semantics of, 130–135
  syntax of, 127–130
  vocabulary of, 125–126
Cantor, Georg, 200
Carnap, Rudolf, 14, 15, 216
Cartwright, R. L., 177
Categories, 107–108
  canonical notations and, 122
  commitment to, 109–110, 111–112, 130
  Quine's, 185, 200
  reductions among, 212–213, 217–218
Causa sui, 77
Causality. *See also* Mechanism *and* Teleology
  conditionals, and, 169–170
  as constitutive, 93–94
  events and, 199–200
  in Leibniz, 81–82, 84
  in Spinoza, 78–79
Change, problem of, 34–35, 36, 102
Chemistry, 95–96
Christianity, 37–38
Clarke, Samuel, 57 fn., 82 fn.
Classes. *See* Sets
Classical atomism. *See* Atomism
Clerk Maxwell, James, 97
Cohesion, 86, 88
Collision, 47, 48, 51–52, 53, 88–89
Color, 3–4, 64–65, 66–67, 72–73, 74
Complete notion, 83–84
Compresence, 213
Concrete particulars. *See* Particulars, concrete
Conditionals
  counterfactual, 167–168, 170–172, 181
  factual, 168, 172–173, 180
  material, 125, 166
  open, 167–169, 180–181
Constant proportions, law of, 95
Constructions, passive, 114–115
Contingency, 7–9. *See also* Necessity
Continuity, principle of, 84–85
Copernicus, Nicholas, 44
Copula, 109
Corpora simplicissima, 79. *See also* Spinoza
Corpuscles, corpuscularianism. *See* Atoms *and* Atomism
Cosmology, speculative, 21, 107, 218–219
Countability, 48–50
Cresswell, M., 164 fn.
Cross reference, 121–122, 134, 142. *See also* Reference
Curvature of space, 103

Dalton, John, 95, 98
Darwin, Charles, 3
Davidson, Donald, 195–199
De Broglie, L., 100 fn.
Democritus, 3, 45, 60
Demonstratives, 119–120, 152
Dennett, D. C., 165 fn.
Descartes, René, 2
  cosmology of, 6
  on God, 38
  on matter, 71 fn., 90
  on method, 5
  on the void, 56
Descriptions, definite, 119. *See also* Singular terms, definite
  theory of, 115 fn., 142–147
Deus-sive-Natura. *See* God-or-Nature
Dispositions. *See* Sentences, dispositional
Domain, 130–131, 176
Donellan, K., 145–146
Dynamics, 45–47

Eddington, Sir Arthur, 69
Egocentric particulars. *See* Indicators
Einstein, Albert
  atomic physics and, 101
  general theory of relativity of, 51, 103
  quantum theory of, 98
  special theory of relativity of, 40, 154
Electric charge, 97
Electricity, 96–97
Elements, 44–45, 95–96, 98
Empiricism, 9, 11–12
  logical, 14–16
Energy, 100–101, 103
Epicurus, 45
Epochs, 153–157, 217
Equivalence, material, 42, 125, 158–159, 160
Error, 2–4, 14–15, 74, 105
Events, 32–35, 101–102, 194–200, 217
Exclusion. *See* Solidity
Extension
  of a body
    in Boscovich, 87–88, 91
    in Leibniz, 83–85
    in Locke, 48–49, 68
    in Spinoza, 76, 78
  of a predicate, 131
Extensionality, 135, 162–163, 177–180
External world, problem of the, 26

Features, explicative, 38–39, 48–49, 93 fn.
  of events, 102
  identifying, 79–81, 83–84, 85–86
  theory founding, 38–39, 48
Feyerabend, Paul K., 20
Fiction, 112–114
Fields, 71, 97–98, 99–100
Figure. *See* Shape
Force, 46–47, 48, 51–52, 68–69
  in Boscovich, 86–88
Formation rules. *See* Canonical notations, Quine's
Frege, Gottlob, 13, 164
Freud, Sigmund, 3

Galileo (Galilei), 5, 44–45, 55, 72
Gassendi, Pierre, 45, 57
Gay-Lussac, 53
General term. *See* predicate
Generalizations. *See* Sentences, general
Geometrodynamics, 103

INDEX 245

Geometry, 5–6, 103, 191–193
Ghosts, 90–92
God
  basic particulars and, 37–38, 194–195
  Berkeley and, 40
  change and, 35–36
  Kant and, 11
  knowledge of, 9, 138
  Leibniz and, 6, 81–82, 83–84
  Locke and, 72
  logical empiricism and, 14
  in philosophy of matter, 32, 72
  sets and, 204
God-or-Nature, 6, 39, 42, 75–78
Goodman, Nelson, 203, 205, 216

Harmony, pre-established, 82, 84
Harré, R., 55 fn.
Hegel, Georg, 12
Heisenberg, Werner, 98–99
Hilbert, David, 115 fn.
Hobbes, Thomas, 5, 6, 57
Holbach, Baron F. d', 57
Hughes, G. E., 164 fn.
Hume, David, 7–12, 16, 41

Idealism, 6–7, 39–40, 48
  in Leibniz, 81–82
Ideas, 4, 8, 10, 66–67
Identity of indiscernibles, principle of, 145, 215
Illusion, 3–4, 7, 41
Impact. *See* Collision
Independence, 29–31, 39–40, 76, 81–82, 84, 85
  of events, 102
Indicators, 151–157. *See also* Singular terms, definite
Individuals, 131–132, 214–216
Intensionality, 162–173
Interaction among substances, 47–48, 50–51, 77, 79–81, 83–84
Interaction patterns for primary qualities, 63–68, 69–70, 71
Intuition, 9–10

Kant, Immanuel, 9–12
Kepler, Johann, 44, 46
Kinematics, 45–46
Kuhn, Thomas S., 20

Lavoisier, Antoine, 95 fn.
Lazerowitz, Morris, 15, 16 fn.
Leibniz, Gottfried Wilhelm
  on atomism, 57–58, 75
  on basic particulars, 39–40, 83–84
  Boscovich and, 86–87
  cosmology of, 6–7, 81–82
  on God, 38, 84
  method of, 6
  monads of, 6–7, 39, 42, 55, 71, 81–84
  philosophy of matter of, 27, 31–32, 71
  on space, 57, 82

Light, 47, 92, 97
Linsky, L., 164 fn.
Locke, John 7
  on atomism, 48
  on individuals, 214
  on matter, 72, 90
  on primary qualities, 48–52, 59–60, 61–63, 66–67, 68
  on secondary qualities, 60, 62 fn., 66–67
  on *substratum*, 77 fn., 214
Logic, 5–6, 7–8, 11–12, 13–14, 219
Logical analysis, 108
Logical atomism, 13–14, 119–120
Logical constants. *See* Particles, logical
Logical construction, 4. *See also* Reduction
Logical empiricism. *See* Empiricism, logical
Lomonosov, Mikhail, 47
Lucretius Caro, Titus, 45

Mach, Ernst, 102
Mackie, John, 171–173, 180–181
Macroproperties, 53–54. *See also* Reduction
Magnetism, 96–97
Martians, mechanical, 90–92
Marx, Karl, 3
Mass, 51, 88, 100–101, 102, 103
Material bodies, 4, 27–29, 32–33, 71
  in Leibniz, 81–82
  in Spinoza, 78–79
Material points, 54–55, 68–69, 86–88, 91–92, 93–94, 99–100. *See also* Boscovich, Roger J.
Materialism, 27, 57, 68, 105, 185, 188
Matter, essence of, 62–63, 71–72
Measures, 189–191
Mechanism, 72, 86
  in biology, 104–105
Metalanguage, 130, 133 fn., 177
Metaphor, 138
Method
  in metaphysics
    assumptions and, 26
    explanation and, 35–36
    mathematical, 5–7, 81
  in ontology, 108, 119–120
  science and, 17–19, 85–86
  in science, 5, 17–18, 19–21
Microproperties, 53–54. *See also* Reduction
Mill, John Stuart, 12, 41
Minds. *See also* Perception *and* Sensation
  in Berkeley, 40
  in cosmology, 105
  in Kant, 10–11
  in Liebniz, 81–83
  in Spinoza, 75
Minkowski, Hermann, 40, 154
Misner, C. W., 102 fn., 103 fn.
Mobility, 48–49
Modality. *See* Necessity
Modes, 6–7
  in Spinoza, 76, 78–79
Monads, 6–7, 39–40, 42, 71, 81–84

Monism, 6–7, 47–48
  in Spinoza, 77–78, 84
Motion, 45–51
  in Boscovich, 86–88
Myth, 112–115
  limit, 192–193

Names
  logically proper, 119–120
  proper, 131–132, 135 fn., 145–146
  in paraphrases, 147–151
Natural kinds, 208–209
Natural law, 170–171
Naturalism, 188
Necessity, 7–8, 9, 164. *See also*
    Noncontradiction, principle of
  in Leibniz, 85
  of sets, 204–205
  in Spinoza, 77–78
Negation
  internal and external, 113, 125
  truth conditions of, 113–114
Newton, Sir Isaac
  atomism and, 47, 55–56, 57
  Boscovich and, 86–87
  Kant and, 10–11
  on light, 47, 92
  physical theory of, 46–48, 51–52
  on space, 49, 57
Nominalism, 207–208
Noncontradiction, principle of, 6–7
Noumena, 9, 11
Number. *See* Countability
Number theory, 202–204
Null class, 131, 204–205

Occam s razor, 111 fn., 185, 204
Ontic Commitment, 111–112, 119, 131, 173–177, 199, 205–206
Ontology, analytic, 21, 107–108
Opaque constructions. *See* Intensionality
Ordered pairs, 130–131

Pantheism, 6, 37–38, 75
Paraphrase, nature of, 137, 158–161
Particles
  atomic, 98–100, 103–104
  logical, 125
Particulars
  abstract. *See* Tropes
  basic, 29–31
  in atomism, 48, 53–54
  in Boscovich, 86–88
  in cosmology, 72, 100
  in Leibniz, 83, 84–85
  properties of, 29–32, 36, 38–40
  in reduction, 41–42
  in Spinoza, 75–79
  concrete, 25, 27–29
  in change, 35–36
  in ontology, 110, 111–112, 135
  in Quine, 186–187
  tropes and, 213–215
  derivative, 36–38, 53–54

egocentric. *See* Indicators
Parts
  material, 29–31, 84–85
  temporal, 32–35, 150
Perceived qualities, 66–67, 72–74
Perception, 2–3, 8–9, 10–11, 60–61, 65, 72–74
Perduration, 35–36, 79–81
  of particles, 100–102
Phenomena, 9–11
Phenomenalism, 41, 48, 119–120
Plato, 2
  method of, 5, 8–9
  on properties, 116 fn., 211–212
Plenism. *See* Void
Pluralism, 100
  in Leibniz, 82, 85
Points, 191–192
Positivism. *See* Empiricism, logical
Predicates
  in canonical notation, 126–127, 131–132
  extension of, 131
  Hume's fork and, 8–9
  in ontology, 109–111
Predication, 109–111
  in Leibniz, 84
Priestley, Joseph, 89 fn.
Primary qualities
  basic and derivative, 62–63, 68–69, 71, 87–88
  as common sensibles, 60–61
  complexity of predication, 69–70, 91–92
  essentiality criterion, 62
  explanation of perception criterion, 61
  interaction pattern criterion, 63–68
  resemblances in things, 66–67
  universality criterion, 61–63
Pronouns, 140–142, 153
Properties, 79 fn., 110–111, 206–214, 216. *See also* Features *and* Universals
Propositional attitudes, 165–166
Psychological verbs. *See* Propositional attitudes
Ptolemy, the astronomer, 44, 45
Putnam, Hilary, 209–210

Qualitative difference, 56
Qualities
  perceived, 66–67, 72–74
  primary, 60–71, 91–92
  secondary, 60–68, 72–74, 104
Quantification, 135 fn. *See also* Quantifiers
  semantics, 131–135
  syntax, 128–130
  tropes and, 217–218
Quantifiers, 125–126, 128–129, 131–135
  scope of, 133–135
Quantum theory, 98–99
Quarks, 98
Quasi-material equivalence, 159–161
Quine, Willard Van Orman
  canonical notation of, 125–136

INDEX

on conditionals, 173
on dispositions, 170
on events, 200
on identity of indiscernibles, 145
on materialism, 188−189
on measures, 189−190
on method, 17−19
minimum domain, 184−185
on modality, 164
on naturalism, 188
on predication, 109−111
on proper names, 147−151
on properties, 207−208
on propositional attitudes, 165−166
rule for ontic commitment, 175−180, 205−206
on sets, 200−201
on tense, 157−158
on time, 153−156
on truth value gaps, 121 fn.
Quinton, Anthony, 214 fn.

Reality, 2−7, 8, 9−12, 41
equivalence, 160
Reduction, 2−4
in atomism, 51−54, 57−58
basic particulars and, 37−38
basic predicates and, 186−187
of categories, 217−218
in logical empiricism, 16
programs, 40−42, 184
secondary qualities and, 64−65, 68−69
Reference, 109, 111, 115, 134−135. *See also* Cross reference
particularizing, 146, 150
Reichenback, Hans, 151
Relativity, theorys of, 40, 51, 57, 103, 154
Rollins, C. D., 64 fn.
Russell, Bertrand
on atoms, 44−45, 50 fn.
on events, 101−102, 194−195
on logical atomism, 119
on logical form, 13−14
on number theory, 201
on paraphrase, 159 fn.
phenomenalism and, 41
on proper names, 151
on theory of descriptions, 115 fn., 142−147
Rutherford, Lord Ernest, 98
Ryle, Gilbert, 121

Scholastics, 5
Scientific realism, 47−48, 67, 68−69
Secondary qualities. *See also* Perceived qualities *and* Perception
in bodies, 60 fn.
complexity of predication, 72−74
identity theory and, 67−68
interaction patterns and, 63−65
mediately perceivable, 62 fn.
in modern cosmology, 104
objective correlate, 66−68
sensation criterion, 60
sense-specific criterion, 61

Sellars, Wilfred, S., 27
Sensations, 60
Sense data, 41
Sentences. *See also* Conditionals *and* Natural law
closed, 128−130
complex, 129−130
compound, 127, 129
conjunctive, 117−118
disjunctive, 117
dispositional, 168−170
existential, 117−118
feature placing, 139−140
form of, 113 fn., 122
general, 116−117, 169−170
open, 126−127
paraphrases of, 138−140
relational, 111−112
simple, 126−129
subject-predicate, 108−122
Sets, 200−206. *See also* Axiomatization of set theory
properties and, 208−209
tropes and, 217−218
virtual theory of, 205
Shape, 49, 68
Simplicity of objects, 29−31, 39−40
in Leibniz, 83, 84−86
Singular terms. *See also* Indicators, Names, *and* Pronouns
definite, 109−112, 115, 142−156
indefinite, 117, 131−132, 140−141
Size. *See* Extension
Skepticism, 2, 8−9, 10−12, 19−21
Smart, J. J. C., 60, 98 fn.
Smell, 64, 67−68
Solidity, 49, 51, 69−70
in Boscovich, 89−91
Sound, 64, 67−68
Space, 6, 10, 56−57, 101
curvature of, 103
in Leibniz, 82
Space-time, 40, 71, 102−104
Spinoza, Benedict, 2. *See also* causa sui *and* God-or-Nature
atomism and, 58, 78−79
basic particulars and, 39−40, 75−78
cosmology, 6
identifying features and, 79−82, 85−86
independence in, 39
interaction and, 77−78, 81
method of, 5, 6, 8−9, 81
modern cosmology and, 103−104
monism of, 37, 84−85
Stebbing, Susan, 69
Stout, G. F., 64 fn.
Strawson, P. F., 121, 145
Subject terms, 8, 108−110
abstract, 115−116
Substance, 57. *See also* Particulars, basic
in Spinoza, 75−78
Substratum, 77 fn., 214
Surface, 48, 49, 69
virtual, 89−90

Teleology, 71–72
Temperature, 52–53, 60, 67, 68
Tense
  in paraphrases, 157–158
  truth value fluctuation and, 121
Texture, 48, 52–53, 60, 67
Thompson, J. J., 98
Thorne, K. S., 102 fn., 103 fn.
Time, 10, 153–156. See also Parts, temporal
Timeless present, 109
Token-reflexive terms. See Indicators
Tropes, 212–219
  compresence of, 213
Truth, 110–111
  analytic, 2–5, 8–10, 11, 27, 41, 82
  conditions, 13–14
  for negations, 113–114
  for relational sentences, 111
  for subject-predicate sentences, 110, 111–112, 115–116
  synthetic, 8, 10, 17–18
  values
    fluctuation in, 121–122
    gaps in, 120–121
Tycho, Brahe, 44–45

Uncertainty principle, 98–100

Vacuum. See Void
Variables, individual, 126, 132–135, 146–147
  bound, 132–135
  free, 132–134
  values of, 131–132
Verification principle, 14–15. See also Empiricism, logical
Vitalism, 104–105
Void, 55–57, 84, 86, 97–98, 103–104
Von Neumann, J., 202–204

Waves, 97, 98–99
Wheeler, J. A., 102 fn., 104
Whitehead, A. N., 13 fn., 33 fn., 194 fn.
Williams, Donald C.
  external world and, 26
  method of, 107
  primary qualities and, 64
  tropes and, 212–214
  universals and, 19, 21, 216
Wisdom, John, 15
Wittgenstein, Ludwig, 13, 15, 113 fn., 116 fn.
World image
  manifest, 27, 59, 67–69
  scientific, 59, 64

Zermelo, Ernst, 202–204